364.
1552

THE
UNUSUAL
SUSPECT

D1376019

THE UNUSUAL SUSPECT

The Remarkable True Story
of a Modern-Day Robin Hood

BEN MACHELL

CANONGATE

First published in Great Britain in 2021 by Canongate Books Ltd,
14 High Street, Edinburgh EH1 1TE

canongate.co.uk

1

British Library Cataloguing-in-Publication Data
A catalogue record for this book is available on
request from the British Library

ISBN 978 1 78689 796 1
Export ISBN: 978 1 78689 797 8

Typeset in Garamond Premier Pro by
Palimpsest Book Production Ltd, Falkirk, Stirlingshire

Printed and bound in Great Britain by Clays Ltd, Elcograf S.p.A.

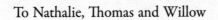

To Nathalie, Thomas and Willow

PROLOGUE

It is early autumn in rural Vermont, the hills and valleys are turning from green to gold, and two federal agents are driving along the tight winding road that leads to the Southern State Correctional Facility. One is a special agent with the FBI. The other is Special Agent Scott Murray, who works for the Bureau of Alcohol, Tobacco, Firearms and Explosives. Both are experienced men who between them have worked to bring down everyone from arms dealers to white supremacist terror groups to heroin trafficking rings. The FBI agent is tall, middle-aged, with a dark suit, a long, impassive face and a steady, methodical manner. Agent Murray is shorter, with close-cropped black hair, and seems altogether livelier and more convivial.

They are driving to the state prison in order to meet an inmate who had been moved there four months earlier, in June 2008. They already know that he is like no criminal either of them have encountered before. He had committed a string of bank heists but escaped the authorities time and time again. In carrying out his crimes, he had utilised flamboyant disguises and elaborate escape routes. He had caused chaos. He had forced the deployment of bomb disposal squads, armed response units, police helicopters and whole teams of detectives. An unpredictable lone wolf, he operated internationally. He was wanted for crimes in the Netherlands and the United

Kingdom. He'd narrowly avoided arrest in Istanbul. Almost untraceable, he would strike, leave with a bag full of cash, and then just seem to vanish. The police had not even known his name. 'There would be a robbery and the area would be flooded with cops,' said one of the detectives charged with capturing him. 'But there would just be no sign of him.'

In May 2008, though, he was finally captured in Vermont. The authorities searched his car and found a diary in which his crimes had been meticulously planned and detailed. Slowly, they began to piece together exactly who he was and what he had done. And as the full scale of his crimes became clear, more and more agencies found themselves involved in his case. Dutch police. British police. The FBI. The ATF. The US Marshals recommended that prison authorities take extra precautions when dealing with him. Possible links with terror groups were investigated. Interpol declared him a flight risk. The use of military personnel to escort him across national borders in order to stand trial was, at one point, seriously explored. Eventually, it was decided he would remain under lock and key in Vermont until all these various agencies could figure out what to do with him.

Murray and the FBI man arrive at the prison and climb out of their cars. The air is cool and fresh with pine. The Southern State Correctional Facility sits at the top of a steep hill surrounded by deep, dense forest, giving it the look of some grim fairy-tale keep. The walls are grey, smooth, and twenty feet high. Immediately behind the walls is fencing, rising to thirty feet and topped with razor wire. Above everything, an American flag cracks and flaps in the wind.

The two agents begin the lengthy process of passing through layer after layer of security. This is because the man they have come to see is not with the general prison population. Instead, he has been placed in Foxtrot Unit, a separate, self-contained wing of the jail. Technically, Foxtrot Unit is categorised as 'secure housing' and is specifically designed for the 'close custody' of particularly disruptive or dangerous prisoners. But these are just euphemisms. To inmates and guards alike, this is simply 'the Hole', a place where men are held in solitary confinement, kept in six-foot-by-nine-foot concrete cells for twenty-three and a half hours a day. Each tiny, claustrophobic chamber is a prison within a prison within a prison.

The two agents are shown to a small interview room, where they wait. Meanwhile, on the corridor of Foxtrot Unit, a pair of large, solidly built prison guards approach a metal cell door and rap on it sharply. One of the guards peers through a viewing slot and tells the figure inside that he is coming with them to meet some visitors. The guard opens a second slot halfway down the door and after a short pause a pair of white hands and their thin fingers come through. For just a moment, it looks like some pale anemone emerging from a rock. Then a pair of handcuffs are firmly clamped around the wrists, they're withdrawn, and the heavy cell door is buzzed open from a central control room. The guards enter the cell, fit a pair of leg irons on the prisoner, and then proceed to walk him to the interview room. The inmate keeps his head bowed low. Together, they pass other cell doors, where the voices of other inmates chatter, sing, shout and whimper. The air is recycled and stale. The noise and echoes and anaemic overhead lights all combine into a low migraine throb.

The prisoner enters the interview room. He is young and skinny, just under six feet tall with short dark hair and deep-set eyes that glance around the room from behind a pair of cheap glasses. As the two agents introduce themselves and sit down opposite him, he remains impassive, staring at his handcuffs.

He glances at a pile of papers the FBI agent places on the table, and for a moment it seems as if he will instinctively reach out to them. But he checks himself, and keeps his eyes down.

'So, Stephen,' says Special Agent Murray, leaning forward and speaking with bright but concerned interest, 'how have you been?'

The prisoner raises his head and looks directly at the two agents for the first time. Seconds pass. He shuts his eyes and lets out a long sigh.

I

It was a cold December morning, the sky was grey and heavy, and a young man stood at the edge of a high clifftop. He looked out to sea as the wind whipped against him, stinging his eyes and making his blonde hair stream and dance. Directly in front of him, just a single stride away, was a 500-foot drop onto a shingle beach where rolling green waves frothed, crackled and vanished. He looked up and down the narrow track running along the top of the white chalk cliffs – it was deserted. He could have been the only living soul for miles around. He shut his eyes and took a deep breath. Gulls cawed beneath him. The sharp smell of the sea filled his nostrils. He thought of everything that had led to this moment: the decisions, the beliefs, the fears, the regrets. He thought about what he was about to do and it left him euphoric with terror, light-headed and weightless. A small, insistent voice inside him was telling him that he didn't have to go through with it. That it wasn't too late to change his mind. He squeezed his fingernails into the palms of his hands and pushed the thought away. He had to see this through. He did not have a choice. He took a few more deep breaths to steady himself. And then he opened his eyes, turned away from the precipice and started to walk, continuing along the high coastal path.

He moved quickly, picking his steps without hesitation

despite the danger. He had known these cliffs since childhood. They form part of Devon's Jurassic Coast – mile after mile of rugged, almost unbroken rock face, 185 million years old. He was heading east, which meant that, directly to his right, the English Channel stretched towards the horizon. To his left were gorse thickets and coarse meadows which, come spring-time, he knew would be dotted with wildflowers: sea lavender and samphire, bluebells and garlic. Beyond were trees – ash, sweet chestnut, rowan, sycamore – which, in turn, gave way to the rich, rolling farmland of south Devon. Beneath his feet was the rock of the cliffs themselves. Formed of strata upon strata of ancient rock, these cliffs draw geologists and palaeontologists from around the globe, home, as they are, to an incalculable amount of ancient life, frozen in time. Fossils of ammonites, trilobites, ichthyosaurs, plesiosaurs, pliosaurs. Again, he knew all this. He knew their names and shapes as intimately as he did the sight of the hovering peregrines that nest along these high rocky outcrops, or the sound of the green woodpeckers in the woodland beyond.

He was slim, wearing a waterproof jacket and with a small nylon bag slung over one shoulder. As he walked along the narrow track, he passed sites he had known for years. The remains of an Iron Age hill fort overlooking the sea. A series of limestone caves and quarries first dug by the Romans. Small coves and seaside villages once home to prolific eighteenth-century smugglers. Eventually, he reached a high headland, and the cliffs which stretched ahead of him in a concave bend were no longer white. Instead, they were a tawny, dusty red. Which meant he had almost arrived. Another fifteen minutes and he was approaching the outskirts of Seaton, a small town with a harbour, shops, churches, pubs, bed and breakfasts and neat rows of white wooden beach huts along the pebbly seashore.

It was approaching noon and, of the few pedestrians who were out and about, none seemed to pay the young man any attention. He made his way towards the centre of town. As he walked, he reached into his bag and pulled out a pair of mirrored aviator sunglasses. He put them on and quickened his pace.

A few minutes later, after seeing off a customer with a brisk smile, a middle-aged female bank clerk was typing a few lines into her computer behind a plexiglass screen in the Seaton branch of Lloyds TSB. A grey stone Victorian building, the bank is some hundred metres from the sea on a narrow street of cafes and charity shops. The bank was quiet. There were only two customers present. One, who was already being dealt with by a colleague, and another, who had just entered the building. The clerk looked up at the approaching figure, and saw that it was a young man with long blonde hair and sunglasses, holding a small zipped bag. He walked straight to her desk and, without saying a word, slid her a piece of paper.

LOADED PISTOL. NO ALARMS. STAY SITTING.

She did not quite know what to make of this. She looked back up at the strange figure in front of her with the wry curiosity of somebody expecting a punchline. The figure, sensing this, placed the small bag on the counter. He partially unzipped it, revealing a black automatic pistol. There was a pause, the cashier absorbing what she'd seen. Then she began briskly taking money from her till before sliding it under the screen, as though she was dealing with any other customer making a large cash withdrawal. She watched the man on the other side of the plexiglass trying to get all the banknotes into his small nylon bag and asked if he would like something bigger. He shook his head and gruffly told her that he did not. She shrugged. 'Well, don't blame me if you drop it all,' she said. Seconds later, he had turned away and was walking back towards the door of the bank. He waited for the piercing sound of an alarm, or for police sirens, or for the wind to be suddenly slammed out of him as he was forced to the floor from behind. None of these things happened. He walked out of the bank and back into the cold sea air.

It had just gone noon. He passed pensioners and local workers starting their lunch breaks, but otherwise the town was quiet. He walked for ten seconds, twenty seconds, thirty seconds, every moment expecting the peace to be shattered by the sudden chaos of pursuit. After sixty seconds, he turned into a small local park and vanished from sight. A minute passed. And then another. And then a different figure emerged. It was a slim young man, but his hair was short and dark rather than long and blonde. He was not wearing sunglasses. He had different clothes and was wearing a backpack rather than carrying a small nylon bag. Leaving the park, he broke into a jog and headed towards the coastal path west out of Seaton, following the track as it rose up and up and up. He jogged back past coves and smuggler villages. Back past Roman quarries. Past Iron Age hill forts. After a few miles he slowed to a walk. Bespectacled and unassuming, he could have been a birdwatcher or amateur geologist. Couples out walking their dogs along the high path smiled and nodded at him, and he smiled and nodded back. Behind him, in the distance, he could hear the sound of a helicopter flying over Seaton. He forced himself not to turn around and scan the horizon. It would simply be the coastguard, he told himself. He kept walking as the English Channel rolled and broke hundreds of feet below him.

* * *

When detectives from Devon and Cornwall Police arrived in Seaton to investigate, they could guess, very quickly, who was responsible. They did not know his name, but they knew that he was almost certainly the same man who had been targeting banks and building societies across the region – and possibly further afield – for weeks. Armed bank robberies in this peaceful, coastal corner of the UK were almost unheard of. And the individual carrying them out had, so far, evaded them, dissolving into the background within moments of striking. As the crimes continued to mount, the investigating officers began to understand that there was something distinctive about their quarry that went beyond an ability to vanish into thin air. He left strange mementos. Pound coins with a single line scratched through their faces were found at the scenes of his crimes. When, at one point, the police had arrested the wrong man, he let them know through an anonymous letter to a local newspaper. In the same letter, he announced that he would be carrying out more robberies. These were not the kind of things that most bank robbers did. It made no sense at all. Why was he doing it? What did it mean? And, above all else, who was he?

That same day, as night fell over Devon, the figure from the clifftop slowly approached a grove of trees at the top of a small hillock. He paused to look and listen before slipping in amongst them. He was still carrying the backpack, which contained, amongst other things, a long blonde wig, a pair of mirrored aviator sunglasses and a black semi-automatic pistol. It also contained £4,830 in cash, most of which he had divided into thick stacks of notes, each wrapped tight in a plastic bag. Taking hold of a large, low branch, he pulled himself up and began to climb one of the trees, moving slowly up through the darkness until he found what he was looking for. Pulling the plastic bags of cash from his backpack, he began to stuff them into a deep nook within the crown of the tree. The lights of a small town shone beneath him.

It was 19 December 2007. Five thousand miles away, the United States of America had just officially entered recession, precipitating what would soon become known as the Global Financial Crisis, a cataclysm of unimaginable scope and scale. It was an event that the figure in the tree, at least, had been expecting and preparing for. His crime that day, like all his crimes, was not random. Nor was it motivated simply by greed. What the police detectives had yet to understand was that they were not hunting a criminal. They were hunting an outlaw. He dropped down from the tree and slipped away.

Later, a homeless man turned to give his dog a stroke. He'd been sitting on his cardboard mat for hours, quietly asking passers-by for any spare change, but was having no luck. As he whispered reassurances into the dog's ear, he heard a light thud and the jangle of coins. Something had landed amongst the pennies in the hat he had laid out. He looked up and saw a man walking briskly away. Then he looked back down at his hat and picked up the dropped object. Holding it close to his face, he realised that it was a tight, thick roll of twenty-pound notes. And as he leafed through it, not quite sure what to think, he noticed something else. Every single note had been marked with the same two letters: RH. He looked for the man who'd given it to him. But he'd gone. Vanished into the night.

2

The name of the young man in the interview room at Southern State Correctional Facility was Stephen George Dennis Jackley. He was twenty-two and came from a small town called Sidmouth on the south Devon coast. He was a geography student at the University of Worcester. As a rule, geography students from Devon do not tend to find themselves consigned to the Hole. Or known to Interpol. Or being interrogated by a pair of US federal agents. Or, for that matter, being the subject of a multi-agency, multinational criminal investigation. But Stephen Jackley was not like most geography students.

'I was told that he had very sophisticated abilities, and that escape should be at the forefront of my mind when dealing with him,' says Southern State's Chief of Security, a large, steady man named Mark Potanas. 'He was considered such an escape risk. There were very few prisoners we worried about to the extent that we worried about him. He was basically on lockdown.'

This was not the first time Special Agent Scott Murray had encountered Stephen. He had interviewed him some months earlier, on the afternoon of his arrest in May 2008. Since then, he had been liaising with British detectives on a case unlike any he had ever encountered. 'I do a lot that involve firearms and explosives,' he says. 'Every case is different, but this one is memorable. I guess that's the best way to put it.'

Stephen Jackley had, like many young people, looked around and concluded that the world was not fair. And like many young people, he had wanted to make a difference. But rather than going on protest marches, involving himself in politics or running sponsored marathons, Stephen ended up robbing banks. Over a seven-month period between 2007 and 2008 he struck repeatedly and successfully. 'You could not expect an educated person in his early twenties to commit a series of armed robberies across the country and internationally,' said one British detective, speaking to the press after Stephen's eventual capture. 'It has been a complex and protracted investigation.'

Agent Murray had spent enough time with the young man in front of him to judge that he was both intelligent and about as far from a typical bank robber as you could get. But there was also something about him that Murray still struggled to understand, a side of his character that remained elusive and hard to associate with the high-security surroundings they both now shared. Stephen was calm, quiet, incongruous. 'I never felt I got a full scope of who he is,' says Murray.

One thing that struck everybody was Stephen's unusual habit of writing everything down. As British and American investigators dug into the evidence surrounding his case, it became clear he had what seemed a compulsive need to commit his thoughts and deeds to paper. Everything he planned, he wrote down. Everything he did, he reflected on in his diaries – page after page after page filled in his careful, steady handwriting. 'He was methodical in the way he wanted to write down what he wanted to do in the future and what he had done in the past,' says Murray.

Back in the interview room at Southern State, the austere

grey-haired agent explained to Stephen what the FBI was and what they did. In a deep, measured voice he said that the agency was helping British police with their investigation into Stephen's crimes. He produced a pile of photocopied papers, covered in writing, numbers, dates and strange codes. He sifted through them slowly and deliberately, found what he was looking for and slid it across the table. It was a photocopy of a British banknote with the letters 'RH' scrawled on it. The FBI man glanced at Murray. Could Stephen tell them, he asked, what it meant? Stephen glanced at it. And he nodded.

What follows is an extract of 'Desperate Times', an essay written by Stephen Jackley from a British prison and posted to several newspapers and one Royal Court of Appeal judge in 2013.

The world is spinning on the axis of oblivion. Humanity stands on the brink of massive change. Within just twenty years, scientists predict the depletion of fish stocks and widespread ecological disasters. Within fifty years it's likely the world population will reach 10 billion people, with subsequent increases in carbon emissions and environmental pressures. Already species are going extinct by the day, ecosystems are being extinguished, and entire habitats are vanishing. Pollution, global warming and overpopulation is pushing the planet beyond its capacity to support life.

The fate of our world is the concern of everyone, yet like all dependable things it is often taken for granted. As different as we are, each of us is a passenger on the same great vessel, members of a species responsible for so much destruction. Despite this, humanity as a whole cannot be blamed. From affluent Western nations to Chinese towns, people are destroying the planet not for survival but to support a system that few even realise exists.

Eighty-three per cent of the world economy is controlled by the richest fifth of the population. Thirty-five of the biggest economic actors are companies and just fifteen are governments. It is reasonable to conclude that the world is being run by and for a transnational capitalist class – a corporate oligarchy that hides behind both democracies and dictatorships. Every government is really a pawn to economic forces, as determined by the elite super-rich minority. Blinded by power and greed, this minority are not really concerned with impending ecological crisis. Perhaps they think they can escape it, just as they've escaped the economic hardships others have had to endure. Or perhaps they believe it will come anyway – that there's no avoiding 'the inevitable' – and therefore the best option is to enjoy life to the full. Either way, whether by intention or inheritance, the global oligarchy is a primary architect of the world's devastation.

People are starting to realise that the Earth is a giant Easter Island, and that it can only endure so much destruction before being irreversibly destroyed. Slow, tentative steps are being made, but they are not enough. It would take a drastic shift in behaviour to avoid the predictions of scientists. And a change in behaviour requires a change in thinking.

Only comparatively recently has humanity realised that the planet is a delicately balanced, interconnected system; that its resources and biological diversity can easily be extinguished; that every ecosystem is a complex web of mutually dependent species. Rather than seeing life as a biological arms race whereby every species competes with another, we are beginning to understand that it is more like a symbiotic relationship, where all species have their special roles in sustaining each other. Humans rely on this symbiosis: from the mitochondrion in every one of our cells (a distinct lifeform that gives us energy) and the bacteria in our digestive system to the food we consume and the oxygen-nitrogen air we inhale. Our very existence is because of other species. Despite this, humanity persists in a relentless path of destruction and blind competition – all in the name of 'progress'.

It's a misleading word, this 'progress'. It's often used interchangeably, if not equivalently, with 'growth'. In today's society it tends to mean only one thing: more. More houses, more roads, more jobs . . . more money. And meanwhile, as these are built and hoarded, the thing on which everything rests is being destroyed. The world is not infinite; its resources are not limitless. If humanity is to survive it must sacrifice the desire for 'progress' and replace it with sustainability. Each time 'progress' or 'growth' is promised, two questions need to be asked: for whom and for how long?

'The economy' is another misleading term. In the present socio-economic system an economy is measured not by the happiness of a population or the ecological richness of an environment, but rather as the flow and accumulation of an esoteric substance known as capital. Possibly this is the greatest con trick of all. Few realise that nearly all money is created more or less from thin air; it is a representation which only bears a vague resemblance to reality. For example, over 90 per cent of the UK's money supply is created by commercial banks from interest-bearing loans – a scenario echoed across the world.

Increasing food prices, taxation and inflation means more pressure for those at the bottom of the pyramid. A parallel could easily be made with feudal Britain, where rich lords increased taxes on the population in order to maintain their luxurious lifestyle. The cost of upper-class greed and folly would always be enacted on the lower class. It became apparent that I could fulfil the role of a hero, following in the footsteps of a man who had lived in similar times – a legend who had broken the law in order to bring wealth and justice to the people.

I could become a modern-day Robin Hood.

3

It's late March 2016, and I'm in a small, drab meeting room above a charity shop in Bristol. Sitting across from me is Stephen, holding a mug of tea in both hands. It is the first time we have met. My initial impressions are that he is quiet, unobtrusive and not particularly big on eye contact. In fact, everything about him seems calculated to deflect attention, from his plain t-shirt and tracksuit bottoms to his cropped dark hair and simple rectangular glasses. Five minutes earlier, a pair of friendly elderly volunteers on the charity shop floor had told me where I could find him. And as they directed me to the staircase at the rear of the building, I couldn't help wondering: do they know? Do they actually know who Stephen is? Do they have any idea what he has done? Or where he has been? How would they respond, I ask myself, if I told them that Interpol, the FBI and police forces in four different countries all have files on the shy young man who works upstairs? By the time I finish this thought, the elderly volunteers have gone back to arranging old boxes of jigsaws on the shelves. So I thank them and make my way up. At the top of the stairs, I see that Stephen is already waiting for me, standing in silence. He wears an impassive expression, but keeps his eyes fixed on me as I climb.

I introduce myself and, as he leads me through the empty

grey-beige office space where he rents a desk, I attempt some small talk. It quickly becomes clear that Stephen is not very good at small talk. Open-ended, conversational questions are answered quickly and directly, often with one word. Silences hang in the air, long and unbroken. I remind myself that this is a young man who spent months in solitary confinement, conditions defined as torture by both the United Nations and Amnesty International, and who experienced the best part of his twenties behind bars. The previous year, in May 2015, he had been released from prison on probation, and from his manner it's hard to know whether he is nervous, suspicious or just ill-attuned to the kind of offhand chit-chat that regular society tends to demand of you. He makes us some tea and we move into a pokey room with just enough space for a round wooden table and a couple of chairs. As he shuts the door behind us, I take out a notepad and place my digital dictaphone on the table between us. He pauses, looks down at it and for the first time a self-conscious smile plays on his lips.

His hands now hugging his tea, he says that it feels strange to finally talk to someone face to face about everything that has happened. About everything that he has done.

'Looking back, the thing that strikes me is my naivety,' he says gently, eyes fixed on the dictaphone in front of him. 'My inability to understand the full impact of my actions. I was someone who not only went off the rails, but who lacked an understanding of both the world and the consequences of what I was doing.' He looks up and pauses, choosing his words. 'I thought what I was doing was necessary and right. But now I can see that, no, no, that was not the case.'

Two weeks earlier, I had cold-called a Bristol telephone number. A quiet, somewhat wary-sounding young man answered, and when I introduced myself and asked if it was possible to speak to Stephen Jackley, the line seemed to go dead before the voice told me that Stephen was not around, but that I could send an email explaining what I wanted. So I sent an email. I explained that I was a journalist who had heard about his heists, his obsession with Robin Hood and his eventual capture and arrest during his attempted US 'mission'. I explained that I wanted to know how a shy, socially awkward geography student from rural Devon had arrived at the conclusion that it was his 'duty' – a word he was to use often – to rob from the rich and give to the poor as the Global Financial Crisis unfolded. I wanted to know how he was able to steal thousands of pounds from banks while evading the police for months, and I wanted to know how and why he ultimately found himself languishing alone in a tiny concrete cell in the high-security wing of an American jail. I finished my email by asking if he would be willing to meet up so that we could talk about all of this. I honestly didn't expect that he would. But you have to ask.

Three hours later, I received a short reply. He would, he said, be willing to do an interview. Which is how I come to be sitting with him in the odd little room above a charity shop in Bristol. Over tea he begins to speak, tentatively at first but then with an increasing composure. He does not rush or mumble, instead talking with the kind of steady, slightly formal precision that reminds me, ironically enough, of a police officer. He has a mild squint. He looks, I realise after some time, very tired. We talk for around two hours, during which time we discuss his crimes, his double life as an unassuming geography student and the methods he employed as a would-be Robin Hood. 'Anyone with half a brain can rob a bank,' he says, levelly, on more than one occasion. 'Without wishing to encourage it, it is extremely easy.'

More than anything, though, Stephen talks about how his bank robberies had, at least to begin with, stemmed from a genuine desire to do something good. To change the world for the better. 'I was portrayed in the press as a mad university student that suddenly decided to rob banks,' he says. 'But it wasn't a sudden process. It was gradual, and it happened due to different factors.'

He is remorseful about his actions and the terror he caused, and I get the strong impression he is still trying to comprehend exactly how and why his previously quiet, solitary existence had exploded into such wild, unpredictable drama. It is only when I listen back to our interview that I realise what the strangest thing about Stephen is. Hearing him talk in his steady, measured voice about events which were frenetic, dangerous and daring, I realise that I had expected someone different. Given the scale and scope of his crimes, given the chaos he had caused, I had imagined that he would somehow be larger than life, a charismatic savant, fizzing with energy and vision. An actual Robin Hood. Instead, Stephen seems . . . normal. Or if not quite normal, then something very close: just a half-step behind normal, an individual who could have easily passed his life in the same quiet, anonymous way he seems to be doing now.

Prior to his heists, he did not have a criminal record or even a passing, prurient interest in crime. Instead, he liked hill-walking, natural history, astronomy and philosophy. He liked *Star Trek*, *The Lord of the Rings*, *A Brief History of Time* and writing poetry. He wanted to get a geography degree. He wanted to get a job. He wanted a girlfriend. These are normal things. He was, as he entered his late teens, increasingly anxious about humanity's disregard for the environment and increasingly angry about the inequality perpetuated by global capitalism. Today, these concerns are so mainstream as to be uncontroversial beliefs shared by millions. To be anxious and angry about these things is normal.

The interview ran in *The Times*. Over the weeks that followed, we remained in touch. I kept asking if he would do another interview, and he eventually agreed. We spoke on the phone for a couple of hours and made plans to do so again. As the months passed, we spoke regularly. Sometimes he would come to London and we would arrange to meet at cafes or vegetarian restaurants or at the *Times* offices so that I could ask him more questions. I tried, on these occasions, to construct a picture of his life, although this was not easy. His living situation seemed transient and precarious. He lived in Bristol. Then he moved to Glasgow. He spent long periods of time in southern Europe, leading an ascetic life and working as a farm labourer. He never mentioned a girlfriend. He never mentioned any friends full stop. He barely had any family. An only child, his father died in 2008 and his mother would pass away in 2018. Most relatives had more or less disowned him after his crimes had been discovered. I knew he had a parole officer but, beyond that, I don't think I had ever met someone so alone.

I would sometimes email him questions or ask for more details on certain topics and his responses would be thoughtful and highly detailed, often essay-length. He thinks that he might have something close to a photographic memory, as he is often able to recall long sequences of numbers and sketch intricate floorplans of American high-security prison wings. At times, when talking about the terror he had deliberately caused in order to get bank staff to hand over the money, he'd shut his eyes and almost seem to shrink into himself with self-reproach. One wet winter evening, we are eating veggie burgers in an East London cafe and discussing his crimes, and at one point it becomes too much and he breaks away from the conversation. He puts his head in his hands. 'What was I doing?' he quietly asks himself. The rain outside beats down and we both sit in silence for what seems a very long time.

One day we arrange to meet up and Stephen arrives holding several large plastic bags. Some of them are transparent and have 'HM PRISON SERVICES' printed on them in large blue letters. These bags contain dozens of notepads, sketchbooks and cardboard envelopes filled with sheets and sheets of correspondences, prison paperwork, legal documents and more. The notepads date back to his early adolescence, when he first began keeping a diary. This was one of the reasons why, upon his eventual capture, securing a conviction was not particularly difficult: he had already confessed to everything. These notepads also contain pages and pages of poems, essays, short stories, cosmological theories and pencil sketches of landscapes. As well as all these papers, Stephen gives me old family photo albums and rolls of undeveloped film. These rolls turn out to contain dozens of photographs of the Devon landscape, from rings of Neolithic standing stones on high, windswept moors to blurry snaps of rock formations, the significance of which only Stephen can know.

I take these bags home and begin, very slowly, to work through the contents. Ring-bound notepads. A5 workbooks. Thoughts and feelings scribbled on the back of photocopied sheets of prison regulations. A quiet young man's life in the form of hundreds of thousands of mostly handwritten words, stacked in rough piles on my bedroom floor.

I pull, at random, some stapled sheets of paper from one of the plastic bags and find that they are a copy of a complaint he made to the UK Ministry of Justice in 2013, while in jail.

The nature of his complaint? That the prison had been built on a lapwing habitat and yet he has not seen any nesting boxes provided for them. He wrote the following in the box provided on the official complaint form:

> You must ask the question, what was this location before it was a prison? If another building, what was it before then? A marshland? Forest? Arable fields? In any case its rightful residents (native wildlife) have been dispossessed and as a public body you should be taking steps to help existing species, i.e., the lapwing population.

I put this paper down and reach for a small black hardback notebook with a red spine. Opening it around the middle I see that it contains pages of what appear to be theories relating to cosmology and time, of contracting and expanding universes, the possibilities of different dimensions and of light-speed travel. It dates from 2001, when Stephen was fifteen, and is written out longhand, in blue fountain pen. It is dense and hard to follow. One page starts with a quote – 'Time is the ultimate motion of existence' – and a small diagram with 'Beginning', 'Nothing' and 'End' all joined together by a series of arrows forming an infinite loop, like some endless Scalextric track. He's jotted a thought next to this:

> Nothing is keeping the beginning and end apart, therefore they are the same 'event'.
>   There is a fault in my model of the universe: all evidence points towards there being a big bang, so how can the universe expand and contract if the end is the same as the beginning? This needs to be sorted out!

I keep flicking. Phrases like 'gamma rays', 'general relativity' and 'supermassive black holes' flash and vanish amidst the stream of scratchy blue handwriting. On one page he writes about how, at 9 p.m. on 14 December 2001, he observed a 'spectacular meteor' appear above Devon: 'I was able to see a green-white streak go across the lower sky and could also see it burn up. Very lucky indeed.'

There are, in and amongst the piles of notepads, wads of what seem to be photocopied extracts of diary entries. Stephen has explained that these are copies made by the police, and were used as evidence during his prosecution. When I contact the Crown Prosecution Service to ask about retrieving the original diaries, I am told they have almost certainly been destroyed.

One evening, going through his mass of papers, I find one of Stephen's old university essays, entitled 'Social Harm and Social Justice'. One paragraph in particular has been highlighted:

> The notion of what constitutes a crime needs to be re-evaluated in terms of the social harm it causes. In many ways power and authority are the greatest legitimising forces on Earth. They determine right from wrong, justice from injustice, business transactions from outright crime. The wealth, power and influence of global corporations and governments provides a screen to their more nefarious activities, which often go right to the heart of causing social harm and injustice ... In this way what can be seen as 'just' in one place actually causes massive social harms in another. To truly measure what is socially just, we must look at things on a global scale.

In a short note at the end of the essay, Stephen observes that this topic covers 'issues I had strong feelings about, but I've tried to present the discussion objectively'.

He is not joking about the 'strong feelings'. Stephen had, on one occasion, walked breathlessly into a university lecture having come directly from the scene of a bank robbery. He took a seat towards the back of the hall and sat upright and attentive. Unlike the other students around him, however, he did not pull out a pad and pen and start making notes. Instead, he kept his backpack on the floor, firmly between his feet, because it contained thousands of pounds he had just stolen from an international banking system that was, in his view, already collapsing under the weight of its own avarice.

4

From a young age, Stephen would take the thirty-minute bus ride from Sidmouth to the small, pretty cathedral city of Exeter, to spend the day at the public library. Stephen went there in order to find a quiet corner where he could research whatever particular subject happened to be his passion at the time. Archaeology. Astronomy. String theory. Steam engines. Jet planes. Tanks. Fossils. The library is a large, mid-1960s modernist block: a long concrete rectangle three storeys high with a frontage made almost entirely of glass. Bright, peaceful and airy, it is a popular refuge for many of the city's homeless, who sit and read until closing time. Sometimes, the ten- or eleven-year-old Stephen would steal glances at these tired-looking men and women. When they smiled at him, his eyes darted back to his books. This building remained one of his favourite places throughout his adolescence and into his early adulthood.

On Friday, 7 September 2007, aged twenty, Stephen caught the bus to Exeter and walked to the library he knew so well. He was wearing a black three-quarter-length woollen coat, blue jeans and a white t-shirt, and was carrying a white plastic bag. He stopped within view of the library, near a narrow, empty back street called Musgrave Row. He checked his watch. He was early. He loitered by a corner, hiding his face from any passers-by. He checked his watch again. He glanced up and saw a van park on Musgrave Row. It was 5.35 p.m. He knew exactly what was going to happen next. A sturdy middle-aged man got out of the van and walked towards a secure door. This door was the service entrance to a large branch of Lloyds TSB. The man was a courier, operating on a timetable, and he was about to unlock the door and enter the bank. From behind his corner, Stephen watched him vanish into the building.

A minute passed. Stephen shivered. The bright early evening sun reflected on the library behind him. There was nobody around. On the other side of Musgrave Row, he could hear the sound of people walking up and down the busy high street. Suddenly, the bank service door reopened and the courier stepped out, heading back towards his van. Stephen took two shallow breaths and then stepped forward.

The courier heard the footfalls behind him and instinctively turned around. He saw a figure with his coat collar turned up and a black woollen hat pulled low over his face. He saw the barrel of a black automatic pistol. 'I have a gun,' the figure told him with urgent clarity. 'Let me back in.'

This would be Stephen's first ever bank robbery. It was a moment he had been preparing himself for. 'In my mind, I couldn't see how it could go wrong,' he said later. 'But of course, it did go wrong.'

One week earlier, Stephen had spent the afternoon at the library. He was on the top floor, sitting at a table by one of the large windows. As his mind began to wander, he let his eyes drift to the view outside. But there was really not much to see: just part of a narrow, secluded back street full of bins and the service entrances of the shops and businesses which open onto Exeter High Street. The shops. And businesses. And banks.

Stephen can't remember what he was reading when he looked down and saw a man walking towards the secure rear entrance of a Lloyds TSB and enter. A few moments later, he saw the same man leave with a bag before getting back into his van and driving away. Stephen looked at his watch and made a note of the time in his notepad. It was 5.35 p.m.

He returned to the library the following afternoon, took the same seat by the window and waited. Eventually, the same vehicle arrived, a man got out and entered the bank via its rear entrance and returned outside a short time later. Stephen checked his watch and made another note of the time in his notepad. It was almost exactly the same as the previous day. The following day, Stephen was back, sitting in the same seat, looking out the same window while doing his best to appear inconspicuous. 'I was reading continuously as well as making notes of the time the guy arrived,' he says. And the timings, he began to realise with each passing day, were remarkably close. Which made them remarkably predictable. Stephen – anonymous, bespectacled and surrounded by books in a public library – sensed an opportunity. An opportunity to help change the world. Right under his nose.

Which was why, on Friday 7 September, just after 5.35 p.m., Stephen was aiming a gun at a startled courier and demanding to be let into a bank. He says he remembers feeling anxious but, beyond that, finds it hard to describe what was running through his head in the run-up to the confrontation. 'I am good at recalling physical details, but I am not good at recalling emotions, unfortunately. I had been just around the corner looking at my watch, and I can remember being too early because I just sort of hung about for a bit waiting for him to arrive. Then I just stormed up to him and that was that.'

Only, that wasn't that. Stephen's whole plan was founded

on one fatally flawed assumption. Namely, that the courier worked for Lloyds and that he would, if threatened, be able to open the security door and let Stephen into the bank where he could then demand money from cashiers or, even better, force them to take him to 'the vault' where he could fill his bag with hundreds of thousands of pounds. But the courier, whose name was Raymond Beer, did not work for Lloyds. He was just an external delivery driver who collected post and who had to be buzzed in like anybody else. When Stephen demanded to be let into the bank, Beer simply replied that he couldn't do it. Stephen was not expecting this and hesitated for a split second. And then the next thing he knew, the man he had just been threatening with a gun was now charging directly at him.

Raymond Beer acted bravely. But he also wasn't stupid. He could tell that Stephen's pistol was not real. It was, in fact, a cheap pellet gun he had bought from a sporting goods shop. 'That prompted him to try and get it off me and apprehend me,' Stephen tells me, shrugging. 'Which is fair enough.'

Beer wrenched the gun from Stephen, kneed him in the groin, kicked him in the shin and then hit him in the face with the butt, opening up a bloody gash on his left cheek. Despite the shock and creeping panic, Stephen knew that even if he couldn't force his way into the bank, he absolutely had to retrieve the gun. If he couldn't, it would be used to hunt him down.

And it wasn't just that it now had his blood – and thus DNA – on it. There was something equally incriminating about the black BB gun. Beer may not have noticed it in the struggle, but sellotaped to the handle was a piece of paper covered in writing. In planning for his first robbery, Stephen realised that if he was going to demand access to a vault of money, then he was probably going to have to talk to several members of bank staff, possibly a group of them. As a child, talking to groups of people had always made him incredibly anxious and now, as a twenty-year-old, he was no better at it. So, thinking ahead, he wrote down the things he wanted to say and stuck the little script to his gun with all the nervous care of a schoolboy preparing to cheat in an exam.

'When I thought about how things would go after entering the bank, I worried I could get so overwhelmed and distracted that I would say the wrong things,' he explains. 'It wasn't a convoluted script, just something I could glance at very quickly. "Armed robbery", "no dye packs", that sort of thing.' He'd read online that it's important, when robbing a bank, to make sure that no tracing devices or exploding packs of dye are placed inside the bags of cash that you have just been handed. 'And I thought there was a risk of me forgetting about that, which is why I wrote it down.'

After receiving the blow to his face, Stephen retreated to the other side of Musgrave Row. He then made a decision that would have profound consequences on the rest of his life. He produced a combat knife with a seven-inch, partially serrated blade and demanded that Beer return the pellet gun.

Stephen says that he was holding the knife as Beer made a second attempt to apprehend him. 'He kind of came towards me and it connected with him,' he says. 'I didn't thrust it at him but I was obviously aware that it had come into contact with him.' He managed to disentangle himself from Beer, gave up on recovering the gun and, instead, turned and ran, dropping his white plastic bag on the floor as he fled. Later, Stephen says he felt sick with fear that the courier had been badly injured. 'I was just really scared that he had been hurt. You might think,

Well, he is going to say that. But I was.' In the moment, however, his sole focus was on fleeing the scene.

But at that point, escape seemed incredibly unlikely. He had just attempted to rob a bank, in broad daylight, in a compact and bustling city centre. He was armed and dangerous. Within a minute or two, he could hear the sound of police sirens. Then came the ominous thrum of a low-flying police helicopter. He was sprinting for his life, holding a commando knife as blood ran down one side of his face. As he fled from Musgrave Row, he ran past several members of the public.

Stephen was not running blindly, though. He raced past the library and towards Rougemont Gardens, a large and leafy public park containing the partial ruins of a Norman castle. He came to a shady grove of trees and thick bushes and, fighting to catch his breath, slipped into the foliage and out of sight. Concealed amongst the branches was a plastic bag containing a change of clothes. Stephen quickly tore himself out of the black overcoat, jeans and t-shirt he wore for the robbery, stuffing them into the empty bag before covering it up with leaves. Pressing a handkerchief against his cheek with as much discretion as he could manage, Stephen stepped out of Rougemont Gardens and began to walk back through the city centre towards the University of Exeter's St Luke's campus. With the campus just closing for the day, the route he took was thick with other young people coming and going. He took his place amongst them, walking calmly away from the city centre.

The stop-start wail of sirens still echoed behind him. The helicopter was hovering in the sky, scanning the streets below. Every part of Stephen's flight instinct was screaming at him to just get away, to break into a sprint and to not stop until he was safely amidst the woods and valleys he had grown up exploring. He fought the urge, beating it down with each slow, steady step. For a few moments, he believed that the helicopter was following him. He examined the possibility and then discarded it: 'I thought it was illogical because I couldn't see how they could possibly know it was me.'

After ten minutes, Stephen turned off the busy pavement filled with students and into a public leisure centre called the Pyramids. Walking into the male changing rooms, his senses were hit by the hot chlorine tang and the distant sound of splashes and screeching children. He took a key from his pocket and opened a locker. Inside was a second change of clothes. Shielding his cheek, he moved to a shower cubicle and washed the blood from his face before changing into his third outfit of the day, one which happened to include a pair of large sunglasses.

Stephen had stashed other changes of clothes around Exeter too. One was hidden in a small park next to the city's medieval cathedral. Another was hidden in a locker at a second nearby leisure centre. He had arranged these contingencies well in advance, and had practised walking to them, memorising the fastest routes. He had timed himself to see how long it would take to reach each one and to see whether he could change clothes in public without drawing attention to himself. It turned out he could.

After leaving the Pyramids, he waited at a bus stop, his cheek starting to swell up behind his oversized sunglasses. He was anxious and impatient. The bus route back to Sidmouth took him down one of Exeter's main arterial roads and he was concerned that he would run into police blockades or patrolling officers looking for a tallish, youngish man with a bloodied cheek.

What Stephen didn't know was that the police had a much

bigger problem than an at-large armed robber – Stephen's plastic carrier bag. When the police arrived at the scene, they looked inside. They found a device comprised of two clear chambers, each filled with a strange greyish effervescent liquid and connected by an ominous jumble of electrical wires. It was a bomb. Immediately, commands were issued for the street to be cleared.

A mass evacuation got under way. Shops and businesses were quickly emptied of staff and customers. Police officers helped to usher away members of the public before cordoning off and guarding the area to make sure it remained clear. A specialist bomb disposal team arrived and, very slowly and very carefully, approached the device Stephen had left behind. The surrounding streets were now silent. An officer in a blast suit reached out to open the bag. Seagulls cawed overhead.

Finally, upon close professional examination, it became very clear that this was not a bomb. It wasn't really anything. Just a couple of plastic bottles filled with Coca-Cola and milk. Stephen had made it with the vague idea that it might be a useful way of distracting the police if he had to make a sudden getaway. Which was exactly what happened. 'It was just what I intuitively thought a bomb would look like, from films I suppose. I just made it from stuff around the house. Wires. Tape. Used bottles.' He had hoped that, if it was noticed and taken seriously by any pursuing police officers, it might buy him a minute or two. 'Although the extent that it was taken seriously I was surprised by.'

So not only did the 'bomb' do exactly the job he had hoped it would, it did the job better than he had dared imagine. Detective Constable Alex Bingham – now a detective inspector – was the man who would effectively lead the Devon and Cornwall Police investigations into Stephen's crimes, and he says that this ploy absolutely helped him to escape that day: 'Yes, because our priority isn't to catch someone who has committed a crime. It's people's safety. One person gets away from an armed robbery? We can risk-manage that. But doing nothing and a bomb going off and there being numerous injuries? We cannot allow that to happen.' The fact that Stephen's DIY effort with the bottles and wires caused this amount of alarm is not something to criticise the police for. The point, says Bingham, is that homemade bombs do tend to look homemade: 'If it looks like a bomb, it will be treated like a bomb.' By the time the truth was uncovered by the bomb disposal team, 'most of Exeter town centre was starting to be evacuated.'

Less than an hour after confronting Beer, Stephen was on a bus heading back to Sidmouth, rumbling down tight country roads hemmed by tall, dense hedgerows, past fields and farms and patches of woodland. Rather than getting off at Sidmouth, he disembarked a few miles up the road as a precaution and hiked through the countryside, finally arriving back at his home as darkness was falling. His mother and father were both in, and wanted to know why he had a swollen, bloodied cheek. Stephen told them he'd gotten into a fight, then went to his small room and fell onto his bed.

Stephen's first attempt at robbing a bank had ended in failure. He had convinced himself that he would enter, come out with a bag full of money and then make his getaway. The attempted robbery and bomb scare made the local news, and Stephen says he remembered being relieved to hear that Raymond Beer had not been badly hurt. He would later learn that his knife had left a scratch, but nothing more. Nevertheless, Stephen believed that he had now passed a point of no return. 'I had crossed the line. There was no going back. And due to the failure, the onus on me was now even stronger to make a successful heist after that. Rather than deterring me, it did the opposite.'

Alone in his room, Stephen did what he had always done when trying to process his emotions. He picked up a pen and he wrote.

A Bank Robber's Dream

Deep in this vast sprawling hoard, wealth flows into the banks and money counters, flowing like a serpent's tail through shops and up to corporate boardrooms – for every lump of gold, a grain to the masses. An endless cycle of paper and metal, ruling life for everyone, breaking or making dreams, cementing the status quo. For every Western sunset, the same sun rises halfway round the world, and under those Eastern rays, millions starve and struggle, forced onwards by an invisible hand of money worship. No god of any age bore such allegiance: it is an idol worshipped night and day, an aim of insurmountable immorality.

Inches of steel separating piles of accruing currency, flowing into protected shells of glass and brick. But for some, such barriers can be broken. With the gun and mask as tools, a cunning and ready plan outlaid – the rebels wait in ambush. To take from the rich and scatter to the poor, to pinch the serpent's tail, to smash the corruption and injustice.

The dream of the RH is to break the status quo and release those in poverty from a hidden slavery established by the rich and powerful. To steal from the rich and give to the poor. To create new possibilities and equality.

The day will be ushered in when the legend of RH will

be known across every horizon, when the people of Earth live in a new era of justice and opportunity, no longer to suffer under the yoke of corruption and exploitation.

To fight, to suffer, to die for this dream – this I will do.

5

S idmouth is a quiet seaside town in on the south Devon coast. A pretty tourist resort for much of the nineteenth and twentieth centuries, it has a long shingle beach, distinctive red cliffs and, to the north, sits surrounded by miles of gently rolling hills, fields and greenery. In the semi-imagined Wessex of Thomas Hardy, it provided the inspiration for the town of Idmouth which, if nothing else, suggests there wasn't much about it he'd change. And because Sidmouth was never too bustling or grand even in its summer-season heyday, it doesn't have much of the sad, faded pathos you find in so many English seaside towns today. There are narrow streets of pretty whitewashed Georgian buildings leading to half a dozen Victorian-era seafront hotels lining the town's esplanade. Stephen moved there with his mother and father when he was eight years old. 'I can remember the day we arrived,' he says. 'We took a scenic route and it looked really beautiful. It was the spring, I think.'

It was just the three of them and it was not the first time they had relocated to a new town. During his early childhood, Stephen's parents, Peter and Jenny, moved around Devon several times without ever managing to settle. At Sidmouth, Stephen started at his fourth new primary school. Prior to this move, they had lived in a small village where he remembered being incredibly happy. 'I remember being really upset when we left,' he says. 'I didn't know why they moved so often.'

The Jackleys moved to the north of Sidmouth, a mile or so away from the seafront and historic town centre. This was not Thomas Hardy's Wessex so much as semi-rural post-war suburbia: a sleepy world of bus stops, bungalows, privet hedges and cul-de-sacs. Sidmouth is a relatively affluent town thanks to the number of people from across the UK who choose to relocate there for retirement. But the Jackleys had never been wealthy and moved into a house on one of the town's two council estates. 'We always lived in council houses,' says Stephen. 'It would be fair and accurate to describe my parents as "working class".'

For a couple with an eight-year-old child, the Jackleys seemed unusually old. His mother was fifty-two. Peter Jackley was almost sixty when they moved to Sidmouth and, over the course of his life, had held down various jobs at different times, working in care homes, as a gardener or in the local motor museum. Stephen thinks his father may have once worked as an engineer of some sort, but isn't entirely sure. Peter blamed an old back injury for keeping him out of regular work.

His mother went through spells of employment, taking on low-paid menial work now and then, but she would also spend hours engrossed in arts, crafts and poetry. She painted, sketched and crocheted. She decorated large pebbles from the beach or from the banks of the nearby River Sid with floral patterns or smiling faces, and much of the Jackley's ramshackle interior decor was Jenny's handiwork. She cared for their indeterminate number of cats. Their new home was a neat two-storey, two-bedroom 1960s terrace on Manstone Avenue, a quiet street of identical council houses with gardens front and back. From the end of his new street, Stephen was able to see green hills and meadows.

Stephen began at Sidbury Primary School, a tiny institution located in a village about two miles north of his home. A decade later, he wrote down a definitive list of every school he attended over his academic career, rating his overall experience at each one with a mark out of ten. There was an accompanying key which set out this system in more detail. A score of ten, he wrote, meant his experience had been 'Excellent'. A score of one meant it was 'Totally Awful'. He gave Sidbury Primary a rating of six: 'Bearable'.

Upon arriving there, he met a boy named Ben Weaver. Like Stephen, he lived in Sidmouth. And like Stephen, his family lived in a council house. 'I remember Stephen transferred in a bit late,' says Weaver. 'I don't know where he had come from before, but we were in a really small school with maybe eight people in our year. There weren't really many others to talk to. We sort of hit it off there.'

Weaver, who is now a PhD candidate at the University of Helsinki, would go on to form a ten-year friendship with Stephen. It was a relationship that would not always be straight-forward. But to begin with, at least, he remembers a boy who was easy-going and sociable. More than anything, though, he remembers Stephen's imagination.

'He had this game that he used to play. It was called "International", I think. It was a space game that he had conjured up and it was incredibly vivid for him. We would go into the woods, or even just in his bedroom, and suddenly the things around us would come to life for him. There might be a space-craft flying in or, like, there might be a peace treaty that needs to be negotiated. So we'd be in the woods and then suddenly we'd have to sit down on the floor and deal with this,' says Weaver, who recounts all this warmly. Stephen, he says, had a way of drawing him into this world with him. 'I was kind of enraptured by it. Back then he was very charismatic and it was just a fun thing to do because I never really had an active imagination. It wasn't something that I thought was strange. I thought it was fun.'

As the two boys continued their friendship into their early adolescence, however, Weaver began to observe things about the Jackleys he found odd. First and foremost was their social isolation. Sidmouth may have been a conservative town with a disproportionate number of elderly inhabitants – Weaver describes it as 'a cemetery with street lights' – but it was still, at the end of the day, a friendly place to live. In 1977, for example, Sidmouth made the Guinness Book of World Records by staging the world's largest conga-line, with 5,562 residents dancing along the esplanade. Neighbours held conversations over garden fences or stopped to bend your ear if you passed on the street. 'It was a very sociable neighbourhood,' admits Weaver. But the Jackleys? They seemed to exist apart from it.

'They just never saw anyone,' Weaver continues. 'Stephen's father would sit at home pretty much every day in front of the television. They had this massive wall of VHS videos and he would watch and rewatch the same things over and over again. His mother would go off into this area of parkland and do her own thing and come back with a new pebble. But Peter isolated himself. I can't remember there being times when you would see him talking with somebody. They never really spoke to anybody. That was the impression I got as a kid.'

They were unlike other families. In Sidmouth everybody took a degree of pride in their front gardens, but the Jackleys simply allowed theirs to become messy and overgrown. 'Which was like a crime against the town,' says Weaver. And the strange thing was that they actually took great care of their back garden. They just ignored the one that needed to be tended in public view. The apparent unwillingness of Peter Jackley, in particular, to show his face invited 'distrust'. They carried out unusual bits of home improvement. They threw together a kind of rickety conservatory at the rear of their house which Stephen describes as a 'greenhouse', though Weaver recalls it being made from 'some kind of plastic sheeting'. A rumour went round that the Jackleys had converted a small garage at the rear of their home into a spare bedroom, which was in fact true. Later, when Weaver was in his teens, Stephen's father sometimes encouraged him to use it: 'He would say, "You can come and stay any time you want. You can sleep in the bedroom and you don't have to tell Stephen". Which, now that I think about it, is a bit weird.'

Weaver remembers how the frenetic and intense games of make-believe ceased almost overnight. 'When he was about twelve suddenly he was like, no more. That's done. It was as if this was no longer what we do. I remember being a little bit confused and thinking . . . well . . . what do we do?'

Instead, the two boys played on their computers, talked about their shared interest in science and astronomy or went on fossil-hunting trips. The two of them would set off on long walks, ranging around the countryside that hems Sidmouth or trudging the high coastal footpaths that rise and fall with the cliffs.

It was always just the two of them. This, Weaver began to realise, was non-negotiable. He had other friends and would sometimes suggest to Stephen that they go and meet them or see if anyone else would be interested in coming on one of their walks. Stephen would always make it clear that he did not want this to happen. 'For him, it really did seem that bringing anyone else in would sort of . . .' he tells me, before trailing off for a moment. 'He wasn't able to cope with it.

Looking back, you can see that he wasn't able to connect with people well, and definitely not in groups.'

By the time he started secondary school, Stephen had become increasingly withdrawn. He began to play truant. He would go whole days barely opening his mouth and spent hour after hour sitting on his own under the sympathetic supervision of a middle-aged home economics teacher called Angela Thompson. 'He would come into school in the morning and he'd be wound up like a spring,' she says. 'We had a little office and he would spend most of the day in that. Very often he would go missing in the day and then I would have to go find him.'

Often as not, Thompson would find him sitting alone in a field next to the school. 'He often didn't have lunch money and we would have to go get him lunch. I remember once he came to school and his glasses were broken. So I took him to get new ones from the opticians in town.' She gives a sad, fond sigh. 'He was blind as a bat.'

It was not just Stephen who struggled to settle. A gentle presence, Stephen's mother Jenny was, unlike her husband, generally well-liked. 'I just remember her being really kind but always really busy,' says Weaver. 'She and Peter seemed to be very separate from one another. And she existed quite separately from Stephen as well. She would cook and clean and provide for the family. But she was in her own world.'

As the months passed, though, Jenny was increasingly known around Sidmouth for her erratic behaviour. She would do things that left locals unsettled. She went through a spell of posting sinister pictures through the letterboxes of her neighbours – 'Strange, abstract images based around eyes,' says Stephen – and was sometimes convinced that she was being watched or followed. She visited local shops, purchasing as many items as she was able, and then attempted to give them away to people she passed on the street. She would sometimes play records at very high volume or drag furniture around the house at strange times. On one occasion, she was found trying to place a lit firework underneath a parked taxi. When a number of bicycles went missing and were found dumped in a nearby stream, the finger of blame fell upon her.

Weaver describes how, as they entered their teens, he would often go round to see Stephen at the weekends only to be greeted by his father. 'Peter would say, "Oh, come in and have some tea", so I would sit down in the living room.' This would be at noon and Stephen would still be asleep. The whole time, says Weaver, he would be stuck downstairs with Peter, who talked nonstop about how worried he was about his son not fitting in at school or, increasingly, failing to keep regular hours. 'He'd be railing against him, going, "I don't know what to do with Stephen" and offloading emotionally onto me, a thirteen- or fourteen-year-old kid.'

Stephen says that he does not know how his mother and father met. 'I think I asked them once,' he tells me during one of our conversations, frowning slightly. 'But I can't remember.'

They had in fact first encountered each other at an Exeter hospital, where they were both patients on the psychiatric ward. Jenny Symons was schizophrenic. Peter Jackley suffered from manic depression. That their relationship began under these circumstances does not seem to have been a secret. Or at least, not by the time the residents of Sidmouth had done some detective work. Angela Thompson, for example, knew all about it. 'From what I can gather his father was in a psychiatric hospital, where he met Stephen's mother,' she explains with a chatty matter-of-factness. 'They got together. I think they both had severe mental problems. Stephen was the product of that relationship. So he had interesting genes on both sides.'

Peter's half-brother, Jolyon Jackley, frames things a little more romantically. 'They were two kindred spirits,' he says. Jolyon has spent much of his life working as an actor and theatre manager. After I approach him several times, he agrees to a brief email correspondence. He confirms that Stephen's parents had, indeed, met on a psychiatric ward. 'Jenny was a long-term resident and Peter had signed himself in following the break-up of his first marriage,' he explains. 'Their meeting was the road to recovery and Stephen was the blessing and happy fruition of their true love for each other.'

'Road to recovery', though, was perhaps wishful thinking. Both Jenny and Peter struggled badly with their illnesses throughout Stephen's childhood. Which is not to say that he did not experience the same fierce love and dependency that most young children feel for their mum and dad. When describing his mother, Stephen always emphasises her kindness, gentility and compassion. 'She was very creative, she did lots of artwork, she was very into gardening and nature and she loved animals. Honestly, it's hard to think of many other people who were that kind.'

But she was only like this when she was well. 'When she became ill it was a very chaotic environment. Furniture being moved about randomly usually marked the beginning, followed by loud music, all the windows being left open and things being chucked out.'

The loud music, in particular, distressed Stephen. She would often play The Beatles at increasingly higher volumes as she built towards a psychotic episode ('Which is part of the reason I'm not too keen on their music today'). As well as paranoid delusions which saw her fixate on the idea of eyes and the sense that she was being watched, his mother's episodes involved auditory and visual hallucinations, a distorting of reality that left her fearful, angry and manic. Listening to Stephen describe it, you get the distinct sense that his younger self was somehow privy to fragments of what his mother was experiencing. That, just as he was able to draw Ben Weaver into his own vivid imaginary world, he couldn't help but follow his mother into hers.

'A peculiar thing I recall was how some of the music itself had a warped feel to it,' he says. 'Does that make sense?' When his mother was ill, he describes sometimes hearing and seeing things as a young child that simply didn't seem natural. 'Banging noises when nobody was there. Once I'm sure a picture frame and cup moved by itself.' And when he says that she would rearrange furniture, he means that she would be able to move heavy cupboards, beds, tables and dressers around their house with a speed that didn't seem possible. He would come home after being out for what only seemed a short amount of time to find literally everything had been moved. As a result of his early experiences of his mother's illness, he says that he remains open-minded when it comes to the supernatural. Looking back, he says, 'There was definitely the sense of an energy present.'

His mother had conversations with invisible people. To a young child, this was incredibly unsettling. 'As a kid, I found that really scary. Obviously, I thought there was someone else there. Sometimes my dad had to explain that there wasn't. But I couldn't understand.' Even if she appeared to the casual observer to be 'normal', Stephen would pick up on the slightest signs that his mother was, yet again, beginning to slip away from him. 'I mean, living with someone you love and who is your mum, you notice a change in voice tone or saying things that didn't make any sense. While it wasn't visible to other people, they were visible to me.'

The fact that his mother was usually so loving and gentle only made the pain more acute when that loving and gentle mother vanished. It wasn't just that she was behaving oddly or hearing voices. She would look at Stephen as though she had never seen him before in her life. 'When she got ill, our connection just evaporated. So if anything, I would have preferred it if she was *less* kind when she was well. Because then it wouldn't have affected me so much when she was ill.'

Jenny, like Stephen, wrote poems. Her verses are light and airy, full of trees, woods, animals and nature. They are often melancholic, sometimes hopeful, though always with an under-current of soft, gentle pleading that can verge on the eerie. Her own schizophrenia is constantly alluded to, as are her feelings of isolation and inability to connect with those around her. One such short poem is called 'Drop Out?'

Out of where?
In a land of dreams
which are apart from your world
Your world exists like mine
Your reality is strong and hard
My reality is weak
I cannot be so real
because reality frightens me
Please don't condemn me
for what I am . . .
~~~

Eyes watching, waiting
in the corners of my mind
Piercing, striking . . .

then retreating steadily
when they find nothing is there

Stephen remembers his mother being forcibly institutionalised. 'The one characteristic of her illness that I remember the most was how it could come and go. For months she could be well, then for no apparent reason that I knew then, she lapsed, and had to be hospitalised,' he says. 'Several times the police came and dragged her off.' He remembers the doctors and psychiatrists who would treat her, but as far as he was concerned, they were just as bad as the police. The former were taking his mother away. The latter were keeping her from him. He began to see authority in a negative way. Many years later, during the height of his crimes, there was a part of Stephen that enjoyed the fact he was, in his mind at least, making the police look foolish. It was a measure of revenge for the times they took his mother away.

Stephen says that his father, Peter, was a stubborn man, argumentative and prone to shouting. The first few times we speak about his father, I come away with the impression that this stubbornness was somehow plucky and pugnacious, a simple function of the fact that he seemed to be the one holding his small family together. He was the one dealing with everyone, from disgruntled neighbours to psychiatric doctors. He was the one always trying to provide Stephen with some semblance of normalcy, taking him away on father–son holidays while Jenny was institutionalised or taking him on trips to the local observatory in Sidmouth as Stephen's fascination with the cosmos developed. He was the one who, ultimately, chose to marry and then start a family, at the age of fifty, with a schizophrenic woman. To do any of these things, a degree of obstinacy probably doesn't hurt.

Stephen has, initially, talked about how his father had also seemed a generous man, always on the side of the underdog, insisting on picking up hitchhikers they'd pass on Devon country roads or allowing the Samaritans in for a chat 'even when me and my mother asked him not to'. Again, it's hard not to hear all this about a man who would sometimes be forced to jump into a car with his young son in order to go looking for his missing wife and not feel that, ultimately, he must have been decent. Difficult, perhaps. But decent.

But the more Stephen – and others – discuss Peter Jackley, the more this image changes. His stubbornness seems to morph into more malign characteristics. On the one hand he could be controlling, manipulative and arrogant. On the other, he could be needy, wheedling, eager to ingratiate himself to others. Stephen says that his parents saw a lot of a local couple, Ken and Judy, who were born-again Christians, but that otherwise, they did not seem to attract many friends. There seemed to be something about Peter's character that just made some people uncomfortable. 'He was vile,' says Angela Thompson, flatly. 'He would come into school and I would have these meetings with him. I didn't like being in a room alone with him. He was horrible. A horrible man,' she says emphatically. 'He was creepy. He would touch your knee. He was horrible.'

'There was just something really off about him,' says Ben Weaver. 'Even as a kid I remember feeling uncomfortable with him. I remember my stepmother asking, "Has he touched you?" Because there was that kind of weird vibe from him. He never did. He was always very, very kind to me.'

It had always seemed to Stephen, on the other hand, that his father was very good with people: that he appeared able to act with a confidence and assurance that seemed alien and impossible to him. But he also talks, consistently, of how 'controlling' and 'domineering' his father could be. The truth of this is a very hard thing to gauge, for a couple of reasons. For a start, when asked for examples of his father's controlling nature, Stephen tends to cite things that don't seem that big of a deal. He complains that when his father carried out DIY work around their small home – such as putting together their odd jerry-rigged kitchen extension – he would only allow Stephen to help under very close supervision. 'Everything had to be done "just right" and his way,' he remembers with frustration. But this, I tried to explain to Stephen on more than one occasion, isn't really that weird. If you're going to let your child help with a household construction project or allow them to have a go with some power tools, you are, as a parent, going to want to supervise them closely. It's not being controlling; it's being responsible.

What's more, Ben Weaver says that as Stephen entered adolescence, it was clear that he 'ruled the roost' within his house. He kept his own hours. He was allowed, it seemed, to come and go as he pleased. 'I think he became aware quite quickly that he could do whatever he wanted and within reason it would be allowed to happen.' Stephen would sometimes try and make weekend plans with Ben, and Ben would have to explain that his parents had said he couldn't spend his entire Saturday going on a hike because they had made other plans. 'And he would be quite surprised that my parents would impose these limits on me.'

So why the insistence that his father was controlling? Part of the answer may lie in a phenomenon that has been observed across a number of studies involving the children of a schizophrenic parent. Specifically, that it is not uncommon for boys or young men with a schizophrenic mother to report having a difficult relationship with their fathers because they believe them to be too authoritarian. It's not hard to imagine why this may be the case: as the father in this situation you are the one who is often having to initiate the hospitalisation of the mother. You are the one having to do the bulk of the day-to-day parenting while your wife is either physically absent because she has been institutionalised or emotionally absent because she is at home but so highly medicated that she is barely there at all. Either way, she's not telling anyone that they can't help with the DIY. So your son either perceives you to be controlling relative to his mother, or when faced with the stress and chaos of a schizophrenic wife and a family to raise, you do actually end up being more controlling than the average father. You can't really win.

But on the other hand, at one point during his recollections of Stephen's family life, Ben Weaver makes what seems like a strange observation. 'This is going to sound like an awful thing to say,' he begins, 'but I always got the impression that the father liked the fact that Jenny was ill.'

By which he means, for all the upheaval her schizophrenia could cause, in the long run, it made her easy to control. Ben remembers Stephen's parents having arguments – or at least, he remembers the feeling of just having walked in on an un-resolved dispute – and something telling him that these confrontations were being deliberately instigated by Peter as a means of pushing his wife towards some kind of breaking point. 'Sometimes I wondered if the arguments that would then cause an episode were engineered by the father so that she would go away. They would fight over something and she would then be sent away for treatment and come back high on whatever meds they had given her. But malleable.'

'I would agree with that,' says Stephen. 'And I have many times established that connection to when my mum got ill.

Yes, she did have mental illness. But how much of it was ex-acerbated or brought on by my father's behaviour? I think it played a big part in her being hospitalised and possibly exacerbating the schizophrenia.'

Money was another constant source of tension at Manstone Avenue. Because of her illness, Stephen's mother received some state benefits. His father worked occasionally, but during his periods of depression work was impossible. His mother did have a small allowance left to her by her parents and which continued after they died, but her habit of just buying things and handing them out to strangers meant that her husband would hide the credit cards from her. As with so much of Peter's behaviour, this can be interpreted in two very different ways. Was he protecting her? Or was he controlling her? Or was it just convenient that one felt very much like the other?

Peter's first marriage – the failure of which ultimately caused him to suffer a nervous breakdown – took place in the late 1960s. Though born in London, he had found himself living and working in the north of England, married to a Yorkshirewoman and running pubs in the Lancashire towns of Preston and Blackpool. In 1969, they had a daughter, Lisa. Ben Weaver remembers that there was always a small photo-graph of Lisa in the Jackleys' living room, although he also remembers that when he asked who she was, nobody seemed to want to talk about her.

Lisa – Lisa Watson, Stephen's half-sister – is today a mother of two. She lives on the Wirral, near Liverpool, and speaks with a gentle sing-song Merseyside accent. She says that she doesn't remember growing up with Peter as a father for the simple reason that her parents' marriage ended when she was two years old. 'One of the reasons my mum and dad divorced was because, I don't know what job he had at the time but he had lost his job,' she explains. 'And he didn't tell her. He would pretend to go to work. My mum didn't have a car so she would get on the bus, take me to nursery, then go to work. It would have been hard to tell her, but it would have made my mum's life easier. But he didn't tell her. He was quite selfish in some ways like that. Lots of things happened like that and my mum, who is a very strong, independent woman, just wouldn't put up with it any more.'

Lisa fell out of contact with her father during her teenage years, but during her twenties she recommenced her visits to Devon, by which point Stephen had been born and grown into a young boy. 'He seemed like a happy little kid, but I did feel sorry for him. His parents were quite old and I thought it would be difficult to meet other kids because of his circumstances,' she says, meaning that the Jackleys were notably insular and antisocial. 'I just felt that the way my dad and Jenny were, they wouldn't encourage him to mix with other children or take him to clubs or things like that. I think he was quite isolated.'

She is right. By the time Stephen was at secondary school, he found socialisation virtually impossible. 'I wanted friends,' he says. 'It wasn't that I disliked people. It was just very hard. A part of me was also quite scared that if I did make a friend, I would only lose them through moving house. Or they would come back to my house and they would see the state of my mum and my dad. That was the one thing with Ben Weaver, that didn't seem to bother him, so I guess that is why he remained a friend. I'm not sure why.'

Because of his mother's schizophrenia, Stephen was placed under the care of Child and Adolescent Mental Health Services, who monitored how he was coping with her illness. He was seen by a succession of child psychiatrists and social workers who all did their best to encourage him to open up about how he was feeling. 'Sometimes they took me out to different places, to do activities like walking, going to shops and cafes. I think they just wanted me to talk, to get me to say stuff. Emotions,' he says, a little impatiently. As a child Stephen was instinctively wary of psychiatrists thanks to his experience of them in relation to his mother, and also because his father had a habit of dismissing them as 'quacks'. 'They just dug and dug and dug. They were not satisfied unless you told them everything about how you were feeling.'

He was eventually diagnosed with a 'social phobia'. Then, in 2000, at the age of fourteen, Stephen was made the subject of a Child Protection Plan. This was for a combination of factors: the stress that his mother's illness was causing him, the increasingly fraught relationship he had with his father and his inability to cope with school. Stephen's medical records include the minutes of a Child Protection Plan meeting dated 23 October 2000. One of Stephen's teachers had made a report:

The teacher gave a disturbing account of how Stephen does not interact with people at all to the extent that he will not sit opposite them. Stephen never utters a single word to any of the youngsters. Fellow people are not unkind to Stephen and are very patient with him. If people brush past Stephen this is dreadful for him. He will utter abnormal comments about other children, for example 'they sit behind me and they hit my chair'. Stephen also refuses to sit in the dining room on most occasions saying he does not wish to eat. Staff are finding it very difficult to cope with this disturbing and distressing behaviour. Stephen is slightly more relaxed with women teachers. He

cannot bear any shouting. When Stephen has attended
lessons he has displayed elements of bizarre behaviour.
This consists of killing ants even when not in existence,
turning around in circles in the classroom, pacing up
and down, banging his head against walls and breaking
his spectacles.

In a letter to Stephen's GP, dated 21 October 1999, Julia Lee,
the head of Year Nine at Sidmouth College, echoed many of
these concerns. Stephen, she wrote, appeared depressed. He fell
asleep in lessons. He twitched and scratched the desks and
floors. 'On 19 October 1999, he had to be taken to the health
centre by the school health sister after losing control in school,
snapping his glasses and banging his head against the wall,
tearing his hair out, mumbling and shaking'. That same day,
wrote Lee, Stephen expressed a desire to get away from his
home for a while. Angela Thompson, the teacher who spent
so much time looking after Stephen at school, says that
Stephen's mother seemed to agree this was a good idea. 'One
day she came and we had a meeting with the headteacher, and
I can remember [Jenny] saying to me, "Could he come and
live with you?". I said, sorry, no, I don't think that would be
appropriate. But she said, "He would be happy if he came to
live with you."'

Throughout this period, Stephen's great fear was that he too
suffered from schizophrenia. It was a fear shared by his parents,
although whenever the possibility was raised, they were assured
that their son was not schizophrenic. 'But part of me would
have been relieved to have had it,' says Stephen. 'Because then
I would have understood why I wasn't so good with social
interactions. But everyone I saw was adamant I didn't.'

Uncommunicative, anxious and alone, around the age of

twelve, Stephen took to writing down his thoughts. He acquired a black hardback A5 notepad with a red spine and wrote 'Stephen Jackley, Writing Book' on the front cover. From this point on, Stephen kept a regular journal, writing for nobody but himself. As he got older, these writings would take the form of diary entries reflecting on the events of the day, but to begin with, he seems to jot down whatever is on his mind. On the inside front page of that first black 'writing book' he elaborates: 'Ideas, stories, notes, poems, handwriting practices, theories and other things'.

It's impossible to neatly characterise the contents of this first book, which all roll into one another in a flow of free association. They are equal parts touching, funny, strange, mundane and, occasionally, unsettling. He wrote a short poem about the family dog, a yellow Labrador named 'Hammy', in which he declares his love for it but accepts that it will one day die. He noted various astronomical distances. The Sun is 93 million miles from Earth. Jupiter is 600 million miles from Earth. The Andromeda Galaxy is 2.2 million light years from Earth. He wrote episodic fantasy stories about a hero named 'Memo' and his companion, a creature called 'Mingo Platypus'. He practised his joined-up handwriting relentlessly, copying out the alphabet many times or reproducing certain sentences and phrases over and over again.

But some of these phrases, you start to notice, seem oddly misanthropic: 'England lacks proper people' or 'People are extremely stupid nowadays and do not understand the meaning of life'.

Much of what twelve-year-old Stephen wrote to himself was highly didactic. He produced regular bullet point lists of instructions to himself.

- Practise your handwriting and <u>spelling</u> every-day
- Eat an apple everyday
- Win all English competitions
- Don't watch TV too much instead read a good book
- Be a bookworm!

Elsewhere, he veered from grammatical rules – 'I before E except after C' – directly into motivational fantasy – 'Continue to read and write and you'll find yourself in a millionaire's mansion'.

At one point he wrote a news bulletin that seemed to echo the arguments his parents had about money ('We have just been informed that 1 million credit cards have mysteriously disappeared') and, every few pages, jots down a joke ('What makes a tree noisy? Its bark').

It's also possible to observe Stephen's own concerns about his mental health. He wrote a poem called 'The Boy Who Said No'.

> Their was once a boy who
> Said no all the time. He arrived
> At school one day and went mad
> Just to put you in the picture
> The first signs of madness
> actually I don't no the first
> signs of madness

The poem ends there. But Stephen later returns to the final line and, in a different coloured pen, adds an annotation: 'But they should be somewhere in this book'.

6

In May 2008, Stephen crossed the Atlantic in order to carry
out a very specific objective. This mission – he always
referred to it as a 'mission' – had taken him weeks to plan and,
if executed successfully, would have allowed him to take his
crimes to dangerous new levels. But this is not what happened.
Instead, the mission ended in disaster and Stephen was held
in a high-security prison unit. While he would go on to spend
132 days in the Hole at Vermont's Southern State Correctional
Facility, this was not where his experience of the US penal
system began. Instead, he started off by spending a little under
a month at the Northwest State Correctional Facility. A short
drive from the town of St Albans, Vermont, NWSCF is
surrounded by field after field of farmland and occasional
patches of thick forest. Set back a hundred yards or so from a
quiet country road, a row of plump conifers are supposed to
soften the view, but it's clear that the buildings they are
supposed to hide form a compact prison of low red-brick units
ringed by fencing and razor wire.

Stephen arrived at NWSCF on 22 May 2008, escorted by
a pair of US Marshals. The two men had judged his behaviour
in their custody to be both erratic and suspicious and they
had called ahead so that, when they finally arrived and pulled
Stephen from their secure van, there were already eight prison

guards standing there waiting for him. No chances were taken. 'They were really cautious of me when I arrived,' he says. 'I think they strip-searched me about eight times.' Handcuffed, legs shackled and under constant observation, he was processed, given a red prison uniform and assigned a cell in Echo Unit, the prison's 'close custody' wing. He was to be kept apart from the general prison population. He couldn't eat his meals in the canteen. He was not permitted to go outside. Instead, he was locked in a six-foot-by-nine-foot prison cell. Aside from Stephen himself, the only things taking up space were a metal toilet and sink plus a hard, narrow cot. The brick walls were painted a creamy off-white which only exacerbated the swampy glow of the single ceiling light as night began to fall. Once an hour, a guard peered through a small square window in order to observe him. Trays of food were passed through a slot in the door three times a day. As a precaution, he was kept in his restraints, which meant his wrists and ankles were still bound.

Stephen very quickly became an object of curiosity at Northwest State. Baby-faced, insular and English, he was unlike other inmates usually consigned to Echo Unit. After a few days of solitary incarceration, during which time he was repri-manded for scribbling poetry on the walls, he was finally allowed a brief period of time away from his tiny cell. A guard escorted him to a small 'rec room' – a bare space where three other inmates were sitting around a table playing cards. For the next three weeks, these men were the only other inmates Stephen encountered. One of them was a tall man in his fifties with swept-back grey hair, a deep voice and eyes that seemed to have a kind of opal glow. He told Stephen that he was involved in drug trafficking and that he was waiting to stand trial for three counts of murder. His name was Trevor and

Stephen was immediately frightened of him. 'I was pretty convinced he was some sort of psychopath.'

The second man was young, loud and ridiculously muscle-bound. His name was Paul and he had arrived at Northwest State on drug charges. He had been moved to Echo Unit after assaulting a guard, and would react angrily whenever he lost a hand of cards, though this was almost entirely for show. The third inmate was thin, fortyish and pallid, with a receding hairline. Stephen did not know what he was doing there and the man did not discuss it. For an hour or so every day, Stephen was escorted from his cell to this same small room to stand awkwardly in the corner while these same three men played cards or watched the wall-mounted TV.

After a few days of this, Stephen picked up a local newspaper during one of his enforced visits to the rec room. His heart skipped as he saw that on the front page there was a photograph of the thin, middle-aged inmate currently sitting across the room from him playing cards. His name, he read, was Brian Rooney, and he was a construction worker who had just been convicted of the rape and murder of a twenty-one-year-old student at the University of Vermont named Michelle Gardner-Quinn. Stephen felt something like vertigo upon realising who he was locked in a room with.

But at the same time he felt something else. Deep inside him, be began to realise, was this bubbling urge to understand how somebody could rape and kill an innocent person. Very quickly it became essential to know what had driven this man to do what he had done. 'I just couldn't get my head around it,' says Stephen, frowning. 'I didn't understand the logic to it.' He bit his tongue. Finally, during one of the other men's endless games of cards, Stephen could no longer contain the burning wish to know. So he snapped. And he cleared his throat. And he asked.

'Why did you kill that girl?' he called over to Rooney.

The three other men all stopped what they were doing and looked at him. Instantly, Stephen knew that he probably should not have asked this question. He would go on to learn that, when in prison, it is both pragmatic and polite to play along with the fiction that all inmates are innocent of the crimes that landed them inside. 'You don't ask, "Why did you do it?"' he explains. 'You ask, "Who set you up?"'

But Stephen had only been in prison for a few days and did not yet know this. And in any case, he had always been direct when dealing with other people. When someone behaved in a way that he couldn't understand or which did not seem rational, he questioned or challenged them regardless of whether it was a good idea or not. A confrontation was only averted by Paul and the sudden arrival of a guard. Stephen felt a wave of relief as he was escorted back to his cell. For the remainder of his time at Northwest State, he did not say another word to Rooney and Rooney did not say a word to him, 'Which was a perfectly acceptable arrangement.'

The days at Northwest State Correctional Facility passed by in dull, soupy nothingness. Stephen couldn't accept the fact of his capture nor the reality of solitary confinement. He could walk the length of his tiny cell in just a few steps, the sole of his foot banging into cold whitewashed brickwork before he planted it a fourth time. He crossed the cell's breadth in one stride. When the sun was high in the New England sky, he got, at best, up to two hours of natural light through his barred window. But either side of that, Stephen's world was one of muted, flickering fluorescence and walls that seemed ready to squeeze the life from him. For the first few days he mostly slept, curled up on a thin plastic mattress. 'In my dreams I was always running, trying to get out, often along a corridor,' he remembers. 'But it was always blocked by a dark figure.' This figure mocked and threatened him in the voiceless language of dreams.

Anonymous eyes sporadically peered through the viewing slot. He could hear the voices of other prisoners up and down the corridor – men shouting, whispering, complaining to prison staff, even singing – but never saw their faces. They were each confined to their own cell for twenty-three hours a day. The only other prisoners at Northwest State he ever actually met were the psychotic Trevor, the musclebound Paul and Brian Rooney, the man convicted of raping and killing the young woman. He continued to write snatches of poetry on pieces of paper while the other men played cards or cursed at the TV. Then, after a time, guards came and walked each of them back to their cells. It became a routine that, after a week, seemed to have been in place forever.

Stephen had not spoken to his mother since before his arrest and he had no desire to do so now. The idea of calling home and hearing her soft, cautious voice on the other end of the crackling line and not knowing whether she would understand or how she would react was too much to bear. He sat in his cell and, even though it was agonising, he shut his eyes and pictured the vast, open spaces of his childhood: from the high cliffs of the Jurassic Coast to the coarse, sweeping wilds of Dartmoor, where the wind would whip around ancient druidic stone tors and seem to whisper and sing for him while he stood there, terrified and enraptured.

The prison staff were, for the most part, courteous. The two agitated US Marshals who had delivered him to NWSCF had insisted that Stephen be subject to nightly strip-searches. The staff did not do this. The Marshals had wanted him to remain shackled, but Stephen had already had his chains removed in exchange for a promise to stop drawing on the cell walls. Some of the guards gloated and teased him for his accent and his glasses and his incessant scribbling but, by and large, he seemed to be treated with polite interest.

On one occasion, Stephen was given a disciplinary write-up when a prison officer saw that he had been removing the white caulking from around his cell window. Stephen tried to explain that he was not trying to escape, he was just bored and fidgeting. 'The windows had thick metal bars over them and a metal mesh. Even if I had managed to get the plexiglass window off by removing the caulking, it wouldn't have made any sense whatsoever.'

He continued to ask questions that led to trouble. In the rec room, he casually asked the other two inmates he was still in communication with whether anybody had ever escaped from this prison. And, if so, did they know how they went about doing it? The question was dismissed with irritation by Trevor, who told him to shut the fuck up. A few more minutes passed in relative silence, as the other inmates played cards and Stephen glanced at them from over a newspaper. Then he piped up and wondered aloud what the best way to kill yourself might be.

He didn't actually want to kill himself. It was just that the question had been on his mind for a while and he couldn't help asking. 'I was just curious how people do it.' He shrugged when he explained this to me. Same with escape. He would have loved to escape but appreciated it was very unlikely. That didn't mean he didn't want to find out more about how it might, theoretically, be done. The fact that other inmates might not want to discuss either of these topics did not occur to him.

In response to his last question, though, Paul did something that surprised him. He got up and began to fiddle with a radiator in the recreation room. Grinning, he managed to retrieve a disposable shaving razor from behind it. Inmates were permitted to use these in the main prison, but in segregation, they were forbidden. 'He had obviously deposited it there for whatever reason.' He handed it to Stephen with a smile. Stephen couldn't tell if this was all being done in jest or whether the large, loud inmate was genuinely trying to provide the means for him to end his own life. Stephen had struggled since childhood to identify when people were joking with him. But right then, in the rec room, he thought it was probably best to just take the razor. He hid it in his uniform and later placed it on a ledge above his door.

That evening his cell was searched and the disposable razor quickly found. As a punishment, Stephen was placed in an observation unit. It was just as small as his usual cell, but the lights were on constantly and there was a video camera mounted in one corner. The lights gave him a headache. Sitting on the bunk, he put a t-shirt over his head while he tried to read a paperback. When a guard saw this, he immediately barked at Stephen to stop. So Stephen let the t-shirt fall around his shoulders and continued reading. Moments later, the door of his cell clanged open as several guards stormed in.

The whole episode irritated him as much as anything. 'They were all shouting, "He's making a noose! He's making a noose!" They took me to this shower room and strip-searched me. Then they gave me the blueberry suit.'

A 'blueberry suit' is prison slang for an anti-suicide smock used in US prisons. It is a heavy, padded, tear-resistant gown into which prisoners can be tightly and securely fastened. It is designed to be impossible to tear or otherwise be turned into a noose. They are often blue and give wearers the swollen, shuffling appearance of the character Violet Beauregarde in

Charlie and the Chocolate Factory, the little girl who eventually
swells up into the shape and colour of a gigantic blueberry. A
naked Stephen was strapped into one of these and then pushed
back into his observation cell. He couldn't know for certain,
but he was pretty sure one of the three other inmates in the
rec room had told the prison authorities that he had been
talking about escape, suicide and the fact he had a razor blade.
He was chilly. He waddled across the cell to sit down and
noticed, with a sigh, that all his bedding had been removed.
He turned around to see a pair of eyes peering at him through
the viewing slot in the door, then vanish.

After almost four weeks at Northwest State, Stephen was
moved. He gulped down the fresh air as he was loaded into a
prisoner transport vehicle. He was driven south-east through
Vermont, following the Winooski River. It was June and the
sky was vast and blue. Rolling down I89 he passed lakes and
ranges of hills blanketed in dense greenery: the Centennial
Woods Natural Area, the Mount Mansfield State Forest, the
Camel's Hump State Park. Stephen couldn't observe any of this
because he sat within a cage inside the van, and its grilles covered
the thick security glass windows. He sat alone, his body gently
swaying with the roll of the road, the tight cuffs around his
wrists making the tips of his fingers turn numb.

He arrived at Southern State Correctional Facility (SSCF).
Even more guards were waiting for him than when he arrived
at Northwest State. He was strip-searched then half led, half
dragged to the Foxtrot Unit – 'the Hole' – the highest security
unit of the highest security wing of a high-security prison. 'I
went to the Hole under their "Administrative Segregation"
system, which can be applied to any prisoner thought to be an
escape risk, a risk to other inmates, or a risk to themselves.'

Stephen, wearing just a pair of shorts after his strip-search, was escorted by four guards to his new cell in the Hole. Prisoners in their cells heard the boot-stamp of the guards and came to their doors. A slow, slurred chant went up.

'Dead man walking! Dead man walking!'

Metal doors were beaten and banged, making Stephen blink and wince as he was pulled towards his cell. He had never coped well with loud noise and he was, by now, completely disoriented. His head pounded and his breathing was shallow and fast as the guards pushed him into a cell. It was the same tiny size as his last, but filthy. The toilet had shit smeared all over it. One of the guards shouted a command at him, but it didn't register. He shouted again, but Stephen either couldn't hear or didn't understand what was being asked of him. Then, without warning, the four guards rushed him, forcing him to the ground and knocking the wind from his lungs. A flurry of blows rained down, leaving him gasping, half naked, on a cold concrete floor.

The guards marched out and the heavy metal door slammed shut. The shouts and jeers of other inmates echoed and bounced along the corridor and reverberated through his cell. Pale and shivering, Stephen lay curled on the floor and cried. Not the frustrated, angry tears of his first few nights at Northwest State, but rather pathetic, heaving sobs of despair.

The days in the Hole passed in feverish uncertainty. Stephen was never allowed to settle, to establish any kind of routine. Guards appeared at random times and conducted strip-searches. Several times a week, he was moved from one cell to another then onto another. Guards banged on his door in the middle of the night and ordered him to place his hands through a slot so that he could be cuffed before they entered. He slept in fits and starts, but it was hard. It wasn't just that he never knew when he would be dragged to a new cell or be forced to undergo yet another search, it was that there was an atmosphere of delirious mania. Some of the other prisoners seemed unhinged. Some sang strange nonsense verses for hours on end. Others screamed abuse at guards or made loud animal noises. One had a habit of making exaggerated, orgasmic moans. Now and then, Stephen heard teams of guards storming a cell followed by the screams and curses of an inmate.

Stephen's treatment was neither accidental nor arbitrary. If not the blows that rained down on him, but the constant searches, the cell moves, the disorientation and despair . . . this had all been carefully pre-planned by a tall, thick-set man with a dark goatee. Mark Potanas was, at the time, Chief of Security at Southern State. He has a deep voice and a cool, methodical way of describing the demands of the role. Stephen, he explained, was somebody who had been moved to the Hole at the specific behest of the Director of Facilities for the Vermont Department of Prisons. Stephen was an inmate who was under investigation by federal agencies in the US as well as police forces overseas, who had been flagged by the US Marshals as a potential escape risk and who had been found removing the caulking around his cell window as well as being in possession of a contraband razor blade. Potanas says that, in advance of Stephen's arrival at SSCF, he established a programme for him.

'The plan I put in place was very simple. It was not to allow him to become comfortable in his cell. And by "comfortable", I mean not staying in one cell for any period of time. So I gave instructions to the supervisory staff that his cell assignment was to be moved randomly at least three times a week. So this was to happen at any time. Maybe he would come out from a shower or his recreation period and find all his belongings in a new cell.' This, says Potanas, was to prevent Stephen 'working' on any one cell over a period of days, whether that be attempting to loosen window frames or conceal items that could be used as weapons. 'There is a certain psychological aspect to it of course,' Potanas admits, 'when you are not allowed to stay in the same bed for more than a couple of nights. I imagine he was constantly thinking about what would happen.'

Still, he says that it was important not to emphasise the fact that Stephen was subject to extra measures. 'We tried to avoid giving any inmate any kind of superstar status. Obviously, other inmates knew he was getting a kind of special treatment because they weren't getting it themselves. So the security staff, the supervisors, were aware of his history.'

On one occasion, Stephen was made to share a small exercise space with a large man who the guards gleefully informed him was a known 'snapper', someone who was in segregation for raping other prisoners. Stephen spent thirty minutes awkwardly doing squats and press-ups while doing his best to keep the tall, silent man in his line of vision. Guards occasionally peered in and sniggered. Sometimes, depending on which cell he found himself consigned to, Stephen could press his face to the barred window at night and catch glimpses of the stars in the night sky. He strained to identify constellations. To find comforting familiarity in the heavens above as everything around him seemed in constant, terrifying flux.

In 1912, the British astronomer Norman Lockyer won support for the construction of an observatory on a wooded hill overlooking Sidmouth. Lockyer had, amongst many other things, discovered the element helium and after a distinguished career retired to the Devon coast. When he died in 1920, the white, one-storey facility with four large grey domes was renamed in his honour and became home to an amateur astronomical society.

It was to the Norman Lockyer Observatory that a shy and socially isolated Stephen would often retreat after moving to the town. Stephen had always experienced obsessive interests as a child, but astronomy would prove to be the most profound and long lasting of all, doing more to shape him and his view of the world than any other. He practised his handwriting by copying out words like 'Milky Way Galaxy' and 'Andromeda'. On the door of his family's small living room, he tacked a poster of the Horsehead Nebula, a photograph of a beautiful and eerie intermolecular dust cloud, taken by the Hubble Space telescope, swathed in pink and grey and punctured by the iridescent light of countless stars.

In one journal entry, from 6 January 1995, he wrote about a visit to the observatory and how he had looked at the Orion Nebula. Six months earlier, at the age of eight, Stephen was at the observatory to witness the Shoemaker–Levy comet impact Jupiter. Peering through one of the giant lenses, he observed the surface of our solar system's largest planet and was left awestruck by the sight of the gas giant's red-brown atmosphere being whipped by supersonic winds. An object 600 million miles away and observable in fine detail from the top of a hill a mile or so away from his council house in a quiet corner of Devon.

For Stephen, it was not a simple feeling of euphoria and wonder. The Shoemaker–Levy impact was the first time humanity had been able to directly observe an extraterrestrial collision: in this case, huge pieces of rock and ice over a kilometre in diameter slamming into a planet at 134,000mph, disrupting the gas giant's atmosphere and leaving prominent scars on the surface, visible for months afterwards. Stephen saw this entire event play out before his eyes and, as he travelled back down the hill to his home, he felt leaden with existential dread. What if that had been Earth instead of Jupiter? How many giant chunks of rock were out there, flying through space at incredible speeds? Life on this planet had come close to eradication after an impact before. Why not again? The prospect, to Stephen, didn't just seem possible. It was probable. Inevitable.

It was a 'seed of doom' planted in his mind. The more he learned about the vastness of the cosmos, and the more he was able to directly observe everything from the rings of Saturn to the very heart of galaxies, the less significant Earth seemed. We were vulnerable and life on this planet could not be more precarious, he concluded. It was sheer chance that we had ended up orbiting the Sun at a distance which allowed humanity to evolve. The smallest shift in this orbit would mean the end of everything. Death by heat. Death by cold. He began to read about the phenomenon of geomagnetic reversal, random events whereby a planet's magnetic north and magnetic south swap positions. He visited Exeter Library and borrowed books detailing theories about how a magnetic reversal led to the loss of Mars' protective atmosphere, stripping life from its surface and leaving it a barren wasteland.

He read about how there have been an estimated 183 reversals on Earth over the last 83 million years, and about how they have been linked to mass extinctions. The last such reversal took place 780,000 years ago. When would the next one occur? It had to happen at some point. So why was nobody talking about it? Why did nobody seem to want to acknowledge what to Stephen was becoming increasingly clear: that life on Earth is terrifyingly fragile. That we were teetering so close to annihilation that it gave him a headrush just thinking about it.

When he was hiding from his teachers in the long grass of a field by his school, or walking by himself along the banks of the River Ex, or sitting alone in his tiny bedroom at night, these were the thoughts that pulsed through his head.

The danger isn't just from stray chunks of space rock, either. As Stephen entered adolescence he began to understand that the greatest dangers to humanity are man-made. Nuclear weapons. Greenhouse gasses. A short-sighted disregard for nature in the pursuit of productivity. On 9 October 1998, twelve-year-old Stephen produced an untitled poem for National Poetry Day. It was written in blue fountain pen in his determined cursive.

At a time the world had
beautiful trees sparkling water
and fascinating animals but
then a species arrived they
cut down the trees and built
horrible factories they made
the water black and smelly
they polluted the air with
there smoking choking fumes
and they killed and hunted
the other animals how could
a species do this?
the species was

Man!

These concerns only deepened as Stephen moved into his teens. His mother still had Campaign for Nuclear Disarmament pamphlets, and decorated their home with pebbles painted with the CND logo as well as her own pencil sketches of hedgehogs or paintings of trees. At night Stephen looked up at the sky and wondered why, despite the overwhelming odds in favour of there being intelligent extraterrestrial life amongst the billions of stars in our galaxy, humanity had never made contact with an alien race. He read about the Great Filter theory, which solves this paradox by positing that all advanced races at some point acquire the technological means to utterly destroy themselves. And that most galactic races unwittingly do this before they are able to master interstellar travel. Hence the lack of alien contact.

'This concept worries me,' he wrote. 'Do all races destroy themselves when they reach our technological level? This may be a "natural defence" against beings advancing further and further until they have the power of gods.'

On the final page of one diary, Stephen wrote that he believed that humanity will destroy itself in 2039. It will be, he concluded, 'the year of self-annihilation'.

For all his pessimism, though, the teenage Stephen never descended into nihilism. In fact he did the opposite. His appreciation of nature – of existence itself – intensified. His long, solitary walks around the wilds of Devon produced in Stephen a kind of bliss state. The plants, trees, birds, streams, fossils, rock formations all took on an almost spiritual significance. He appreciated, when viewed on a cosmic scale, how miraculous it was that the world around him even existed.

'Nature is perfect,' he scrawled in his diary at the age of sixteen. 'When you gaze up at the night sky you are looking at the most beautiful thing anyone will ever see. It is the universe, all that there is. Galaxies, stars, time, everything.'

He developed an overwhelming urge to travel, to see the world beyond Devon, to escape the stress and chaos of life at

Manstone Avenue and enjoy the planet while he was still able. He wrote a short poem in his journal called 'I Want'.

> I want to climb to the top of trees.
> I want to swim in the deep blue sea.
> I want to smell mint in the forest.
>   And I want to lie in the desert at night looking up at
>   the stars.

He spent hours looking at the globe, tracing journeys he might one day make. He frustrated his maths teachers by spending lessons drawing maps in his exercise books. Stephen allowed himself to imagine that when he was older, he would play a part in helping Earth avoid ecological disaster. To sidestep the Great Filter. He imagined cities built underwater and the colonisation of distant stars. To Stephen, this was not science fiction. This had to happen. It was necessary forward planning.

From the age of sixteen, Stephen found himself becoming more and more angry about the state of the world. He began to view his existential concerns through a social lens, writing in one journal entry:

> Why does 'the greed of the few outweigh the needs of the many'? – this seems to be what the human race has lived by. As certain individuals or groups gain power, they eventually abuse it . . . power is the medium of corruption, all power in the hands of anyone is bound to corrupt them to a certain extent.

During their long country walks together, he pontificated to Ben Weaver about these things. The existence of poverty and the divide between the rich and poor started to become something he found intolerable. In hindsight, Ben wonders whether this was a result of Stephen's gradual realisation that he came from a poor family. 'I think a lot of the poverty stuff came from his father, because they didn't have much money and there just wasn't really a way for him to get work.'

Stephen held forth on these issues as the two teenage boys rambled across fields or sat in front of Stephen's PC playing strategy games like *Command and Conquer* and *Civilization* long into the evening. 'It always seemed like there were only absolutes for him,' Ben remembers. 'There was a right answer and a wrong answer, and grey areas never existed.' Stephen's concern for humanity always struck his friend as sincere but also detached somehow. 'When he talked about issues like poverty he had empathy for people, but only on an abstract level. It was like "this is happening and it's bad". But on an individual level, he wasn't really able to have empathy for other people. He wasn't able to relate to others on that level. There was this emotional barrier.'

Which I don't think is necessarily true. It may have seemed like that to his friend because of the way Stephen expressed his emotions in person, but Stephen's concern for those worse off than him goes beyond the abstract. In a red spiral-bound notebook, the seventeen-year-old Stephen wrote a meandering prose-poem about a homeless man who approached him in Exeter that evening, asking for some spare change. Stephen describes how he walked past him without responding, but then turned around to see the same man asking other pedestrians for whatever they could spare. Seeing this scene play out in the third person, Stephen was horrified. Not just by the pathos of it, but by his own hypocrisy in simply putting his head down and striding past the outstretched hand.

How can one have the heart and soul to refuse? Yet in my rush I did just this, while in my bag was tucked pounds, pennies galore. Why did I not stop? Guilt wracks my heart even now. Pray that this man approaches me again.

Knowing the right thing to do in these situations – when faced with poverty or somebody in immediate need – was something that Stephen struggled with. He knew it was right to give money to those who needed it, but it seemed to him that there was no perfect way of doing so. 'I can often remember that feeling, the feeling that I did something wrong, whether it be not giving money to someone on the street, or not giving them enough, or giving it to the wrong person because I'd then pass someone further down the street who could have needed it more,' he remembers. It was a dirty feeling that, as the years passed, never quite left him. If he was ever going to make a real difference, he was going to need more than his own pounds and pennies. Much, much more.

7

On 8 September 2007, Stephen woke from a restless sleep and winced. The area beneath his left eye was swollen and painful, and there was a rust-red bloodstain on his pillow. He sat up, touched his face and quickly looked around. He was in his bedroom at Manstone Avenue, back in Sidmouth. Downstairs, he could hear a kettle boil and the faint sound of a radio news station. As everything rushed into place, a deep lurch in the pit of his stomach pushed him back to the mattress. He had failed. After all his planning, after all his belief, he had failed to force his way into the Lloyds TSB opposite the Exeter public library and make off with the hundreds of thousands of pounds he was convinced he would. Yes, he had succeeded in utilising his stashes of clothes and his fake bomb to help him escape the police. But by allowing his replica pistol to be taken from him by the courier he had attempted to ambush and who then promptly used it to bust open his cheek, he knew he had provided the police with a sample of his DNA. He could have cried with frustration. The same blood covering his pillowcase would, by now, be in a forensic laboratory. It would be sampled, analysed and kept on a police database. A sword of Damocles, hanging over him forever.

He had found the whole thing terrifying, the act of approaching Beer with his replica gun a queasy, out-of-body experience. He did not want to do it, but felt he had to do it, like a young man volunteering for war because he couldn't live with himself if he didn't. 'I felt like it was a duty,' he says. 'I felt as if . . . I don't know how to describe it, but I felt I had this obligation. And that by not doing it I would be failing people and failing myself as well. That was the mindset I had.'

Stephen told himself that he couldn't lose momentum now. Which was why, at 9.15 p.m. that same day, he burst into a branch of Ladbrokes bookmakers on South Street in Exeter city centre. He had entered through a rear door which he accessed via a back street. He knew that round the back there was an outdoor toilet for customers.

He pushed open the door and strode across the empty shop floor towards two startled male members of staff who were counting up for the night. Stephen threw a small, hard object at the wall behind the men then quickly rushed towards them. He was wearing a black balaclava, a black leather jacket and black gloves. He was holding a commando knife and a hammer. He shouted and screamed at them, instructing them to empty their tills. He forced the branch's assistant manager to fill his backpack with cash before running out of the same rear door. The whole thing was over in about ninety seconds.

Stephen walked briskly. It was a Saturday night, dusk had passed and the streets were busy with people going to pubs and restaurants. Groups of young men and women shouted and laughed at one another. He sprinted away from the area surrounding the bookmakers and into some gardens adjacent to a block of flats. Just like the day before, he had already planted a change of clothes. Street lights cast a dull glow, but it was dark and quiet enough for him to tear himself out of his clothes and into some new ones without being seen. Walking back through Exeter, Stephen tried to regulate his breathing and kept his eyes on the ground. The sounds of shouting revellers and of half a dozen different upbeat pop songs blaring out of half a dozen different pubs assaulted his ears. But he breathed deeply and sat at his bus stop, impassive and anonymous. An hour later, he was home. His parents were sleeping. In his room, he took the cash out of his backpack and counted it. He had stolen exactly £886. He put it in a large envelope, which he would later stash in a tree. Then he climbed into bed and fell asleep.

By Monday 10 September 2007, the Exeter *Express and Echo* newspaper was carrying stories about the attempted Lloyds TSB robbery as well as the successful Ladbrokes heist. Within these reports the Devon and Cornwall police made appeals for information, offering descriptions of the suspect who was in both cases described as slim, young and around five feet ten inches tall. Stephen was relieved to read that Raymond Beer had not been hurt, the courier describing to the *Express and Echo* how he disarmed the masked man before forcing him to flee.

Detective Constable Alex Bingham of Exeter CID was the officer on duty when Stephen robbed the South Street Ladbrokes. He was sure that they were dealing with the same man who had attempted to rob the Lloyds TSB a little over twenty-four hours earlier. The sites were less than 200 yards apart and these kinds of crimes were relatively rare in this part of England. 'In Devon it is very uncommon,' he says. 'It is still a great place to live and we don't have high crime stats. We have a very low rate in knife crime. We don't have that kind of organised criminal living down here.'

Bingham is cordial and systematic, though there are hints of a police officer's black humour when he discusses the case. As Stephen's crimes mounted, he was the man who led the attempts to find him. The official name of this investigation was 'Operation Gandalf'. There was no particular reason for this. Bingham says that each month a new theme was chosen for the naming of new operations. In September 2007, it just so happened to be 'famous wizards'. So, unbeknownst to Stephen, he was now being hunted by a character from one of his favourite books.

The Southern State Correctional Facility was, at the time of Stephen's incarceration there in June 2008, a state-of-the-art prison. It had only been open for a few years and it was one of the most secure federal facilities in New England. Constructed on a twenty-seven-acre site hewn from thick forest, it sits surrounded by trees about half a mile from the Connecticut River, the border between Vermont and New Hampshire. It can accommodate up to 370 inmates. The majority of these are categorised as 'general population' and held together in the main prison building known as Alpha Unit. There is a communal canteen and a gymnasium with basketball hoops and volleyball nets. Outside, there is a baseball diamond, chalked out in a large grassy field within the high perimeter fencing.

Stephen, however, was not in Alpha Unit. The cell in which he was left shivering and sobbing by the group of escorting guards was inside Foxtrot Unit, a separate, smaller, self-contained building within the prison grounds. As the weeks passed and Stephen's random cell moves continued under the specific direction of Chief of Security Potanas, he gradually began to piece together a picture of his surroundings. Foxtrot Unit was divided into three wings: F1, F2 and F3. Stephen was in F1, which was reserved for prisoners on 'disciplinary segregation'. Here, the concrete slab which served as a cot came without blankets or pillows, just a thin plastic mattress. Each wing contained two storeys of cells. On the ground floor, these opened onto a wide grey corridor. On the upper floor, they opened onto floating walkways, seven or eight feet high. The concrete-block walls were painted a dull cream, the heavy metal doors and railings the kind of pallid sage green you only ever see inside institutional buildings. Despite the overhead lighting, there was something intensely soporific and numbing about the environment. This, Stephen would eventually conclude, was probably not an accident.

The three wings of Foxtrot Unit extend away from each other like the north, east and west points of a compass. The southern point is the Secure Housing Unit's entrance, while at the centre there is 'the Bubble', a secure control room from which prison staff can view each wing, monitor the corridors via CCTV and electronically lock and unlock the cell doors. Stephen, like all the inmates in the Hole, was consigned to his cell for twenty-three or more hours a day. Unlike his time at Northwest State, there were no supervised trips to rec rooms or the chance to interact with other prisoners face to face. At the end of each unit is an outdoor metal cage which, in theory, allows prisoners to get fresh air. But in practice these seemed to be rarely used and were never made available to prisoners in F1. Instead, Stephen found that his daily exercise would at best involve being allowed to walk his unit corridor in handcuffs and leg irons. Each inmate took their turn to clank up and down in this manner. There is a yellow line on the floor of the corridor, half a metre from the other cell doors. To cross this line – to stray too close to another inmate's cell door – was prohibited and can result in punishment if spotted by the guards.

Punishment was an unavoidable feature of life there. The

SSCF Inmate Handbook is forty-seven pages long and contains dozens and dozens of rules and regulations, a minefield of potential infractions and misdemeanours. Solitary confinement fosters both woolly headed slow-wittedness and festering, rebellious anger in equal measure. Allow either of these to subsume you and you will, inevitably, find yourself breaking rules and facing the consequences. Stephen sat on his bunk and listened to the different noises echoing up and down the corridor and reverberating through his cell: the electric buzz of cell doors being unlocked by guards and the harsh, heavy clang of them being thrown open, the stamp of guards' feet, the fuzz and crackle of their walkie-talkies and the various moans, screams and songs of the men all around him, each held in their own little concrete boxes.

There was something delirious about the atmosphere in the Hole, hyper-real yet interminable. Stephen heard voices of men talking to one another from their cells, but never saw their faces. Snatches of conversation drifted into his cell and into his dreams and he dozed, only to be woken by guards who told him to place his hands through a slot in the door so that he could be cuffed and moved, yet again, to a new cell.

During his thirty-minute daily walks up and down the corridor, other inmates called out to him. Some were goading, others asked questions, eager to know who Stephen was and why he was subject to what even they could deduce were special security measures. The fact he was English was of intense interest to some – it didn't take long before he was simply referred to as 'English' by guards and inmates alike – and he was peppered with questions: had he ever met the Queen? Did he know an inmate's niece, who lived in London? Was Big Ben taller than the Empire State Building? What was the food like? What was he doing thousands of miles from home in the high-security wing of a federal prison? Being scrutinised in this way made him feel self-conscious and anxious, but he answered them as best he could.

As the days passed, Stephen came to know some of the voices on his wing. One belonged to Gene, a squat, round-faced man in his late twenties with a deep, sad singing voice. At the encouragement of other inmates, he would often sing for the unit as evening came, performing Kenny Rogers' 'The Gambler' in a graveside delivery.

A man named Howie showed Stephen how to play games of chess and battleships with other inmates, by drawing grids on prison notepaper with the tiny, unreliable flexi-pens and then shouting coordinates to your opponent down the corridor. Howie and several other voices in Foxtrot Unit communicated in Pig Latin, which left Stephen baffled until the concept was explained to him. There was a tall, handsome Native American inmate the guards simply referred to as 'Bothways' and who seemed imperturbable, a kind of real-life Chief Bromden from *One Flew Over the Cuckoo's Nest*. The man who kept making the loud, exaggerated orgasmic noises was called Solomon, a wild-haired young man about the same age as Stephen. Everyone in the Hole just called him 'Stinky' because of his refusal to shower and horrific personal hygiene. Stinky was a compulsive masturbator – one afternoon Stephen took a paperback from the book trolley only to open it and discover that Stinky had ejaculated on several of the pages. Instinctively, he flung it across his cell with a cry of shock and disgust, then rushed to scrub his hands in the small metal basin. Stephen developed an anxiety that, with all his cell moves, it was only a matter of time before he was forced to move into a cell in which Stinky had been kept for months on end. He imagined what it must be like – the accrued filth,

the state of the toilet, the smell of that cramped airless chamber
– and it made him retch.

Stephen struggled. Life in segregation within a federal prison
is hard. The special regime that he was subjected to – the
calculated disorientation, the constant changes, the sudden
strip-searches and deliberately disturbed sleep – made things
even harder. This would be the case for anybody. But for
Stephen it was particularly unbearable. Since childhood, he'd
had a very specific and very intense need to know what was
going to happen in the immediate future.

He remembers, as a child, complaining to the BBC when
the scheduled episode of *Star Trek: The Next Generation* did
not air one evening. *Star Trek* was his favourite TV show. He
deeply admired Patrick Stewart's Captain Jean-Luc Picard and
he would watch it religiously every Wednesday. Only one night,
there was something else on. Perhaps it was a sporting event
that had gone on longer than expected, or a special news report,
or some other kind of one-off broadcast. He can't remember.
All he can remember is becoming hysterical, having a meltdown
and sobbing uncontrollably in his small, ramshackle living
room.

But Stephen's response to his favourite show not being on
TV would not have come as a shock to his parents. He had
always responded badly to changes in routine. Specific meals
had to be served on specific days. Specific TV shows had to be
watched at specific times. Amidst the chaos and stress of his
parents' illnesses – his mother's schizophrenia, his father's
manic depression – and their repeated house moves, Stephen
was a young boy who seemed obsessed with regimens and
clockwork predictability.

'The *Star Trek* thing happened when I was about eight, but

there are loads of different examples really,' he says. 'Looking back, I can just remember feeling really anxious when these things changed. It's like I had this overwhelming need for them to be the same, when most other people would have been that way.'

What nobody knew during his childhood, and what nobody knew during the course of his crimes and what nobody knew during his entire period of incarceration in the United States, was that Stephen had Asperger Syndrome. Stephen himself did not know this until it was conclusively diagnosed in February 2013 following a series of psychiatric appraisals, undertaken while he was in British jails.

'Part of me always sort of knew that I had this . . . thing,' he tells me one day over a plate of salad in the *Times* canteen, brows furrowed, his hands stretched out before him, seeming to wrestle with something heavy but incorporeal. A form of Autism Spectrum Disorder (ASD), those with Asperger Syndrome see, hear and feel the world in a way that is unlike most other people. And because it is a spectrum disorder, it means it affects individuals in different ways and to varying degrees. But individuals with the condition often have difficulties in a few key areas.

Social communication and social interaction are problematic. If you have Asperger's then you may find it hard to express yourself emotionally and struggle to read other people or pick up on subtle social cues. You do not always intuitively understand gestures and facial expressions, or know when to start or end conversations. You will sometimes employ what to others seem like needlessly complex words and phrases. Figurative language can be confusing, and you will often interpret what others say to you very literally. Jokes, colloquialisms and sarcasm do not always register. Socialisation can be very challenging.

You may wish to form friendships but you don't seem to know the best way of going about this. Often, if you find yourself in a large group of people – a classroom, for example – you will feel overwhelmed and experience the urge to seek out time alone, or to soothe yourself by rocking or swaying. Others may come to regard you as aloof or insensitive. The world will often seem confusing and unpredictable, which is why you may be so predisposed to routines, rules and timetables. It is likely that, from a young age, your interests are highly focused, sometimes obsessive, and it may be that you end up with a deep knowledge of the subjects which interest you. You may also have certain sensory difficulties. Strong smells, loud noises and bright lights can cause you anxiety, distress or even physical pain.

Dr Sajid Suleman is the consultant psychiatrist who, in 2013, produced a thirty-seven-page report confirming that Stephen has Asperger Syndrome. Then the lead clinician at the Lewisham Adult Autism Spectrum Disorder Clinic, Dr Suleman interviewed Stephen for several hours over the course of two visits to HM Prison The Verne, Dorset, in December 2012. The first interview was not a success. Dr Suleman remembers that Stephen had not expected the interview to take place in the prison's busy visiting room, around other people, and as such was 'extremely anxious'. At one point, according to the report, Stephen 'required a toilet break to escape from the situation' and the interview could not be completed on account of his restlessness. The second interview, a few weeks later, was more successful for the simple reason that the visiting room was almost empty.

Over three dozen A4 pages of densely typed paragraphs arranged under various headings and subheadings, Dr Suleman describes Stephen's psychological landscape in short, clinical sentences. As you scan the pages, the words flow with a kind

of terse, maudlin rhythm. A litany of difficulties tapped out
like telegrams.

> He cannot initiate conversations and his communication
> is not to and fro. He is only interested in talking about his
> interests and cannot do small talk or social chit-chat. He
> has informed me that he finds it difficult to understand
> other's emotions. He informed that once his mother was
> upset but he thought she was happy. He therefore said
> something to her which made her upset even more. He is
> too direct when talking to others and is socially naive. He
> informed me that he has got himself into trouble in prison
> on several occasions due to this. He gave me an example
> that in prison there is a procedure of turning chairs on the
> dinner table after finishing. He felt that by doing this, tables
> get dirty again and need cleaning again so he told them
> that this was stupid which offended others.

Cleanliness and hygiene is a preoccupation of Stephen's. He is,
writes Dr Suleman, 'obsessed' with numbers and described how
he gives them unique shapes and attributes. The number two
is in Stephen's mind square and dark blue. Three is longitudinal.
He explained to Dr Suleman how, when he did calculations,
he imagined in his mind how the shapes of different numbers
intermingle with each other. He would sometimes invent
words. For example, 'gratolucowocun' described 'when someone
is happy in a situation but the happiness is due to an unrelated
external event'.

Stephen's mother told Dr Suleman that as a child her son's
speech was often monotonous. When travelling in the car he
would repeat the phrase 'we cycle sometimes'. He would not
point at things which interested him and he did not make use

of conversational gestures, such as waving goodbye. He did not share things with other children or engage in social play. Amongst a pile of old photographs there is one taken at what looks like his sixth or seventh birthday party. Five other children look at the camera, standing on either side of a home-made puppet theatre replete with stage, curtains and sign ('Stephen's Puppet Theatre' beneath a rainbow and smiley-faced star). A real effort seems to have been made. There are balloons on the floor and his mother and father stand behind the theatre, both with awkward half-smiles. His father even wears a paper party hat. But Stephen is just sitting on the floor, face turned away from the camera, looking pensively at a stuffed puppet in his lap. You could draw a small bubble around him. There may as well be nobody else there. He was also sensitive to loud noises. Once he and his parents were visiting Dover Castle and a cannon was fired. Stephen became extremely upset by this. He kept screaming, his mother explains in the report, 'for a long time'.

The report concludes with Dr Suleman stating that 'there is little doubt' that Stephen suffers from Asperger Syndrome. In a prison diary entry from the time, Stephen reflected matter-of-factly about the possibility that this had been the elusive *thing* which had made him different for so long: 'If I have Asperger's, then this makes perfect sense.'

The temptation is to shout, 'of course it does!' It is easy, with hindsight, to observe the sweep of Stephen's life and conclude that there was something crying out to be diagnosed. From his behaviour at school to his inability to form friendships with anyone other than Ben Weaver to his constant journal keeping, obsessive interests, hysterical responses to changes in routine and everything else detailed by Dr Suleman. Had this been your child, you tell yourself, you would have intervened. You would have done more to understand what was wrong and how it could be addressed. But Stephen was not neglected. He had regular contact with mental health professionals during his childhood, both on account of his mother's schizophrenia and also because of his own difficulties coping with school. He was under a Child Protection Plan. He was seen by family therapists and social workers. He was the subject of meetings between his teachers and doctors and social workers. Angela Thompson recalls one such conference when Stephen was fourteen or fifteen.

'I can remember we had this multi-agency meeting,' she says. 'I think this might have been after something had happened at home with his mother. She'd set fire to cars and she also stalked people. I remember she stalked one of the people who worked in the chemist in town. But there was a meeting, and a doctor was there, a social worker, I was there, school's headteacher was there, it was a room full of people including a psychiatric doctor who knew the parents.' Thompson says that the possibility of Stephen suffering from a mental condition beyond a social phobia was raised at this meeting, but the psychiatric doctor dismissed the idea. 'They said, "Well he's far too young to have a diagnosis. I don't want to label him at this age."'

It is also important to know that many people go through childhood with their Asperger's undiagnosed. Dr Suleman – who is in person the very opposite of his report in that he is warm, lively and effusive – says that he wouldn't have the job of diagnosing people in adulthood if this was not the case. There are reasons why the adults around Stephen may not have sought to confirm that he was on the autism spectrum. For one thing, we simply knew less about Asperger's twenty years ago than we do today. It was less well known and less understood. It's also the case that children with the condition are generally high-functioning, meaning they are of at least average intelligence and able to develop intellectually and academically without any issues. Children who are not able to do this, perhaps because of more severe forms of autism or conditions such as dyslexia, generally receive a lot of attention because there is something demonstrably 'wrong' with them.

But in the case of Stephen, it seemed to most observers that the only thing wrong with him was his home environment. That whatever behaviour he exhibited was the result of the stress, conflict and social isolation that came with life with his mother and father. Even at the age of nineteen, after years of contact with mental health services, an evaluation carried out by a consultant psychiatrist did not flag the possibility of Asperger's. Dr Suleman, summarising this evaluation in his own report, writes that it described Stephen as being 'an insecure young man who on account of his mother's longstanding mental health problems and the consequent marital conflict had been inadvertently psychologically traumatised through his childhood.'

So if Stephen seemed anxious, depressed, unable to socialise with other children, then, given his home life, this all stood to reason. If Stephen was weird then, well . . . look at his parents. The problem was Stephen's nurture, not his nature.

The truth is that it was both. Asperger Syndrome is a developmental disorder which means that it begins to manifest in childhood not because of environmental factors, but because of biological ones. You are, as far as we know, born with it. You do not start to 'get' it because your mother keeps being admitted to psychiatric wards and because your father seems to have a compulsive desire for control and never leaves the house.

In other words, Stephen could have had the most well-adjusted parents and stable home life in the world and still grown up with Asperger's. The fact he had neither of these only made things that much worse. 'It was a double whammy,' says Dr Suleman. By sheer coincidence, during the period of their friendship, Ben Weaver's father was an intervention worker with autistic children. Although perhaps this is not a coincidence at all. The fact that Stephen's only friend had a parent who knew about autism and who had educated his son about it is probably the reason Ben was able to maintain his friendship with Stephen for so long. He was able to accept him for who he was. 'I was aware of there being people who are slightly emotionally different and my family were also very aware of that,' he says. 'My father said he was probably on the spectrum, but there wasn't much discussion beyond that.'

Given that Stephen would shortly embark on an international criminal career that would see him rob a string of banks while successfully evading teams of police detectives, it would be easy to view his Asperger's as some kind of superpower, a means by which an unremarkable young man can operate as a daring criminal savant. This is not what it is. He did not do anything in a 'fit' of Asperger's. He did not come round from an 'attack' of Autism Spectrum Disorder to find he was somehow in possession of thousands of pounds of stolen cash. These kinds of interpretations play into the idea that, inside someone with Asperger's, there is a 'normal' person. And that if it were possible to somehow isolate and neutralise the condition, as if it were a cancer, then there would be a normal person left behind, blinking in the light of their newly normal world.

Instead, Stephen's Asperger's is woven into him. He cannot be separated from it. It is not the only thing about him, but it informs everything about him: from how he has developed to how he sees the world to how he forms relationships. Dr Suleman says that in order to appreciate the depth to which Asperger's forms part of someone, it sometimes helps to regard it as a type of personality rather than a condition. 'Sometimes I say to patients it's like living in a foreign country where you have to live by that country's rules. You have to keep learning those rules while, for others, it just comes naturally,' he says. 'It's not something that "covers" them. It's just how they are.'

And while it's true that none of this would have happened if Stephen did not have Asperger's, it did not happen simply because he did. If that were the case, then everyone with Asperger Syndrome would be out there robbing banks or otherwise breaking the law in a ceaseless wave of crime. But they are not. Instead, the majority of them do their best to mitigate and manage the effects of their condition in order to live day-to-day lives in which their Asperger's does not dominate. 'I wish I knew earlier because then I could be in a better position to handle it and maybe seek support,' says Stephen. 'Just understanding helps. It really does.'

Only he never had the opportunity to do this. His condition did dominate. The consequences of which would, in concert with his own choices, change his life forever.

8

B y the time Stephen reached the age of fifteen it was clear that if he was going to receive an education and sit his GCSEs, it couldn't be at Sidmouth College. Things there had become untenable. His anxiety and social phobia meant that he could barely stand to be in a classroom with other children. He spent as much time hiding out in nearby fields and woodland as he did in lessons and, even when he was present in school, his behaviour – the rocking, the walking in circles, the mumbling and screaming and shaking – were judged to be increasingly disruptive to other pupils.

Eventually, it was arranged that he would attend a small specialist unit at Exeter College for children who were school-phobic, a diagnosable phenomenon also known as 'school refusal' and which disproportionately affects children with mental health issues or whose home environments are marked by dysfunction and upheaval. Divorce or bereavement, for example, can cause school refusal as a child internalises anxiety that something bad will happen to a parent while they are at school. That the same psychological process could take place in a child who has often returned home to find that his mother has been removed to a psychiatric ward does not require much explanation.

The classes at Exeter College were small, with only seven or eight pupils present, and often fewer given that on any day several would simply not show up. It was here that Stephen met John Paige, a cheerful and eloquent maths tutor then in his mid-forties. The pair very gradually formed a friendship which continued after Stephen completed his A levels at eighteen. Although to begin with, Paige was struck by just how awkward Stephen was around the other teenage children.

'He found it almost impossible to talk in any group setting, or to even look you in the eye,' he says, and described how Stephen would physically shrink back into his cheap plastic school chair during class discussions. It was not unusual for Stephen to just get up and leave the room if he found things too overwhelming. 'If things got too intense he would sort of physically cringe and just walk away very quickly. He found face-to-face contact with anyone almost impossible. He was immensely tense.'

Stephen and Paige tentatively bonded over a shared interest in space and time. 'We struck up a relationship because I was teaching maths and he hated maths, but he was completely caught up in cosmology and Stephen Hawking stuff, which I was also slightly caught up in. We used to talk about that and I'd have discussions or arguments with him about maths being relevant to the sort of science that he was interested in,' says Paige. 'He was writing quite a lot of stuff of his own about the Big Bang and the Big Bounce, and they were very sophisticated. I asked to see his stuff, so he would bring it along and we would talk about it and then we would do a bit of maths. It worked.'

While the other teenagers in the special educational unit may have been school-phobic, they did not struggle socially with one another. They chatted and joked, read magazines and listened to music and did all the normal things that teenagers do. All of this was foreign to Stephen. He did not understand the references they were making. He had no interest in football, no interest in soap operas, no interest in the charts. To be honest, his lack of fluency in basic pop culture remains impressive to this day. He thought 'The Beatles' was spelled 'The Beetles'. When pushed, he says he can recall quite liking the Spice Girls. 'I remember a few of their songs. But apart from that, I was an alien in that respect.'

The sheer volume of adolescent life was also a problem. The sound sensitivity he experienced as a result of his undiagnosed Asperger's meant he struggled to process the noise of people talking at him from different directions, the pace of it, the laughs and screeches and hoots all too much for him to process. He went to an outdoor rave but it was a disaster. 'I can only focus on one thing at a time, so when I have noise and then someone trying to talk to me at the same time? I can't handle it. I'm overwhelmed.'

He continued to yearn for friends and friendship without being quite sure how to go about achieving them. Bonding with his maths teacher over cosmology was one thing, but it wasn't the same as what all the other teenagers around him seemed to have with one another. It wasn't even that he was shunned or rejected by his peers. Often it was the opposite. 'The shunning was more from my side in many cases,' he says. He remembers once doing surprisingly well in a school sports day and other children then coming to congratulate him. But he would not engage. 'I was just suspicious. I thought they weren't genuine, I suppose.'

As far as John Paige could make out, Stephen's world consisted simply of his home and his parents. Which was a problem, because his relationship with Peter was by now verging on the toxic. 'He used to be pretty angry about his father. Very angry about his father,' says Paige. Stephen would say 'terrible'

things about him, although Paige says he remembered the force
of the grievances more than the specific nature of them. Peter
would shout at his wife and son. He would argue with Stephen
about his need for specific food on specific days and he would
argue with Jenny about Stephen, about what was wrong with
him and what should be done about it. 'As they got older I
think they became increasingly unhappy,' says Stephen. 'He
[Peter] ended up practically living in the shed at the end of
the garden.'

To the people involved in Stephen's care during this period,
it wasn't the on–off presence of his mother that was a concern
in itself so much as the knock-on effect this had on his family
dynamic. In 2000, when Stephen was fourteen, both his GP
and his social worker observed this in their notes. Dr Suleman's
psychiatric report includes summaries of these. For instance,
Dr Suleman described how in July of that year, John Perry, the
Community Psychiatric Nurse of Child Adolescent Mental
Health Services, Exeter, wrote to Stephen's GP, Dr Morris.

John Perry wrote that his outstanding difficulties appear
to be in his intense difficulty around peer relationships . . .
Stephen had very little social confidence with people of
his own age and struggled to communicate with them at
any level. John Perry also felt that there was a high level
of family conflict particularly between Stephen and his
father.

Earlier that year, in April, Dr Morris had already observed the
strain Stephen was under at home, believing that:

Stephen was at risk of psychological and emotional abuse
due to continuing uncertainty of psychiatric illness exhib-

ited by his mother and the constant stress and difficulty that it places on her relationship with her husband and the domestic arrangements.

Stephen occasionally wrote about this in his journals, although he dedicated far less space and time to it than he did to, well . . . space and time. Or to poetry. Or to phrases and expressions he would try to memorise and learn, or to righteous screeds about impending ecological disaster and man's insatiable greed. On 25 December 2001, aged fifteen, he wrote an entry in which he reflected proudly on the new Waterman fountain pen he received for Christmas – 'which I am writing with now' – and which he hoped to use for all his subsequent journal entries. He then described how that day he and his parents went for a walk, but that it was 'spoiled' by a large row with his father. 'I have calculated that each day I will argue with my dad at least three times. It will soon be 2002 – why does that sound bad? Perhaps it is the thought of another year of stress, worry and argument. Still, life goes on.'

Then, at the age of seventeen, something significant happened. A relative came to stay. Julian Jackley arrived in Sidmouth midway through Stephen's A-levels and lived in the room at the bottom of the garden for over a year. Julian was Peter's cousin. He was a skinny, shaven-headed man in what Stephen guessed to be his mid-forties. He came from London, preferred to dress in black and wore large sunglasses and a leather jacket. It was not made clear to Stephen why Julian was suddenly staying with them, and to this day he still does not know exactly what the circumstances were that led him to decamp from London in order to come and stay in a glorified shed with a family of people each with their own fairly severe psychiatric

concerns. All Stephen's father said was that Julian worked in
the building trade and that he was a 'black sheep of the family'.
One of Stephen's older relatives describes him as a 'blackguard',
though this doesn't particularly register with his nephew. 'I
didn't know the meaning of that term then.'

But what Stephen did conclude was that Julian was cool.
He smoked. He gambled. He spent whole days sat in a pub.
Where Stephen was naive and idealistic, Julian was cynical and
sarcastic. Stephen loved the outdoors, but Julian would cross
the road just to avoid being in the sunlight. He had a nihilistic
outlook on life. He listened to The Doors and read a lot of
Spike Milligan. Very quickly, Stephen found that he was in
thrall to him and came to view him as an older brother type
figure. Having spent his entire adolescence almost completely
insulated from socialisation and friendships, Stephen was
malleable. Open to suggestion.

'Whenever a strong character crossed my path and conveyed
a certain viewpoint, I was inclined to adopt it,' he says today.
'When you are younger, you're like that anyway. But perhaps
it was even stronger with me because of the limited social
interactions I'd had. It was like . . . this is it. This is how normal
people should think.'

Julian let Stephen tag along with him. He introduced his
teenage cousin into what Stephen called 'the drinking scene',
by which he simply meant that he took him to the pubs of
Sidmouth and Exeter. They drank beer and whiskey, a disin-
hibiting experience which Stephen enjoyed. Julian also took
drugs, something he made no attempt to hide. Stephen started
to notice that he always seemed 'happiest at night, ideally after
a few drinks and lines of cocaine'. This really stood out to him.
The fact that people, in general, often seem happiest after
drinking or taking cocaine didn't seem to occur to Stephen. It

was not long before he was smoking cannabis with Julian as
well as experimenting with cocaine, snorting it in pub toilets.
Almost immediately, Stephen observed something interesting.
The drug seemed to wash away his social awkwardness and
anxiety, allowing him to inhabit the noise and jostle of a busy
pub on a Friday night in a way that would have seemed impossible a few weeks earlier. 'It had the effect of numbing that side
of me, making me more confident and letting me do stuff I
otherwise would not be able to.'

Julian introduced Stephen to betting on horse races. And it
was that, more than anything, that the pair bonded over. For
Stephen, gambling became an obsession. He was shown that
money could be made from . . . nothing, a concept which
fascinated him as much as anything Stephen Hawking had
written about dark matter or black holes. In fact it quickly
superseded his more esoteric interests. 'I moved from being a
studious but socially awkward A-level student to reading the
racing pages of newspapers in classes, and skipping them in
favour of reading the form in dark pubs or bookies where I
could.'

It didn't help that, at least to begin with, Stephen did very
well as a gambler. It seemed he had a knack for picking winners
at long odds. His family's money problems were more acute
than ever, which meant Stephen never allowed himself to place
bets of more than £20, though he developed a 'formula' for
picking which horses to back, one that incorporated and
accounted for a host of variables: the horse's previous record,
the success rates of its jockey and trainer, its preferred ground
and distance, its handicaps and the odds. It wasn't an infallible
system, but Stephen won hundreds of pounds using it over the
course of a year or so. One accumulator won him £800, his
biggest single take, and he began to entertain the fantasy that

he might be able to simply gamble his way out of his family's poverty.

Stephen completed his A levels in physics, geography and classical civilisations, but all that time spent with Julian in the run-up to his exams meant his results were not what he had hoped for. Still, they were strong enough that he could have applied to university if he wanted to. But he didn't. Instead, he was set on getting a job. So, at the age of eighteen, he began the process of applying for dozens of different positions with different companies, ranging from energy suppliers to land-scape surveyors. Initially, few companies even acknowledged his application, although as the weeks passed he did get invited to some interviews. Stephen says that, on reflection, this may have been a result of the fact that he forgot to put his date of birth on his CV, which meant that potential employers who'd overlooked his lack of job history still didn't know they would be interviewing an eighteen-year-old until a skinny figure walked into their offices in a school shirt and borrowed necktie.

The majority of these interviews did not go well. Stephen's Asperger's made it very hard for him to connect with the people in front of him, or to adopt the appropriate tone when speaking to them. It was not that Stephen was always withdrawn, although he did have 'a lack of confidence and self-esteem', but rather that he could sometimes be too direct. He told one interviewer that they were 'ageist' for not wanting to employ him, which didn't go down very well. Rejection followed rejec-tion. He couldn't seem to make a good impression on anybody. The only piece of positive feedback he got was one interviewer telling him that he was obviously a very curious young man because of all the questions he kept interrupting them to ask. But beyond that? Nothing.

Stephen couldn't understand why this was, which only made it worse. He was intelligent and motivated and full of questions, but none of these employers seemed to want him. Months dragged by and Stephen felt increasingly embarrassed and upset that he couldn't find employment. What was so wrong with him that meant nobody wanted to at least give him a chance? 'I felt rejected. I felt discarded by society.'

He was also thinking, increasingly, about the opposite sex. He would have liked a girlfriend, although he never actually used that word, referring instead to his desire for a 'soulmate' when writing in his journals. He wrote ever more romantic poems in which nature is personified as a woman and Stephen takes the role of her chaste and faithful servant. At one point he noted down his 'life objectives', which consisted of three wishes:

- To set foot on another world
- To spend just one night and one day (preferably more!) with a soulmate, alone, and in total bliss
- To build a new society in another world or beneath the oceans

None of these objectives seemed particularly achievable to Stephen as he languished in Sidmouth. Winter came and the days were dark and wet, with cold winds rolling in off the sea. He drifted through the small town like a ghost, hiking alone in grey shadowy valleys and passing the time in dingy pubs studying the racing pages. But his winning system seemed to have stopped working and he was starting to lose more and more. The stockpile of cash that had kept him afloat since the previous year had dwindled to almost nothing. Julian had moved back to London as abruptly as he'd arrived, Ben Weaver had left for university in Wales and the stress and conflict of his home life was constant. To make things worse, his father had been diagnosed with prostate cancer, news which Stephen struggled to process the implications of, and so pushed to one side. He refused to sign up for unemployment benefits because he maintained that he'd get a job any day. But the call never came. Stephen stood on the high coastal path above the cliffs outside Sidmouth and looked out to sea, fantasising about being somewhere else. Somewhere far away. And never coming back.

One day, Stephen visited John Paige in Totnes. During a long walk through the countryside, he told his former teacher that it was quite possible that they would never see each other again. With a cautious but convivial curiosity, Paige asked him why. Stephen told him that he intended to travel around the world. His friend bit his tongue. The idea that Stephen – *Stephen* – a teenager who was barely able to make it to school on his own, might be capable of travelling around the world seemed beyond unlikely, never mind the fact he clearly could never afford to do it. Paige smiles at the memory. 'I remember thinking, *Fuck that. That's ridiculous.*'

Only, a few weeks later, Paige came down his stairs one morning to find that there was something bright and gaudy peeking from beneath the pile of post on his hallway floor. He bent down to investigate and found a postcard. From Stephen. And he was, somehow, in Bangkok.

Just when it seemed luck had completely deserted him, Stephen hit a winning streak with the horses. His betting system suddenly began to fire again, like an old car engine that finally purrs into life after the twentieth twist of the ignition. In early 2006, over the space of a week or so, he made several hundred pounds in profit. Then he did some research and discovered that, for £700, STA Travel – a travel agency catering for students and young people – offered round-the-world plane tickets, with stop-offs in various places across south-east Asia, Australia, New Zealand and the USA. The prospect of such a journey was daunting, but after an entire childhood spent looking at maps and globes, fantasising about smelling mint in the forest and lying in the desert looking at the stars, he knew that he had to go: to do whatever he could to put half the world between himself and Manstone Avenue. He told John Paige that they might never see each other again because he wanted to believe it, and that his dream of running away and never coming back might come true.

His parents did their best to discourage him, particularly Peter, who didn't like the idea of his son being 'out of reach'. In the end though, it was Peter who gave his son the last few hundred pounds needed to make the trip practicable. Which was how, in January 2006, Stephen found himself walking through Bangkok with a large backpack and an expression of tentative happiness on his face. It was like nothing he could have imagined: the skyscrapers, ornate golden temples and wooden buildings built cheek-by-jowl. The Buddhist monks in their bright robes paying early morning visits to shrines. The noise and organic chaos of the traffic and tuk-tuks. Street vendors hawking everything from tropical fruit to dried snakes to bright and shiny trinkets while, overhead, monkeys skipped from tree to tree, sometimes pausing to peer down at him with blank, appraising eyes before vanishing with a jump.

None of this overwhelmed him in the way he had feared it might. Instead, he felt energised and alive. In Sidmouth, he was isolated, unwanted, invisible. In Thailand, strangers smiled at him and said 'hello' as they passed. He didn't always know how to respond but there was no pang of awkwardness. He did not find himself bowing his head or averting his eyes. Staying in backpacking hostels, he travelled along Thailand's coast, heading east towards Cambodia. He passed through resort towns, teeming with traffic and tourists, and spent nights on empty beaches off the beaten track. More than anything, it was the sense of freedom that made him feel giddy. He was not in his bedroom peering at a map and imagining all of this, or fantasising about it in his diaries. He was here, in real life, diving in tropical seas and exploring ruined temples in the jungle. The sadness, stress and fear of the last ten years hadn't left him; he had left it. Far away. On the other side of the world. He had escaped.

One night in Thailand, Stephen was sitting by himself in the quiet bar of a hostel. He was writing in his journal when he heard a voice and looked up. Standing by his table was a Thai woman in her early twenties. She introduced herself to Stephen as Chailail and, in perfect English, explained that she worked behind the bar and thought that she would come over and say hello. She smiled. Stephen blinked. There was a pause before he put down his pen and quietly introduced himself. Chailail sat down beside him and started to ask questions about where he had been in Thailand, what he had made of her country, where he planned to go next. And Stephen started to tell her.

Stephen was naive, but he was not stupid. He had already seen enough of Thailand to know that, in some places, Western men automatically attracted attention from local women. 'You could be a hunchback dwarf with horns coming out of your head and still have approaches.' But this did not feel like that. She was not some teenage girl just coming up to him with a fixed smile while softly repeating the word 'hello'. Instead, she was a university student from Bangkok. She seemed smart, curious and genuinely interested to know where he had come from and where he was going. Stephen was attracted to her and she was attracted to him, a slim, reserved young man who was spending the evening writing in a journal rather than getting shitfaced and trying to round up girls for skinny-dipping or beach parties.

Ever since he started to experience an interest in the opposite sex, Stephen's problem had been that talking to girls he liked was even harder than talking in front of his class.

'I think a lot of times girls tried to form a relationship with me or just be friendly,' he remembers. 'But I would just automatically feel quite awkward and shy and then they would assume I wasn't interested because I wasn't maintaining eye contact and I wasn't smiling back.'

But tonight, in the quiet backpackers' bar, Stephen did maintain eye contact. Or at least, he tried his very best to, harder than he'd ever done before. They spent the rest of the night talking. They arranged to meet the following day. And the next day. And then the day after that. Chailail taught Stephen some Thai words and he repeated them so solemnly and precisely that she laughed and he didn't understand why. At some point, they kissed. And for a while after that, they barely stopped kissing. Stephen lost his virginity. He and Chailail arranged to go travelling together, and for the next few weeks the two of them explored eastern Thailand, rattling around the lush countryside in old buses and cramming against one another in the squeaky single beds of hostels. Stephen asked lots and lots of questions. They visited temples and shrines and he began to develop an interest in Buddhism, buying cheap paperbacks on the subject as they moved from site to site and town to town.

He absorbed new words and concepts: dharma, karma, the idea that pain and suffering stems from mankind's desire to crave and cling to impermanent things, be they wealth or love or sensory pleasure. He thought about Sidmouth and the endless days spent in pubs and bookies with Julian, the bullet-point lists of wishes he wrote down for himself, the yearning to have his mother simply stay his mother and not keep turning into a stranger, cold, distant and frightening. He turned his past over and over in his mind. Beside him, Chailail snuffled and slept.

These weeks were a learning curve for Stephen, who had never been in any kind of romantic relationship before. Sometimes he upset Chailail with his directness. Sometimes he made what he felt were innocent observations about Thailand or Thai people which made her angry or, even worse, go completely silent for hours at a time. 'Sometimes she would not talk to me and I would say, "Why are you being like that?" I couldn't understand. I just said whatever was on my mind, really. Even now I sometimes wonder whether I can read people in the same way most people would,' he says, discussing how his Asperger's appeared to jam his ability to pick up on nuance, inference and subtle, non-verbal social cues. He says that he'd probably learned these things in the same way a computer would, by adhering to pre-learned patterns rather than by intuition. 'I've got it wrong many times. Many, many times.'

In the case of Chailail, how much of this was because of Stephen's Asperger's, and how much this was because Stephen was a nineteen-year-old and in his first relationship is hard to gauge. As they explored the beaches, jungles and villages of south-eastern Thailand it became clear that Chailail was not the 'soulmate' Stephen had dreamed of meeting for so long. After two or three weeks of travel, she had to return to Bangkok and Stephen wanted to press further east, into Cambodia. They said goodbye and agreed to stay in touch, possibly even meet up later in Stephen's travels. They swapped emails for weeks afterwards, and Stephen even went through periods of missing her as he travelled alone. But despite some half-baked plans to eventually reunite, they never saw each other again.

Stephen crossed into Cambodia, riding buses eastwards, towards the city of Siem Reap and the sprawling twelfth-century temple complex of Angkor Wat. Passing through towns and villages, often stopping off for food or to spend the night at a small hotel or hostel, a sensation began to grow inside Stephen, a tension in his head and chest that made him feel flushed and uncomfortable. These places and these people were poor. Incredibly poor. Unlike anything Stephen had ever seen or imagined. Many of the houses appeared beyond flimsy, made of nothing but rusty sheets of corrugated metal and bamboo. There were skinny children, shoeless and dirty. Whole families doing nothing but sitting on the roadsides in silence, looking weary and resigned, seemingly waiting patiently for something, though he couldn't imagine what.

He began to fixate on the poverty he saw in Cambodia. Thailand had been exciting: a release, an adventure. But seeing the conditions these people lived in made him feel impotent and ashamed. The other Western backpackers and tourists he met all admitted, with a sigh, that when travelling through parts of Asia it takes a while to get used to the poverty. Stephen, however, couldn't get used to the poverty. He didn't understand how anybody could. He had always thought that he and his family were poor and disadvantaged, but he started to under-stand what a naive and self-pitying outlook that was.

Whenever he had the opportunity, he used hostel computers to search the internet and find out about where he was. Around 40 per cent of Cambodia's rural population live below the poverty line. Around a quarter of all children are engaged in child labour. Thanks to the legacy of civil war, it is a country with millions of unexploded landmines littering the country-side. Because of these mines, there are more amputees per capita than anywhere else in the world and a disproportionate number of these are children. Sometimes when his bus passed through a village, Stephen glimpsed a child playing by the roadside with other children, and he just had time to register that something was wrong with the picture and that one of those skinny kids should have had four limbs but didn't. He looked around at his fellow passengers and saw a British gap year student down the aisle dozing contentedly, or singing along to a pop song while sharing iPod headphones with a friend, and he balled his fists and drove his knuckles into his forehead.

In big towns and cities, it was even worse. The contrast between luxury and poverty was as vivid as it was raw. In Siem Reap, the gateway to Angkor Wat, there were a dozen luxury hotels aimed at high-end travellers. Staying at the Amansara resort, Stephen learned, cost $650 a night. Some hotels charged over $1,500 for their most opulent suites. Visitors paid $1,375 per hour for helicopter tours of the Angkor Wat complex. One or two streets away from these oases, Stephen could see Cambodians sifting through piles of rubbish, or begging on the streets, blind or limbless. Initially, he wasn't sure what to do – he felt exactly how he had felt when he passed that home-less man in Exeter – but this time he didn't put his head down and ignore the outstretched hands. He went out and gave away some of his cash to street children and beggars. He explored the possibility of volunteering for a landmine NGO, but his own meagre supply of travel money was almost spent and he realised that there was no way he'd be able to afford to work in Cambodia for free for a year.

He drifted back towards Bangkok in order to catch a scheduled flight to Singapore which would then take him onto Australia. As he travelled he was sullen, his mind replaying what he had seen over and over. His planned route back took him through the Khao Yai National Park, a lush landscape of forests, lakes, waterfalls and hiking paths. He stayed in a comfortable log cabin and, for a day or so, the sheer beauty of his surroundings soothed him. One afternoon he hired a mountain bike and explored some of the trails. The bicycle chain snapped, so he dismounted and continued to explore the jungle on foot, skirting great fallen trees and climbing over boulders. At one point, he stumbled across a small hamlet and, just like that, the sight of poverty snapped him out of the reverie of his hike. The barefoot children. The chickens strutting the dirty street. The rundown, ramshackle homes. Hot anger and embarrassment flushed through him and he turned away, feeling like a gormless voyeur.

He retreated back into the jungle, walking quickly, breathing hard. After an hour or so, he began to realise that he had no idea where he was. Whatever trail he had taken into the jungle had just . . . vanished. The map he had with him was no help at all. The sun was beginning to set, the temperature was starting to drop and black clouds of mosquitoes were hounding him. Trying his best to remain calm, he attempted to retrace his steps back to the village, but couldn't. He shouted for help but as the echoes died, the only response was the low buzz and chatter of the jungle. Eventually, he accepted the inevitable. He was completely lost and would have to spend the night in the jungle darkness. On a large, flat rock beside a small stream, Stephen curled up in his shorts and t-shirt and tried to sleep. He couldn't. The sound of creatures moving around him, close but unseen, kept him awake. So did the cold. So did the sensation of being utterly alone in nature, of being the only human being for miles in any direction. He looked at the stars and it only reaffirmed to him just how remarkable it is that we exist at all. But it also made him afraid. In twenty years' time, will this jungle even be here? Just a morning's drive away was the concrete and traffic of Bangkok. 'It made me realise how much the world is changing,' says Stephen. 'There are not many places left like that, and it just gave me a feeling of, *what is humanity doing to the world?*'

Dawn came and, shivering and exhausted, he managed to find his way back to a path. He followed it and arrived back at the village he had stumbled across the previous day. Despite his awkwardness and embarrassment, some villagers approached him. They could see he was cold and tired. They invited him to sit. They brought him food and bowls of rice. Some handed him small gifts. One man had a cheap mobile phone and called the park ranger's office to explain that they had a lost Western man in their village who needed collecting. A jeep arrived soon after and took Stephen back to his comfortable lodge.

The night in the jungle had changed him. He had ordered his thoughts and emerged with a clear sense of conviction. Everything he had ever suspected about the unjustness of the world and the inbuilt inequality of modern, global society was true. He had seen it with his own eyes. He thought of the children scrabbling through rubbish piles for something to eat and then considered the fact that the largest component part of America's gross domestic waste is food. Food! In fact, America burned so much uneaten food it would, in 2006, account for almost 15 per cent of the country's carbon emissions. Man's greed means that Earth does not just face ecological catastrophe, but humanitarian disaster under a system that forces more than half the world's population to survive in poverty while the rest live in a state of complacent, selfish plenty. The backpacking

trustafarians he met who railed against capitalism despite travelling with their parents' platinum cards and the rich couples
who bragged about haggling-down local traders enraged him.
But they were only doing in microcosm what their societies
have been doing to the developing world for decades.

As he sat on his flight to Singapore and then onto Perth, he
churned this over and over in his mind. He wanted to make a
difference. But the problem was money. A whole system of
international finance, banking and mutual corporate interests
locked this all in place. What could he do when faced with
that? He stared out the window of the plane and thought.

At almost exactly the same time that Stephen was alone and
shivering in the jungle, something happened in America that
would affect the lives of billions. The Federal Reserve raised
interest rates to 5.35 per cent. This represented the latest in a
series of hikes that had seen interest rates rise by 4 per cent
over two years in an ongoing attempt to slow inflation. This
final rise caused an existing slowdown in the US housing market
to pass a point of no return. People who could only just afford
their mortgages when interest rates were low now started to
default on their debt. And the millions of Americans who had
been sold subprime mortgages – high-interest loans sold by
banks to those with low incomes and little or no credit history
– started defaulting in droves.

This had not been the banks' plan. The logic of making
subprime loans available in the first place had been straightforward. By making home-ownership more accessible, banks had
hoped that they would increase demand for housing. This increase
in demand would, in turn, cause house prices to rise. As prices
rose, it would grant the lending banks greater security because
the value of the real estate on their books would rise accordingly.

For a while this is exactly what happened, with banks encouraging millions of low-income Americans to stump up for a subprime loan in exchange for their own little slice of the property market. But when interest rates began to rise, the cost of repaying these loans became impossible for many and the defaults began. Houses poured back onto the American market, increasing supply and driving down price. The US housing bubble, inflated over and over again by banks, finally popped.

This was a tragedy for the families who were left homeless and ruined, but also had huge consequences for the global financial system. Banks buy and sell debts. There is an international, intra-bank debt market worth trillions of dollars. In a process known as 'securitisation', the bank who sold you your mortgage may decide to take a tiny slice of your debt and combine it with many other slices of many other customers' debts until they have a big bundle of these fine slivers. They can then sell these bundles on to other banks as a complex financial product called a Collateralised Debt Obligation. Selling CDOs in exchange for cash allows the bank to clear these debts from their books and raise capital. Buying CDOs allows patient investors to create a huge, slow-burning return as the debts are repaid with interest.

And because CDOs are made from so many different tiny slices of debt, they felt safe. This was their primary appeal. Banks could slip in slices of risky subprime debt amongst slices of more stable debt without devaluing the overall product. It's like being attached to a hot air balloon by a thousand small strings. If one or two or even a hundred people default on their debts, thus snapping their strings, it's not a huge deal. You are still held safely by the perfectly healthy debts of the thousands of other people who are still able to service their mortgages. Those strings remain strong.

Banks and their shareholders, however, do not like taking risks. Or at least, they don't like facing the consequences of it. Which is why CDOs and similar products are a thing. You encourage ordinary people to put themselves at risk by taking on a debt to you and, in the case of subprime mortgages, a debt which you know perfectly well may ultimately exceed the real value of the home they are buying. And while this ordinary person may have their life ruined when they cannot repay this debt, you, the bank, have inoculated yourself against any such outcome. Thanks to CDOs, the actual consequence of a few customers going broke is diluted to almost nothing. It is expected and it is allowed for. It's clever. Individuals take the risk, the banks reap the rewards. They keep floating serenely upwards, on warm swells of interest, far removed from the occasional repossession or bankruptcy back on earth.

But as more and more Americans began to default on their debts, more and more strings began to snap and these CDOs began to look less and less safe. As a result, they lost their value. Not just because they were no longer the sure bet they once were, but because even calculating their value became very difficult. How much of each CDO was rotten, made up of bad, subprime mortgage debt? Because they were such complex products, it was very difficult to know.

This meant that as 2006 continued, banks found themselves increasingly unwilling to lend money to other banks. Why? Because if you're a bank and you lend to another bank whose books are balanced with ever more worthless CDOs, how can you be confident they are going to be able to repay you? Suspicion and doubt spread from New York to London to Singapore. Banks began to nervously draw whatever liquid cash they held close to their bosoms. The money market – literally, the international market for the buying and selling of money

– began to stall. These financial institutions were now feeling the same anxiety about money that ordinary people around the world feel every single day. They felt nervous and exposed and uncertain. Having set this chain of events in motion, though, they did nothing to ease it. In fact, they simply made it worse. By refusing to issue credit to businesses, the spectre of job losses loomed. Bankruptcies. Repossessions. Recession.

There was a crunch coming. A global economic crisis that would define politics, culture and society for a generation. As the full scale and scope of what was unfolding became apparent, popular anger towards banks and those who willingly enabled them intensified. The idea of the 'One Per Cent' and callous, reckless elites would become widespread and accepted across the political spectrum. Countless numbers of people watched the news or looked at the world around them and demanded that these institutions be punished. That somebody *do* something. And before long, somebody did.

9

S tephen landed in Perth in February 2006 and joined the tens of thousands of young Westerners moving around the Australian backpacking trail. As he travelled, he paid for his accommodation, bus tickets and occasional excursions by taking on a succession of different cash-in-hand jobs. He worked as a fruit picker. He worked packing melons on a farm ('surprisingly heavy', he noted in his diary). He worked as a cleaner and receptionist at some of the hostels he stayed in. He worked as a labourer on building sites. In the evenings, he often wrote down very clear to-do lists for the following day. He told himself that, tomorrow, he would first shower and have breakfast. Then he would buy razors and acne cream. Then he would take some rolls of camera film to be developed. Then he would take a bus to a nearby beach. Then he would return to the hostel. Then he would have dinner. And so on.

He stayed in hostels, keeping to himself amidst the noise and chatter of the cramped dormitories. If greeted, he nodded and perhaps said 'hello', instinctively moving his eyes down and away from whoever happened to be addressing him. Casual attempts to include him in games of cards or the communal watching of DVDs on a laptop sent a cold bolt of panic from his stomach to his chest. He would mutter an excuse and exit the room, leaving everyone with nothing more than the sound of his flip-flops quickly slapping down the corridor and away.

As well as his to-do lists, he filled page after page of his diary with reviews of each day. Sometimes he rhapsodised about sights he had seen, sometimes he complained about life as a backpacker ('Last night got under three hours' sleep due to the snoring of an idiot'). He wrote about how he felt lonely and out of place, but also about how he could only get better at navigating the world by exposing himself to it. As the weeks passed, he developed a private mantra he fell back on whenever things seemed too overwhelming.

Through independence comes skills
Through adversity comes strength
Through skills and strength
                    We can create a better world

Reading through his diaries from this period, what strikes you more than anything is the wide-eyed earnestness that runs through every page. Disembarking a ferry after a trip to an island, an Australian couple offered him a lift back to town in their car. 'I've never met such genuine consideration and kindness,' he wrote later that night. 'I _must_ send them a postcard.'

Later, in Sydney, he paid for a cheap seat to see a performance at the Opera House:

Tonight I listened to Bach's (pronounced 'Barks') composition of 'Passion'. So mighty and deep. It instilled peace and calm thoughts . . . when I got back to the hostel, a German girl clearly wanted to go for a date. But I'm useless in social situations! Plus my appearance wasn't excellent.

The poverty he saw in Cambodia and parts of Thailand still ran on a loop in his head every day, and his interest in Buddhism intensified. He became fixated with a particular quote attributed to the Buddha – 'It is your mind that creates this world' – so much so that he wrote it on the front of one of his travel diaries. His notebooks are scattered with poems to the sea, to nature, to mountains and forests. And while Stephen's mind still grappled with the old, comforting and unsolvable questions of space–time, relativity and astrophysics, new ideas and possibilities were starting to form. The more time he spent in the world, the less time he spent asking abstract questions about the universe and the more he asked questions about the individual. He started looking inwards rather than outwards. Having spent years striving to find some kind of objective truth about existence – a Theory of Everything – it began to dawn on him that 'truth' may in fact be subjective.

I cannot deny that my philosophy has become more anthropocentric . . . and questions such as 'who am I?' and 'what am I?' concern me. I am undergoing, or have already undergone, a schema change. The mind has a greater part in 'creating the world' than I previously thought.

Everything is an interpretation.

Every psychological anticipation, expectation and prediction is based upon past experiences.

Should one say there exists a world that shapes us – our bodies and minds, while shaping everything else? Or should we say that our mind shapes the world, that every form is a projection of our thoughts?

I think it is neither of these . . . that we are the world; the world is us. Reality. That when reality changes, we change. If our minds change, so does reality.

In March 2006, Stephen arrived in the small village of Goshen on Tasmania. He had signed up for a popular programme amongst backpackers known as WWOOF, which stands for Willing Workers on Organic Farms. The idea was simple. In exchange for half a day's work, travellers could enjoy free room and board on participating farms. He stayed on a small homestead owned by Billie Astley, a fifty-year-old woman with bright green eyes, shoulder-length auburn hair and a kind, gently weathered face. Billie lived alone – her daughters were adults – and as well as operating her smallholding, she worked as a potter and ceramic artist. She often took on WWOOF participants – 'woofers' – to help tend to her vegetables, maintain the farm's boundaries and generally do odd jobs. She liked having young people around and even had a comfortable log cabin on her grounds where they could stay. Almost immediately, though, she began to sense that Stephen was different from the usual carefree young backpackers who had passed through her life.

'He was a lost soul,' she says. 'It seemed like he was looking for something. Most woofers are just on holiday and loving life. But with Stephen, he was definitely looking for something. Looking for more. But he didn't seem to know what.'

Stephen was delighted with his new surroundings. Everywhere he looked were hills and green forests. The sea was only a short hitch-hike away. He had the cabin to himself and fell asleep every night to the sound of a stream babbling nearby. Aside from Billie and a goat named Carlos, he was alone. Billie cooked him dinner. Talked to him. Asked him questions about his life. Terse and uncommunicative to begin with, something about Billie, her comfortable, homely farmhouse and the remote, natural setting made Stephen relax. He discovered that she travelled regularly to Indonesia, that she was horrified by the poverty there and shared his views about capitalism and global income inequality.

She didn't reprimand Stephen when she discovered him smoking marijuana outside the cabin. Very quickly, she became something like an inverse Julian: his opposite in every way in terms of personality and outlook and yet, to Stephen, just as important a guiding figure. 'Few people I have met have been as kind and genuine as Billie,' he reflected in his diary one evening. 'She is someone who could teach me much.'

A few days after he arrived in Goshen, Stephen turned twenty. To celebrate, Billie made him a big birthday roast dinner. He felt as though his whole body was unwinding itself. Anxieties melted away. 'I have overcome my fear of bees,' he wrote proudly. 'My curiosity and adventurous spirit triumphed.' He threw himself into working around her property, finding jobs for himself, physical jobs that often involved cutting, painting, digging and sawing.

'I can't remember if he told me exactly what it was with his mother, but I knew that there were things happening between them and that he didn't feel close to her,' Billie says. 'I didn't delve into it or anything. But I felt that he took me on as a kind of mother figure. Somebody who he saw as a nurturer, who was looking after him. Even after a few days I had friends who would be round at my house and see how he would act and they'd say, "He thinks you're his mum." A couple of them were a little bit concerned, saying that he was going to find it difficult moving on.'

After a couple of weeks of Stephen staying there, however, Billie started to notice something strange. Her farmstead had always been a popular stop-off point for woofers. But for some time, there had been no enquiries. 'I started wondering, why aren't I getting any phone calls?' she says, frowning. Then one day, she returned from some errands and overheard Stephen speaking on her landline. 'I caught him! He was on the phone to other woofers telling them that there was no space. "No, sorry, there's no room, we can't take any other woofers on."'

She confronted him. 'Steve, how long have you been doing this for? And he said, "Oh, I've only told a couple of people that you've only got room for me. That no one else can stay here."'

Billie calmly explained to Stephen that she wanted other people to come and stay with her. That she enjoyed it. He tried to convince her that she really didn't need anybody else. That he could do all the work that needed doing. If other people started arriving, he explained with increasing desperation, then everything would be ruined. Billie stood firm. And when Stephen learned that he would soon be expected to share the cabin with Nina and Lena, a pair of teenage German girls, he was distraught. After the blonde interlopers arrived, he wrote:

No more conversations of laughter and free thought, or partnership and friendship. I am no longer free here, my privacy and sense of open peace is somehow crushed by the presence of other human beings. Yesterday she brought her two German friends, showering the place with convention and falsity.

The arrival of others finally prompted Stephen to move on, though his admiration for Billie was undimmed and they parted on good terms.

After leaving Tasmania, Stephen managed to find temporary work selling green energy door to door. 'Can I become a door-to-door salesman?' he asked his journal. 'Hahahaha! Surely not.'

He passed an interview and completed a training day. He
was given a polo shirt and an ID badge and joined a team of
other young backpackers who were transported by minibus
around New South Wales, knocking on doors and trying to
convince people to switch their energy tariff. He filled his diary
with notes on how to present himself. Seventy per cent of a
successful sale, he scribbled, is on account of 'Body Language'.
This included 'slouching, drawled speech, crossed arms,
fidgeting'. During the initial introduction and greeting it was
important to ensure 'good eye contact, straight back, smiling
every time'. Standing side by side with the customer demonstrated that you were on the 'same team' rather than having a
'confrontation'. Tone of voice, he wrote, accounts for 23 per
cent of a successful sale ('enthusiasm, louder, energetic') while
the content of the pitch itself accounts for only 7 per cent.

The other salespeople on the team were boisterous ('crude
and bloody obscene!') but they took Stephen under their wing.
The team spent the evenings together in pubs or smoking
marijuana in local parks, and Stephen always came along.

After a few weeks of knocking on doors, he had enough
money to push on. He spent two months in New Zealand,
travelling, working, picking fruit and spending the evenings
on his own, writing increasingly complex notes about dark
matter, string theory, antiparticles and supersymmetry. Against
a backdrop of white mountain peaks, rolling forests and wide,
sandy bays, Stephen fixated on the nature of reality, prising and
pulling at the fabric of it in his mind. At the same time, in
May, he read about how a mobile telephone number – '666
6666' – had been bought at auction for £1.5 million. The
wanton, unashamed extravagance of this seemed specifically
conceived to goad him. One and a half million pounds! On a
phone number! Think of the good that money could do if

distributed to places that needed it! Think of the good it could do in Billie's hands. Think of the good it could do in his.

He wrote about seeing a homeless man and buying him a bag of crisps and a drink. He wrote about how hard it is picking fruit all day, and how little you get paid in return, and thought of the millions of people around the world doing exactly the same as him only without the luxury of choice. He thought about the beauty of nature, but this only made him anxious, afraid for the future of the planet, his mind running over the same existential fears that had dogged him ever since he first placed his eye to a telescope and saw the Shoemaker–Levy comet impact Jupiter. It was winter in New Zealand, and he was cold. On 22 July 2006, he was resting on the shores of Lake Taupo, which sits in a huge crater left by an ancient volcanic eruption. He shivered while writing in his journal.

> It is the strokes of the keyboard which dictate society: from the regulation of power to the electronic transferring of funds. Money is the idol of modern society: the god that constricts each person and the prison which prevents human advancement . . . Humans constantly strive against one another and furthermore domineer over the rest of nature. A species of such power will ultimately use it unwisely, to the extent that it destroys itself.

Four days later, Stephen made another entry. He wrote about missing the height of the English summer and his work as a fruit picker. 'I am contemplating the fruition of unconventional financial gain,' he then writes. 'That is, a project that would see me "stealing". Some bank or financial institution would do.'

I only have this entry in the form of an A4 photocopied sheet. It has the faded look of a copy of a copy of a copy. In the top right corner, a small official stamp shows that it is 'EXHIBIT No. 242'. It is police evidence, used in Stephen's eventual trial. It is the moment when he first allowed himself to entertain the possibility of 'stealing' from banks or other financial institutions. It does not mean that from this moment on his crimes were inevitable. But the seed was now planted. It is your mind that creates the world. And Stephen's mind was now starting to create his own.

10

Stephen stood in a silent, sun-dappled meadow. The air was warm and still, heavy with the scent of lavender and hot dry grass. In one hand he held a long, curved bow. In the other, he held an arrow fletched with white feathers. Breathing slowly, he planted his feet, notched the arrow and then raised the bow to eye level, drawing the string back to his cheek. Holding the pose, his chest rose and fell as his arms began to quiver gently under the mounting strain. Then, with an exhale, he let go. It took a little over one second for the arrow to fly 200 feet and bury itself into a butt at the far end of the meadow with a gentle thud. Stephen lowered the bow and squinted to see how close to the bullseye he had struck. He was not far off. To his right, he heard a pair of hands clapping softly. Stephen turned to the old Japanese man who had been supervising him. He was in his late eighties, wore simple brown robes and large, square glasses. He smiled encouragingly at Stephen, who responded with a small bow of respect. Doing his best to hide a satisfied grin, Stephen reached for another arrow. He took aim. And let fly.

It was the summer of 2007, and Stephen was in central France, living on a rural Buddhist retreat outside the town of Limoges. He was working there as a gardener and groundsman while studying meditation, yoga and receiving instruction in the ancient art of kyūdō archery. Almost ten months had passed since he'd returned from his travels on the other side of the world. Adjusting to life back in the small house in the small coastal town of his childhood had proved incredibly difficult. He had experienced freedom for the first time in his life but then, suddenly, he was back at Manstone Avenue, the site of so much of his childhood trauma, trapped between the looming figure of his father and the distant, distracted figure of his mother. After years of psychotic episodes and long-term stays in institutions, Jenny Jackley's doctors had finally found the right combination of drugs to keep her relatively stable but, at least from Stephen's perspective, painfully vacant.

Peter Jackley seemed particularly distressed that the young man who had returned to the family home seemed so different from the one who had left it. His prostate cancer had continued to spread and there were signs, from early 2007 onwards, that he was beginning to suffer from dementia. His daughter, Lisa, describes how he had called her up one day after Stephen had returned from his travels.

'My dad thought Stephen had been kidnapped while he was away and that someone different had come back,' she explains. 'He used to say that he was worried it wasn't the real Stephen. He was worried that he had been kidnapped and that it was to do with Nazi gold or something.'

Stephen had not been kidnapped. He had just changed. His travels had made him surer of himself and less afraid of the world. Socialisation was still incredibly difficult, but he knew it was possible. He did not bang his head or pull his hair or simply flee when faced with it. He still possessed the same sense of injustice about the world, about capitalism and global income distribution, only now it was underpinned by first-hand experience. And he had returned to Sidmouth with something more empowering than anything he could ever have imagined. He possessed in his mind a possible solution. A course of action he could take. The final weeks of his travels, which saw him fly from Fiji to Los Angeles, only cemented the possibility of robbing banks for some greater good. He wrote in his journal about the homeless buskers and beggars of Santa Barbara, viewing them as the unforgivable collateral damage of a system focused exclusively on the pursuit of profit. 'Money, money, money,' he wrote from LA. 'Here it is the ruling god. The rich grow richer, the poor poorer. There is no equality of justice or opportunity, since money can effectively buy both.'

On his flight from LA to London, he wrote 'Careers' at the top of a page. He began by brainstorming some options under the subhead 'unconventional'. The first was simply 'bank robber ("hustler")' with the further possibilities of 'counterfeit money producer', 'diamond smuggler (Amsterdam–London)' and 'drug dealer'. He also included 'property developer (mortgage low, develop, sell high)', 'stock exchange/share dealer' and 'currency buyer/seller'. Then he moved onto more genteel options: travel journalist, writer ('physics – not philosophy'), writer ('fiction/poetry'), independent retailer ('crafts, books, fossils'), independent tour operator, apprentice builder, landscape gardener, 'UN (military) personnel', astronaut, marine biologist and, finally, geographer.

Arriving back in Sidmouth, though, his priority was to secure some work. And just as before, he struggled. Interviews led nowhere. Rejections mounted. The autumn of 2006 turned to winter and Stephen slipped back into the same pattern of daytime drinking, petty gambling and isolation. He drifted into depression, signed on for £45-worth of jobseeker's allowance a week, and found his mind returning again and again to the possibility of bank robbery as the catalyst to a better world.

He began to think seriously about how this would work. Because to Stephen, it was not a fantasy. If he committed to it, he could make it real. As the Buddha said, it is your mind that creates the world. 'I thought, right, I can make a difference. I had this concept that if something was first an idea and then an action, then it can happen.'

He began to conceptualise a process. He would steal enough money to set up a 'legitimate enterprise' which he gradually came to refer to simply as 'the Organisation'. Once the Organisation was up and running with stolen seed money, he would grow it into a kind of umbrella NGO, funding hospitals, schools and scholarship programmes for the global poor. It would be a banner to which like-minded people across the planet could rally. Its goal was nothing less than the eradication of world poverty and the prevention of ecological catastrophe. Stephen's heart beat fast with thoughts of the different possibilities.

'There were clear steps in my mind,' he says, trying to explain that while this might all sound vague and fanciful to us, it absolutely wasn't to him. 'It wasn't some illusory, cloudy thing. It was something I would create. I just needed the means to do so. In hindsight, I had this target of £100,000 in my mind. Once I hit that point, I would stop. No more robberies. Because the money would then be going into something sustainable that wouldn't overtly break the law.'

By February 2007, with this possibility still dominating his thoughts, Stephen left Sidmouth for a second time. He says that another lucky win on the horses helped him stump up enough money for a cheap trip abroad. Escaping the 'black hole' of Manstone Avenue, he moved through Europe, travelling from Amsterdam to Paris, then down through France. It was here he discovered the Dechen Chöling meditation centre near Limoges. Comprised of a small eighteenth-century chateau plus outbuildings set in rolling green countryside, it attracts visitors from around the world seeking to receive instruction in Shambhala Buddhism, a modern, secular form of Buddhist teaching. Central to Shambhala is the belief that individuals can, through their own actions, help to establish an enlightened society. The mythical hidden kingdom of Shambhala was, in Hindu and Tibetan Buddhist traditions, a place of dignity, equality and compassion. Stephen first stayed at Dechen Chöling as a paying guest before continuing his travels south, into Spain and Morocco. When his money ran out, he returned to the centre, finding work as a member of the community's staff, tending to the grounds, working in the kitchens and doing odd jobs in exchange for room and board.

As the spring of 2007 moved to summer, the Dechen Chöling staff moved from their rooms in the main chateau and into large tents, in order to make room for the hundreds of guests who would soon flock to the community. Stephen found himself sharing a tent with an American named Ralph Williams. Bald, cheerful and with one silver earring, Williams had worked as an exhibition and theatre designer before 'burning out' in 2005 and starting a semi-itinerant life of travel and work at different meditation centres. He remembers Stephen very well.

'He was young and he was socially awkward, but for me not really alarmingly so. Just a little odd,' he says. 'My sense was that the community in general didn't quite know what to make of him. There was always a little bit of uncertainty. I could see in him that he was a really sensitive guy who just wanted to fit in, but who didn't really know how to communicate in a relaxed way with others. He was still trying to figure out the rules for life, and how one is meant to behave and connect.'

Lisa Steckler worked at Dechen Chöling as part of the

human resources team. A chatty Canadian not much older than Stephen, Steckler admits that she has a tendency to ask people a lot of questions, which was something she says Stephen never responded well to. 'The quality I remember which made him distinct is that when I would ask probing questions or just try and check in, there were times when he would just look at me. I would be waiting for him to answer and he wouldn't,' she says. This confused Steckler because, in her experience, the people who came to the centre came in order to unburden themselves, to share their feelings and experiences. But Stephen seemed to be the opposite.

Steckler says that there was also something else. When he arrived, he did not present himself as 'Stephen Jackley'. Instead he told everyone that his name was 'Steve Mason'. Stephen seems to have experimented with alternate surnames since adolescence. In one of his early journals, he wrote the name 'Steve Mason' several times, trying it out, the same way that you or I might repeat a phrase in our heads. He says that in his opinion there wasn't anything particularly unusual about this. 'It sounded better than "Jackley". And sometimes when I had to say my name to people, I had to keep repeating it and spelling it out, which I found a bit annoying.' Mason, he continues, is a surname from his mother's side of the family. 'I thought it was a good sounding name, so it seemed like a good one to pick.'

The diaries I have from this period show Stephen in a state of conflict. He loved Dechen Chöling but still felt isolated. He was torn between his developing plans for the Organisation and living a peaceful life in line with the teachings of Shambhala. 'Rainy days pass by and I am still alone, without a soulmate,' he wrote in April 2007. 'Only dreams of the stars and walks through the forest provide awe and happiness. Last night I got little sleep but felt so "full" and happy – towards everything that exists.'

Later, he wrote about the internal tension he felt at the retreat.

> I want to stay here till August, maybe even longer. They have me doing mostly physical work here and consequently my physique has improved. Regularity and discipline! But what can I do? How can I make a living? I can't foresee a life of one-off heists if I follow the Dharma.

Opposite the tent shared by Ralph and Stephen was another, belonging to sixty-five-year-old Maizza Waser, a German woman who worked for Dechen Chöling organising the workers and allocating jobs. Waser, like Stephen, is autistic. Unlike Stephen, she had long been aware of her condition at this point. She remembers that Stephen was, to begin with, shy and awkward and that he seemed to struggle with many of the physical tasks. 'Most of the work is manual work, either in the kitchen or garden, and he was not very skilled in moving his body,' she remembers. He once accidentally cut down a young sapling. 'He was nice to talk to but when it came down to giving instructions? That was not so easy.'

Waser says that the fact she is autistic does not mean she was therefore able to identify that Stephen was also on the spectrum, though in hindsight, she can see that it would make sense. One morning, she remembers, the pair of them bumped into each other outside their tents and began discussing the dreams they both had that night. As they walked together through the tall grass to the wash block, Stephen described to her a recurring dream he had. 'It was very intense. He said that he was always running. Running away from people. Running,

running, running,' she says. 'I still remember him saying that.'

Ralph Williams chuckles when describing how Stephen would obsessively do intense aerobic exercise routines right in front of the chateau, either oblivious to the onlookers going about their days or, on some level, hoping that they saw him. 'But I also saw his deep love of nature, and there was this one moment that stood out for me in the tent,' he says. 'I was resting between shifts and he came in from having his day off and he had this dandelion behind his ear, and I could see that he had been out in nature for hours in this blissed-out state. When he came back, he was completely at peace. Almost in a trance.'

Lying a few feet apart from each other every night, Williams found that he often ended up listening to Stephen voice his concerns for the planet. 'We had discussions about the injustices of the world, the banking system and corporate model, capitalistic stuff. He did reference wanting to equalise that in some way, that Robin Hood thing of wanting to rob from those institutions. I remember telling him that you can't do that – I was sort of lecturing him in a way – because you'll get into trouble.'

Amidst all of this, Stephen still yearned to meet someone. 'Soon there will be a large influx of people, which I must deal with,' he wrote from Dechen Chöling before the summer rush. 'Perhaps out of the 200+ there will be someone to share happiness with.'

And then, one early summer's afternoon, he saw her. A large group of new guests arrived by coach and made their way to the chateau to find their beds and dump their bags. Among them he describes seeing a tall, slender young woman in her early twenties with dark blonde hair that fell to her shoulders. She walked with a languid, unselfconscious grace. From a

distance Stephen watched, transfixed. Later, after a group meditation session, he did something he had never done before in
his life. As the room started to empty he ignored the urge to
slope his shoulders, look at the ground and move quickly away.
Instead, he put his shoulders back and slowly, calmly, approached
her. He asked her where she was from. She said that she was
from Colorado and then, smiling, asked if Stephen was from
England. He said that, yes, he was from England. Speaking in
a soft, gentle voice, she told him her name was Rebecca. Stephen
said he asked her how she came to be interested in Shambhala
Buddhism and, before he could really process what was
happening, he and Rebecca were having a conversation. And
it was the easiest thing Stephen had ever done. She made jokes.
She asked questions. She listened to what Stephen had to say,
nodding her head slowly, occasionally moving stray strands of
hair back behind her ears. She had a funny, infectious laugh
that initially caused Stephen a bolt of panic when he realised
that, upon hearing it, he was laughing too.

As the days passed, the two of them gravitated towards each
other more and more. Stephen says that their mutual interest
in Buddhism made things easier for him, in the same way a
mutual interest in cosmology paved the way to a friendship
with John Paige and a mutual interest in horse racing served
to bring him and Julian together. When Stephen was not
working, they would go on long bike rides through the French
countryside, play Scrabble or just sit in the long grass and talk.
'She was quite philosophical and a deep thinker, but at the
same time she didn't have that aloofness that many intellectually inclined people have. I wanted to spend all of my time
with her and nobody else. She became the focus of my world.
I guess it's fair to say I was in love. Certainly, I've never really
felt the same about anyone else I've met,' Stephen says. 'She

also revealed much in her past, which had similarities to mine. Minus the crime and Mum being hospitalised bits.'

One hot afternoon, Stephen and Rebecca were lying together by the shores of a lake. They were both wet from swimming and their bicycles were resting against a nearby tree. He turned to her and, finally, told her something he had not told anyone. He was wanted by Dutch police. He told her that after leaving Sidmouth in February, he had travelled to Amsterdam where he proceeded to get very stoned. He was staying in a hostel dorm and, one night, he said he was woken by an angry member of hostel staff insisting that he had not yet paid for his bed and needed to provide the cash. Stephen, groggy, insisted that he had already paid, but the man wouldn't leave him be so eventually he handed over some more money and drifted back to sleep. Stephen said that the next morning, when checking out of the hostel, another member of staff insisted that he needed to pay before he could leave.

'I didn't have a lot of money on me, and this guy was saying that he wanted me to pay three times, which was crazy,' he remembers. He felt that he was being extorted and intimidated. What happened next is not entirely clear. To begin with, Stephen says that he leaped over the front desk, grabbed a fistful of money from the till, and 'stormed out'. Then he admits that he produced a knife. 'I grabbed over the counter, got the money and then he stepped in front of me, so blocking me from leaving the place. So I just opened my bag and he saw this knife, and he just backed away.'

He sprinted away from the hostel. The day was overcast and wet, and raindrops beat against him, dripping down his glasses and steaming up the lenses. He ducked into a taxi and away, but his identity was no secret, because the hostel made a copy of his driver's licence when he first arrived. He sat panting in the back of the taxi, backpack damp on the seat beside him.

Beside the lake, he told Rebecca all of this. He emphasised his deep concerns for the world. 'We talked about inequality. I talked about how the financial system worked and how it created money from thin air, and where the world was headed. And she agreed with me that the destination it was going in was total destruction and suffering for people, and that unless drastic action was taken it would just keep plodding down this route,' he explains to me, talking clearly and with force. 'Yes, there might be ways people could delay it, but those passive ways wouldn't actually change things. They might inconvenience the powers that be a little bit, but they wouldn't result in any significant changes. I think she understood,' he says. 'In fact I am pretty confident she understood. But she didn't want me to do it in the robbery sense. She wanted me to make money conventionally, and then when I had made money, to spend it on building this organisation that I envisioned.'

The weeks at Dechen Chöling passed, Stephen working during the day and spending the evenings with Rebecca. He continued to train in kyūdō archery under the tutelage of the resident octogenarian Japanese master, and to exercise and meditate. But from time to time he sat at one of the computers in the central office, where he researched the careers and methods of real-life bank robbers. Two in particular enthralled him.

One was an American named Carl Gugasian, who stole in excess of $2 million over the course of fifty robberies spanning three decades. Gugasian, Stephen read, is widely considered to be America's most successful bank robber. A neat, unremarkable-looking man from Pennsylvania, he had served in the army before earning a PhD in statistics. In his spare time, he began to plan bank robberies, almost as a hobby. An intellectual exercise.

Eventually Gugasian started to carry these robberies out. They were meticulously planned. He went to the library to find maps of small towns that had banks close to wooded areas and with access to a nearby freeway. He created caches in the woods in order to stash evidence – clothes, weapons, money – in the immediate aftermath of his robberies. He staked out banks for days, learning the comings and goings and habits of employees, before striking at closing time on a Friday night in the belief that this would mean fewer customers and a greater amount of cash. He would burst into the banks wearing bulky clothes to conceal his build, move quickly and in a crab-like fashion in order to make judging his height more difficult, and would wear a gruesome horror mask for maximum intimidation. Brandishing a pistol, he would vault the counter, demand the terrified cashiers empty their tills, and then flee. All in a process designed to take less than two minutes.

Stephen clicked on dozens of articles about Gugasian, absorbing them all, entranced. He learned about how he would keep a dirt bike in the woods near the bank, then use it to flee to a van parked several miles away and then make good his escape, only returning to the woodland cache of evidence and money days later, once the coast was clear. This went on for thirty years until dumb luck saw a pair of teenage boys discover a cache of weapons stored in a drainpipe in some woods near Gugasian's home, which ultimately led to his arrest in 2002.

The other man Stephen spent hours researching online was André Stander, a South African police detective who, during the 1970s, led a double life as a bank robber. Like Gugasian, he was prolific. He robbed a bank at lunchtime using a disguise, a pistol and a lightning-quick entrance and exit. By the after-

noon, he would be investigating the very crime he had
committed. The fact that Stander later claimed his motivations
stemmed in part from his disillusion with South African society
under apartheid only added to the allure of his actions. Sitting
alone in the admin office of a Buddhist meditation retreat,
Stephen allowed himself to conclude that with the right combination of forethought and boldness, robbing banks was
possible. And just as important, he allowed himself to believe
that you could do this while still being a good person. A
mild-mannered statistics professor. A cop jaded by a racist
society. 'I very strongly identified with these people. They
played a massive part in the Robin Hood persona that I
developed.'

In August 2007, Rebecca returned to the United States.
Before she went, Stephen says she invited him to come back
with her. They could live together, enjoying the mountains and
forests of Colorado. Stephen could find work while she finished
college. It was in so many ways the moment Stephen had
yearned for. But he did not go with her. He felt he couldn't.
He knew how much he already depended on Rebecca emotionally, to help guide him through social situations, and that
worried him. What's more, if Stephen couldn't find work there
– and his experience of gaining long-term employment had
not been good – then he imagined himself becoming dependent
on Rebecca in every possible sense. 'Because of my background,
I was scared that I was being wholly reliant on her. I would
feel like I was a leech latching onto her if that makes sense, and
I hated that notion. I also felt like I had an obligation to be
independent, for both her sake and for mine.' It's not that he
didn't love her and want to be with her. He just wanted to feel
as though he was worthy of her.

And there was the Organisation. 'There was this sense of an

obligation as well, about making a difference in the world, that was still digging at me. I thought if I went down the path of being with Rebecca, then I would be turning my back on the obligation I had seen myself as making. After everything I saw on my travels, that seemed really callous and selfish, even. That sounds weird, I guess,' he says. 'The idea that's it's selfish not to rob a bank.'

The pain of letting Rebecca go was 'unbearable'. But they agreed that one way or another, they would reunite within a year. With Rebecca now gone and little else to occupy his mind, Stephen was almost locked into his course of action. He had been turning the idea over and over since New Zealand. Researching and understanding the methods used by successful bank robbers had become an obsession for him. He gave it the same unblinking focus that he gave to global inequality or, previously, the cosmos, or geology, or any number of his past special interests which, as someone with Asperger's, he had always pursued with single-minded intensity. Because of what he had done in Amsterdam, he told himself that he had already crossed a line. That he was already a criminal. But there was still a part of him that wanted to know – or to believe – that his plan to rob from the rich to give to the poor was morally watertight.

Which is why, one day, he approached an old Buddhist monk who was passing through Dechen Chöling. Quietly and respectfully, he asked the monk if it is ever permissible to steal. The old man smiled and shook his head. The teachings of Buddha say that it is not. Stephen absorbed this and then rephrased the question, asking if it was OK to steal so long as you then do great good with the proceeds. Again, the monk shook his head. Stephen smiled and said, yes, but what if people really, really need the proceeds of this hypothetical theft? The monk, increasingly perplexed, said that stealing is stealing. They went back and forth like this for some time before Stephen eventually asked if it would be OK to steal if the money he was stealing had been stolen from the people who would then, effectively, be having the money returned to them and which would, in turn, allow them all to improve their lives immeasurably. The exasperated monk eventually said that, well, yes, it could be that under those precise circumstances, perhaps it would be permissible to steal. It was all Stephen needed to hear. He thanked the old man, bowed respectfully, then walked away, feeling lighter than air.

Around this time, 250 miles north of Dechen Chöling, a decision was made that would accelerate and intensify Stephen's actions. On 9 August 2007, at the headquarters of BNP Paribas, a statement was drafted and issued. The French bank, one of the largest in the world, announced that they were freezing all withdrawals from three of their investment funds. The US housing market was tanking, people were defaulting on their subprime mortgages at a terrifying rate and with BNP Paribas's books full of increasingly rotten Collateralised Debt Obligations, they solemnly explained that they could no longer calculate how much their holdings were actually worth. As such, the amount of money they were willing to lend and invest would be reduced significantly.

For many economists this represents the moment that the Global Financial Crisis began. An admission, from a huge international bank, that because of their own activities, they simply did not know how much money they had. They would receive immediate aid from the European Central Bank but by then it was far too late. Larry Elliot, the *Guardian*'s economics editor, later described 9 August 2007 as having 'all the resonance of

August 4th, 1914. It marks the cut-off point between "an Edwardian summer" of prosperity and tranquillity and the trench warfare of the credit crunch – the failed banks, the petrified markets, the property markets blown to pieces by a shortage of credit.'

Stephen left Dechen Chöling at the end of August. He returned to Sidmouth, but only briefly. Before returning home, he had applied through clearing for a place at the University of Worcester in order to study geography and sociology. If Carl Gugasian could earn a PhD, then there's no reason why Stephen couldn't get some qualifications along the way. Plus he wanted to go to university and experience what it had to offer. A criminal career and a life as a student need not be mutually exclusive.

11

A s Operation Gandalf rolled into life in late 2007 and the
Lloyds TSB and Ladbrokes robberies were investigated,
one of the first things Detective Constable Bingham and his
team did was link the crime directly with another unsolved
robbery in the area. Doing so didn't require much digging – on
31 January that year, the very same branch of Ladbrokes had
been robbed by a man wearing a black leather jacket, black
balaclava and black gloves, who had threatened staff with a
knife and a handgun before making off with what news reports
later referred to as a 'substantial' amount of cash. To Bingham,
it seemed reasonable to hypothesise that this crime was carried
out by the same man he was now looking for. When Stephen
eventually stood trial in the UK for his crimes, he would be
charged with this robbery. 'In the indictment, I was accused
of doing an offence when I came back to England,' he says,
meaning that the alleged robbery took place after his return
from his round-the-world trip but before he left for Europe
and Dechen Chöling. He reminds me that he pled not guilty
to the offence, and was never convicted of it.

Bingham still thinks he did it. 'Effectively, he got away with
one,' he says. Either way, the timeline shows that Stephen left
for Europe not long after the robbery took place. If Bingham
is right, it means that Stephen didn't spend his time at Dechen

Chöling wrestling with the question of whether or not he should turn to crime. Instead, it would mean he had spent his time at Dechen Chöling wrestling with the question of whether to continue down a path he was already taking.

In any case, in early September 2007 Bingham and the small team working Operation Gandalf were trying to find out who their man was. Their approach was methodical. In the past, says Bingham, police detectives would have been encouraged to try and build up a psychological and personal profile of the man committing these crimes. In many ways this mirrors human instinct, to ask and then address the obvious question: who is this person? What can we deduce about them? What might they be like? But Bingham believed this was the last thing they should be doing. Why risk overlooking the real perpetrator by allowing yourself to rush to the conclusion that the robber was a drug addict, or had previous for armed robbery, or was working as part of a wider criminal network?

'Old-fashioned coppers would have had a hypothesis imme-diately about who they think it would be or the type of person. Actually that could take you down some very narrow avenues in trying to find who it is,' says Bingham. 'You shouldn't try and categorise who it is or what they might be like.'

Instead, Bingham focused on the 'Golden Hour' principle, the idea that following a crime, investigators have a limited amount of time to find and preserve material that could other-wise be lost. 'It's not actually an hour, but it's about securing evidence. As a detective, you just naturally do that,' he says. 'So absolutely flood the scene with forensics and go through all the CCTV, because what you do know is that he isn't going to be walking down the street wearing a balaclava.'

Stills from CCTV of both incidents were printed in the local papers, though it was impossible to identify the man in

the grainy photographs. But as soon as it was clear that they
had managed to obtain a sample of his DNA from the replica
pistol, Bingham allowed himself to feel confident. 'We always
knew after the Lloyds bank one that we had forensics on him,
so we knew we would get him. It was just a matter of time. In
this day and age, if you have DNA or fingerprints, you are
confident you are going to get him pretty quickly.'

Or at least this would be the case if Stephen had already
been a criminal whose DNA or fingerprints from past crimes
– solved or not – were already logged on a database and ready
for a match. Only, he wasn't. Even Bingham, normally so
unwilling to jump to conclusions about his quarry, found the
idea that somebody might begin their criminal career with an
attempted bank robbery a little hard to believe. 'It is unlikely,'
he admits. 'It's not a common factor that somebody jumps
straight to armed robbery. They normally build up through
some form of criminality. They try it out first. Very rarely do
you get somebody doing it as their first crime.' He explains
that planning and executing a robbery, never mind knowing
what to do with the money you steal, is generally something
that requires you to be at least in some way connected to an
experienced network of criminals. 'If you go into a bank and
get fifty grand in cash, you can't just go and spend it. It's a naive
person who thinks that if you rob a bank, it's going to be an
easy option.'

As Devon and Cornwall Police searched through CCTV
footage, conducted interviews and analysed Stephen's replica
gun and fake bomb for forensics, there was one small thing
they would miss. When Stephen burst into the South Street
Ladbrokes, he announced his arrival by hurling a pound coin
across the room. He had planned this the previous day, and he
would do this as the prelude to many of his subsequent

robberies. In his mind it was a sort of symbolic act. The banks and institutions he robbed from had the ability to create money from nothing – from abstract ideas like 'debt' and 'interest'. When he stole from these institutions, he was simply taking money they had spun from thin air. By leaving them a simple, solid pound coin he was 'repaying' them with the means to eventually summon all the money back again. 'That's what I told myself anyway.' The pound coins he used for this purpose all had a single line scratched through them, though rarely if ever on the side featuring the Queen's portrait. 'I probably would have seen that as being disrespectful.'

On 15 September 2007, just a week after Stephen's first attempted bank robbery, there was a run on Northern Rock. One of the largest lenders in Britain, the bank had borrowed large sums of money in order to expand and fund mortgages for customers. In order to repay the money they had borrowed, Northern Rock's business model required them to simply bundle together their customer's mortgages and sell them as Collateralised Debt Obligations on the international money market. Only, nobody in the international money market wanted CDOs anymore. Nor did they want to lend to mortgage banks in general. This left Northern Rock in a liquidity crisis. They needed more cash. On 12 September, they approached the Bank of England to act as lender of last resort, and received some £3 billion of initial aid. This was made public on 14 September, after the BBC's Robert Peston broke the story on *News at Ten*, immediately prompting fears that bankruptcy was imminent. The following morning, thousands of Northern Rock customers up and down the country were filmed queuing up outside their local branches in order to withdraw their savings. These queues, often made up of the elderly and retired, remained in place for three days. It was the first run on a British bank for 150 years. When Northern Rock was finally nationalised in 2008, thousands of ordinary people who had put their savings into shares in the bank were left with nothing.

Stephen watched the bank run unfold on the TV in the ramshackle living room at Manstone Avenue. While studio pundits and the customers interviewed on the street were confused and shocked, Stephen was not. As he sat there watching, his mother on the couch beside him murmuring her dismay, it all merely confirmed what he already knew. That banks had created a system in which they could magic money from almost nothing, but when a reckoning came, it would not be the bankers who faced the consequences, but the ordinary workaday people at the bottom of the pile. 'I remember watching everything about Northern Rock, but it wasn't a revelation to me,' he says. The constant news coverage of what was being referred to as the 'credit crunch' simply stoked Stephen's belief. Seeing other people becoming angry at what was happening and, increasingly, expressing their disgust at the banking system's recklessness and greed, made him feel even more righteous.

'There was going to be a recession. And because the recession was caused by the banks themselves, I was justified in what I was doing. That's the thinking I used both morally and logically. That these institutions are effectively stealing the wealth of the world from other people. And if I stole from them and gave it back, in theory, morally you can't say that's wrong. I couldn't see how anybody could say that it was wrong.'

12

S tephen enrolled at the University of Worcester in late
September 2007. He caught the train north and arrived at
the small, functional campus. A former teacher-training centre
and higher education college, Worcester has grown in reputa-
tion but it's fair to say it's not an elite educational establishment.
He took his bags to his new room. If greeted he nodded and
muttered a reply, but kept walking, eyes down. There was still
a bruise on his face from where Raymond Beer had struck him
with the butt of his own pistol.

Once he was settled, he sat at a small writing table and
opened a new notebook. He picked up a pen and began to
write on the first page.

This book belongs to Stephen George Dennis Jackley
Flat 5, Room 5
Wyvern Hall
University of Worcester
Henwick Grove
Worcester
WR2 6AJ
The contents are dangerous. Do not read.

He also included his mobile telephone number. The fact that Stephen wrote his full name, address and contact information at the start of a book in which he would minutely detail over half a dozen separate crimes is worth considering. Why go through all the care and effort of planning elaborate Carl Gugasian-style robberies with pre-planted caches of clothes and multiple pre-planned escape routes only to then just confess to everything, in your own handwriting, in a notebook you've made absolutely clear belongs to you? From a rational perspective it just doesn't make any sense. Only, the possibility of capture didn't occur to him at all. 'I just didn't see that eventuality,' he says. 'It didn't even cross my mind.'

This apparent contradiction, between extreme naivety and surprising efficiency, quickly became a hallmark of Stephen's criminal career. On the one hand he absolutely shut himself off psychologically from the prospect of failure or arrest. On the other, he was able to apply a robust, clear-eyed logic to the question of 'how might you successfully rob a bank?' He had already determined that it was perfectly possible and far more straightforward than most people allowed themselves to believe. On an intellectual level you don't really need anything more than common sense. The hard part – the part that makes most people tell themselves that a bank heist is impossible – is having the conviction to actually do it. To pull on the balaclava and go in there with the replica gun and come out with a backpack full of cash.

Stephen had that belief. By the time he arrived at Worcester, he had already proved that to himself. There was a part of him that wanted to prove it to Rebecca too. He says that he kept in contact with her via email and phone calls, hinting of his actions. 'I didn't tell her directly, but she knew where I was coming from. She knew my intentions. So I sort of said it in a way like "I am continuing with this mission to alleviate inequality" and she knew exactly what I meant by that. I didn't tell her that I had robbed X bank on X date, it wasn't like that. It was more the sense of, "I am continuing with this until I reach the goal", which was the hundred k.'

In his heart, Stephen knew that the chance to have any kind of meaningful relationship with Rebecca died when he opted to return to England rather than go with her to Colorado. He described a coolness setting in as the reality of their situation became clear and he began to entertain the possibility that she was not the long-awaited soulmate he had been dreaming of. 'Also logically, how is it going to work? She's in America, I'm in England and now I've made this choice, I can't just suddenly fly over and stay there,' he explains to me, a note of irritation creeping into his voice. 'I was quite paranoid as well. That she had already met someone and just hadn't told me.'

With each passing day, he sank deeper into a conviction that he was 'at war' with a callous, capitalistic society that was destroying the planet and ruining lives for no good reason. Everywhere he looked, he saw evidence of this. A form of confirmation bias set in. In the university library, he read the work of American academic, environmentalist and activist David C. Korten. In his book *When Corporations Rule the World*, Korten writes about the need to rebalance the power of multinational corporations with environmental sustainability and what he describes as 'people-centred development'. For the sociology modules of his course, Stephen read the work of German political economist Max Weber, who builds on the ideas of Karl Marx and describes how exploitation is hardwired into capitalism, a system which demands social stratification, a division of the weak and the powerful, the haves and the have nots. He made pages and pages of notes. He thought of the children sifting through rubbish heaps in Cambodia, the bare-foot Thai villagers who fed him and helped him get back to his holiday lodge. He thought of the anxious pensioners queuing to retrieve their savings from Northern Rock. He thought of himself, and of his mother and father, in their shabby little council house on Manstone Avenue. He thought about the Organisation constantly. 'I was so obsessive. It was the sole thing on my mind.'

This does not seem to be have been strictly true. Rather, a kind of cognitive dissonance was at play too. Yes, he was committed to becoming the new Robin Hood he felt he had no choice but to become. But he also seemed to know that university represented his best chance at quietly slipping into the conventional, carefree existence enjoyed by millions of young people all over the world. Like everyone else around him, he wanted to get qualifications, to make connections and to experience a rite of passage.

In his new university journal he reiterated this to himself via a short series of bullet points.

3 reasons for staying here come to mind.
- To gain a degree
- To meet friends – or better, a soulmate
- To have a 'base' to commit crime and gain money and experience

True to his word, for the first week or so of term, Stephen did his very best to socialise. Wyvern Hall is a small, modern low-rise complex with a series of shared kitchens and communal living areas. Stephen discovered that most of his immediate neighbours were Chinese. 'They were quite nice and they used to make curries and we sat down to eat on a couple of occasions,' he says. More difficult was getting on with his fellow British students. Within days, the majority of the freshers in Wyvern Hall had fallen into a close group, piling round to one another's flats for drinks before heading out to the student union. Louise Alice Cawood arrived at the University of Worcester from Leeds to study physical education, and quickly found herself a part of this Wyvern Hall mob. 'We all knew each other and we would all go off in groups together, to do laundry or organise stuff,' she remembers. 'It was like a little community within the university.'

Stephen, though, never found himself part of this instant community. 'He was relatively anonymous. Which I suppose in a way is kind of strange, because everyone else in our halls all knew each other,' Cawood continues, frowning. 'We knew what degrees we all did, we knew which friendship circles we all hung out with, which societies we were in and stuff. With him, nobody really asked, I suppose. But he was never there for any of us to ask. I never saw him in town or anywhere else on a night out. Even when we had nights at the student union I never remember seeing him. After the first couple of weeks, people just forgot he was there.' It occurs to her that Stephen often received a large number of packages and parcels, but beyond that minor detail? 'He just melted into the background.'

It was not that Stephen wasn't trying. It was just that he very quickly concluded that the students he encountered had nothing in common with him. His sensitivity to loud noises was a massive hinderance and his Asperger's meant that, for all his experience in Australia and Dechen Chöling, he still struggled with small talk, social cues, body language and jokes. He was struck by how little his fellow students seemed to know or care about the wider world and the threats it faced. Cawood admits that, amongst the Wyvern Hall group, an impending financial crisis and the impact of climate change were not hot topics. 'I don't really think it crossed our minds. Mostly because we were at the start of university. Everything was about what outfit are you going to wear that evening and stuff like that. We were in a bubble.'

Stephen joined one of the university's outdoor pursuit societies, but when he went out on a pub crawl with them, he was struck not just by their ignorance, but by their callousness. 'I remember they were laughing and joking about a homeless guy and I said, "Why the fuck would you do that?" It was like . . . there's something amiss here. There's something they don't get and I do. Because of that, I didn't go to that group any more.'

Instead, he kept to himself. He stayed in his room, planning his next move and doing his best to keep abreast of the police investigations into the crimes he had already committed.

'Read on the internet (I'm continually searching for "armed robbery" related articles) found the police in Exeter are still pursuing the failed Lloyds TSB heist,' he wrote one evening. 'Damn it! But it seems they've got no clear CCTV images of me.'

He drifted off on his own to explore Worcester. He quickly realised that it bore many similarities to Exeter. Both are small cathedral cities with populations of less than 150,000. Both are surrounded by miles of rolling countryside. As he walked around the small centre, scouting for financial institutions he could target, he found himself passing the same department stores and the same billboards advertising the same brands. An historic English town suffocating in a corporate stranglehold. He looked in shop windows and saw mannequins wearing clothes stitched by children in sweatshops to be sold to people who did not need them. He saw banks, cheerfully offering hard-working people loans and the promise of stability and support while quietly magicking billions from their debt and stress.

> The world is being consumed. Eaten up by the greed of an elite few (what David Korten calls the 'stratos dwellers', who live in luxury 'across a vast gap that most of humanity can never cross'). These are the controllers. These are the rulers. I saw it today: people's faces downcast and suspicious, brand shops pumping propaganda, market researchers assailing shoppers, beggars on street corners. And high up watches a camera, like the demented eye of a vulture, each lens seeking out some infraction – a possibility of a rule breaker. All for what? To protect? To maintain order?

In another entry he wrote, 'To take just a drop hoarded by the rich and scatter but a little to the poor. Is it justice to keep millions languishing in poverty as a few hundred enjoy excessive wealth?'

He asked himself this question again and again. One day, he approached a lecturer who had just given a talk about how society's attitudes towards crime change over time. 'We were talking about how crime is relative and how crimes today were not necessarily crimes in the past, and how crimes of the past could be regarded as positive things in the future and how ultimately crime is about harm, and that if you prevent harm, it is the opposite of crime,' he remembers, talking briskly. 'That kind of reasoning.'

It was quite possible that the lecturer who had just been buttonholed by an earnest undergraduate enjoyed the conversation. Perhaps they felt flattered by the attention Stephen had clearly been paying to the themes discussed. What they could

not have known as the young man walked away was that, in
his room, there was a commando knife. There was a balaclava.
There were boxes and boxes of items he had ordered from the
internet. Disguises. Wigs. Fake beards. A portable angle-
grinder. A replica pistol. And pages and pages of detailed plans
for what were, as the two of them had already discussed, argu-
ably the very opposite of crimes.

On 31 October 2008, almost exactly one year after his conversation with the University of Worcester sociology lecturer
about the relativity of crime, Stephen was sitting inside the
holding pen at Strafford County Jail in New Hampshire.
Opposite him there was a man dressed as a Halloween killer
clown, his death-white face and gaudy outfit splattered with
what appeared to be blood. Stephen had, finally, been moved
from the Hole while British and American authorities tried to
work out what to do with him. He looked around anxiously.
The silent Halloween clown was not the only other person
sitting in the pen. There were recently arrested drunks being
booked and inmates who, like Stephen, had just been transferred from other prisons. These men eyed him with interest.
They tossed questions at him and then grinned and shared
glances when they heard his English accent. They edged slowly
towards him, asking the same question that everybody asked.
What are *you* doing *here*? It was the first time Stephen had
been so close to so many other people for at least five months,
and it made him feel tense and afraid. It was not just their
proximity, but the way they shouted questions at him and how
their tones became harder and more goading the longer he
tried to avoid answering them. A prison officer kept watch
from behind a desk decorated with cheap cardboard jack-o-
lanterns.

After a few hours, Stephen was released from the holding pen and escorted by a pair of guards to a secure room where he was made to change out of his red SSCF inmate's uniform and into a strange blue jumpsuit made out of a paper-like fabric. He was then handcuffed and marched through layers of security. Nobody told him where he was going or what was happening, though he assumed he was about to be placed in some form of segregation. Instead, he was taken somewhere odd. It was a brightly lit cell. Instead of a wall, the heavy door was set in some kind of transparent perspex screen. Stephen was shoved inside and the door was locked behind him. He saw that, on the other side of the screen, across the corridor, a prison officer sat behind a desk. It meant that, at least in theory, he was under constant observation. It was like something you might find in a zoo.

He did not know what was happening. Even worse, he didn't know what would happen next. While this would be stressful for anyone, his Asperger's meant that it was exponentially so for Stephen. It took him a few moments to notice that, inside the otherwise empty cell, there were a pair of shapes lying on the floor, each covered in a green blanket. Suddenly, a bald head emerged from beneath one. Stephen almost screamed. The man's face looked pale and weary, his eyes dull and impassive.

Stephen looked down at him and before he could think, he started to speak.

'Why am I here?' he asked the bald man. 'What is this place?'

The figure on the floor looked at him. Then rolled over and drew the blanket back over his head. The other figure sleeping on the floor did not move, so Stephen walked to the perspex screen and banged on it with both fists, attempting to attract the attention of anyone who could tell him what was happening.

Eventually, the prison guard from behind the desk slowly got up and approached the screen. He was a small man who could have been in his seventies. Talking quickly, Stephen asked why he was there. The guard said nothing, just peered at him with only faint interest before turning and walking away. Stephen shouted after him. He wanted to make a phone call. A legal phone call. He wanted to know what was going on. From the other side of the screen the old man pointed a bony finger at Stephen. 'I don't know who you are, and I don't care,' he said calmly. 'Just shut up and fuck off.'

The commotion woke the second figure in the cell. A young man with greasy, matted blonde hair emerged from beneath the blanket. He rubbed his eyes and looked at Stephen. He asked if he'd just arrived. Stephen nodded. The young man's voice sounded beyond weary and strange, as if his whole mouth was numb. Stephen asked him the same urgent questions: what was this place and why were they here? In response, the young man said nothing, but pulled a sheet of paper from under his blanket and, holding it up to the light, began tracing shapes on it with his finger.

A voice came from behind Stephen. From beneath his blanket the bald man was trying to say something. 'You're in the medical section,' he explained, forcing the words out with what seemed like extreme effort. 'Under su . . . sue . . . suzie . . .' He trailed off, and appeared to drift back into semi-consciousness. Under the cell's bright fluorescent light, Stephen looked at the two men. It felt like a woozy, through-the-looking-glass existence of frustration and oblique non-sequiturs. He stood against the cell wall watching the two men in silence.

Suddenly, the bald man shouted. He forced syllables from his mouth in a way that reminded Stephen of dirty water spouting from an old rusty tap in fits and starts. 'We are under,' he strained through clenched jaws, 'suicide watch.'

Stephen was stunned. He looked down at his paper boiler suit and then around the cell, which was stripped of all items save for the green blankets and thin foam mattresses on which the two men slept. His thoughts flashed back to when he first arrived at Strafford County. At one point during the processing procedure he was asked a series of questions about his health and wellbeing by a prison nurse. 'She asked if I'd ever felt suicidal,' he says. 'I just honestly said "yes". I felt suicidal many times in the Southern State Correctional Facility, but never made an attempt to commit suicide or self-harm. When I felt down, I told myself that the experience was only temporary, with escape always being a possibility.'

To Stephen, the fact that he had been placed on suicide watch after innocently admitting to regularly feeling suicidal was a surprise. More than that, it felt like a slap in the face for having been honest and straightforward with the nurse. He sat on the floor with his head in his hands.

It was a dark October evening in 2007, and a nineteen-year-old student named Luke Twisleton had almost finished his shift at the largest branch of William Hill bookmakers in Worcester. Twisleton was in his second year of a business degree at the university, but applied for a job as a cashier in order to earn a bit of extra money. A member of the university's rugby team, he was strapping, confident and affable. After his job interview with William Hill he was offered employment 'on the spot' and that was that. It was gone closing time and after gently encouraging a few lingering customers out the door, Twisleton was now helping empty the fruit machines and cash up for the night.

As he was doing this, he noticed a pair of gloves still on one of the tables. This made him pause and wonder whether there was still a customer on the premises, possibly in the men's toilet. He decided to go and check. He pushed open the door and saw a figure gripping on to both sides of a sink and staring at themselves in the mirror. They were wearing a black balaclava. Beside them, on another sink, was a knife and pistol. The figure spun around and for a split second, Twisleton saw that there was a look of frantic fear in his eyes. Twisleton filled the toilet doorway. He was near six foot tall and weighed sixteen stone. But he was still processing what was in front of him. 'I was a bit shell-shocked and said, "What are you doing?" But he had a balaclava on, so I think I knew what he was doing.'

There was then a race, spanning a matter of milliseconds, to determine which of the two could react quickest. The masked man won by a fraction. Overcoming his terror, he grabbed his weapons and charged at Twisleton. 'He put the knife up to my chest and the gun to my head. Then he told me to get on the floor, which I refused to do. I don't know if you have ever been in a bookies, but the toilets are not that clean. So all I did was put my hands behind my head and backed out. When I got out of the toilet I put my back to the wall and slid down.'

From behind his balaclava, Stephen scanned the shop floor. He saw Twisleton's manager, a middle-aged woman, and he screamed at her to freeze. She ignored him and bolted out the front door, locking it behind her. Stephen muttered a curse. The previous night, he had concluded a diary entry with a rallying call to himself: 'MAKE SURE YOU DO THE HEIST AND DO IT WELL!'

But the heist was not going well at all. His plan had been to force a member of staff to open the safe before an alarm could be raised. Now there would be no time for that. The police would be here in a matter of minutes. So Stephen leaped over the cashier counter and opened the tills, stuffing banknotes into his backpack. Overhead CCTV monitors relayed everything that was happening and he almost jumped when he caught sight of a black-clad figure in a balaclava. It took a second to realise that it was simply an image of himself. From his position on the floor against the wall, Twisleton could see that Stephen's actions appeared manic and unfocused. There was a bag in plain sight containing cash which the manager had been in the process of emptying from the fruit machines. 'You used to pull thousands from those machines,' he says. 'But he completely missed it.'

Instead, Stephen cleaned out the tills and then rushed to the back of the bookies, where there was a fire exit. When he had entered the shop twenty minutes earlier, posing as a customer with his hoodie pulled low over his head, he knew that he would escape via the rear, into the tight warren of alleyways and backstreets he had determined would suit his purpose perfectly. He bolted past Twisleton, through the fire door and into an alley. Twisleton jumped to his feet and slammed the door shut, because he knew that at the end of the alley was a high gate. He hoped that this would leave the robber trapped. Within a matter of minutes, the police arrived at the front of the shop and demanded Twisleton let them in. He explained that he couldn't, because the manager had locked him in, but directed them round the back. Shortly after, the manager appeared with the keys. Armed police and a dog team poured in through the shop and then out through the fire exit at the rear. But the alley was empty. The gate had been scaled. The masked man had vanished into the night. A police helicopter thrummed overhead, scanning the streets for any sign of him.

They found none. Stephen had already changed his clothes.

He had planted a changeover bag and a bicycle in some bushes near an alley. From there, it was a five-minute cycle back to Wyvern Hall. He hurried past his Chinese flatmates as they watched TV in the communal area and locked the door of his room behind him. Hiding his replica pistol before emptying the banknotes onto his bed, he quickly counted them. In all, the robbery had yielded £530. It was not nearly enough. The Organisation would not arise from petty cash smash-and-grabs. Going after the bookies had been, as much as anything, a reflex. A need to prove to himself that he was still Robin Hood. Later, Stephen would take a red felt pen and mark some of these banknotes with the initials 'RH'. 'To begin with, I just didn't bother. But then I saw it as a point of principle that these notes had to be marked,' he says. 'Don't ask me why.'

Marking the notes seems like an act of defacement. As much as Stephen needed money for the Organisation, he also hated it. He hated the fact that we all allow ourselves to believe that banknotes have any actual real, inherent worth. Of course they don't. In the past, you could at least theoretically take your cash to a bank and exchange it for its true value in gold, even though it would have been impossible for everyone who trusted in their cash to do so simultaneously. But today? Today you can't even do that. The banknotes Stephen had stolen only have value because we agree that they do. In his halls of residence bedroom, he stopped scrawling 'RH' for a moment and stared at the pieces of paper in front of him. He let his eyes trace the fine detail of a £20 note, the words 'Bank of England' etched in an elaborate, florid script, the portrait of the Queen looking back at him, festooned in jewels, gnomic and unblinking.

He thought of the words of Milton Friedman, the Nobel Prize-winning economist. 'The pieces of green paper have value because everyone thinks they have value.' It's not just paper money that this applies to. Every hour, billions of pounds appear, vanish and reappear on stock markets and investment bank balance sheets around the world. This money is not real, any more than the cash in your wallet is. But the idea of money – money as we know it today – has been foisted on us. We have constructed an entire society around the pursuit of it, and now Stephen believed nobody wanted to see or say the truth. He wrote in his diary:

> Wealth is the greatest trick ever played. It is a worldwide illusion that enslaves mankind in a conveyor belt of work, produce and consume. An illusion which people give up their lives to pursue. Wealth is the foundation of all inequality – the primary tool of the rich and powerful.

He decided that a portion of his takings should go directly to those in need. Wearing a long coat and doing his best to cover his face, he says that he would go out at night and drop small rolls of his 'RH' banknotes on the laps of the homeless without breaking stride. 'I remember a couple of them shouting after me, just really grateful, like they couldn't believe it.' On one occasion, a homeless man actually got up and chased after him which, in turn, forced Stephen to break into a sprint in order to avoid being identified. 'That was in Worcester,' he says quietly. 'That was funny.'

Luke Twisleton was interviewed by police at the scene of the crime until 11 p.m. He returned to his flat, went to bed, then got up very early to make a 6 a.m. rugby training session. He explained to his teammates what had happened to him the previous night. Some of them were convinced he was joking. He showered and then went to a morning lecture. And then, from nowhere, he crumbled. 'I couldn't breathe. I couldn't think. I collapsed, pretty much,' he says. 'All of a sudden it hit me. What happened and what could have happened.' He went back to his family home in Bristol, where he remained for a month, unable to eat or sleep. He was prescribed sleeping pills. 'Any confidence I had at that point vanished. My rugby went downhill. I gained a lot of weight.'

What Stephen did to nineteen-year-old Twisleton has left a permanent mark. Twisleton says that he felt ashamed for not having been able to stop him. He thought he was about to be murdered by a terrified-looking stranger in a balaclava. He did not fully address the trauma for years.

> I buried a lot of the stress and I probably only dealt with that a few years ago. It was my wife who convinced me. She has known for a long time that I needed to go and speak to someone. I couldn't sleep without a light on. If it was dark, I couldn't get out of bed if there wasn't a light on because I couldn't go into a dark place. I went years of sleeping two or three hours a night. I finally went to see a psychologist through the NHS and I thought it was going to be a complete waste of time, but it was the opposite. I would like to say I am completely over it, but there are still little tics. It had a big impact on my life.

Over the course of his crimes, Stephen's actions and deliberate use of threats and violent intimidation would impact many people's lives like this. Victim statements provided in advance of Stephen's eventual trial in the UK show this. Ordinary working people left traumatised. One statement provided by a bank worker and summarised by police described how Stephen 'pointed a gun at them and that led them to become hysterical.

The victim was taken to hospital after the incident because she was so distressed and was told she was suffering from severe trauma.'

Another of Stephen's victims told the police that 'the effect of the robbery has left her nervous at work and wary of strangers coming into the shop. If she has to face the suspect, it is likely she will become distressed and unable to give her account'. Others talked of feeling physically sick. Of an inability to return to their place of work or simply not knowing how they will cope with day-to-day life.

Stephen says he now understands that his Asperger's made it hard for him to appreciate the emotional impact of his actions on others. When Ben Weaver describes his friend as being able to have empathy with people and their problems in a general, abstract way, but struggling to have empathy for an individual in front of him, this is what he was talking about. In planning and executing his early crimes Stephen understood that pointing a replica gun or commando knife at somebody would, in that moment, make them afraid. It was a shame that he had to do so, but then making them afraid was the whole point. But once he'd made his getaway he did not spend much time worrying about how these people felt. At least, not to begin with. In as much as he thought about it at all he reasoned that their fear would pass, they would see they were not dead and then they'd presumably just . . . continue with their lives. When he later learned that this was not how they felt, it was a shock.

It's a bit like the genuine surprise he felt when, upon telling the Strafford County Jail nurse that he had felt suicidal many times, he found himself being put straight onto suicide watch. Even if he had entertained suicidal thoughts it was obvious, to him, that he was not actually going to kill himself. He couldn't empathise with the nurse who heard him say this and then worried that he might actually do it. To Stephen, it was also obvious that he was not going to kill or deliberately hurt anybody during his crimes. Doing so would make absolutely no sense. But the person at the other end of the replica pistol didn't know that. And on some level, he doesn't seem to understand this.

'I couldn't appreciate that going into a bank and pointing a gun at them . . . they didn't realise it's an imitation. It could have been real to them,' he says. 'And I didn't appreciate what that would convey to them. In a vague sense I knew it would cause fear. But intellectually, I couldn't understand how it would affect them on an emotional level.'

Later, Stephen reflects on how his Asperger's impacts his ability to understand people's feelings. 'I don't know how big the empathy thing with me is, though, because I care about others, deeply. The issue is more relating to their emotions, or rather understanding how things impact their emotions. It's still a guessing game.'

When it came to his crimes, this problem was made worse by the fact that Stephen had come to view banks and book-makers purely as institutions. Faceless, soulless and malign. When Stephen finally stood trial for his crimes he was surprised, confused and then somewhat outraged to see that each charge listed him as robbing from individuals who had actually been given names. 'I remember saying to the solicitor, are you sure the charges are correct? Because all the evidence was that I never saw it as individuals, I saw it as corporations. I wouldn't have any contention saying I wanted to steal from corporations. But I was charged, in effect, with stealing from individuals.'

Luke Twisleton says that Stephen wrote to him from prison, sending a letter to the university which ultimately found its way to him. It was a gesture of contrition, but also an attempt to make Twisleton understand what he had been hoping to achieve.

'He was pretty much calling himself Robin Hood, that was how he saw himself. He was taking on these big corporations and giving back to the people,' says Twisleton. 'It was sort of an apology. He was saying he was targeting these organisations and going after business but not thinking of the people who work there. But I'm not the business. I'm not rolling in money. I'm working there so I can pay my rent. He suggested some reading I should do,' he adds with a brittle chuckle. 'So that I would better understand what he was trying to do.'

Twisleton says he no longer has the letter. He kept it for a long time, but one day his wife uncovered it when they were in the process of moving house. She took it, ripped it up, and threw it away.

13

Breakfast on suicide watch consisted of powdered egg reconstituted into a pallid slop, two slices of soggy toast and a small carton of milk. As he ate, Stephen learned that the strange young hyperactive inmate, the one who talked in his sleep and traced invisible patterns on sheets of paper, was called Matt. The older bald man who just seemed to lie on the floor underneath a blanket was called Steve. Matt was delighted with the eggs and wolfed them down. He then proceeded to help himself to the food on Steve's tray. He asked if Stephen would like the spare carton of milk. When Stephen said he did not, Matt threw it in the air, letting the carton land on his head. He then stashed it under his blanket along with half a dozen other unopened ones, vibrating with a kind of giddy joy.

The bald man was refusing to eat. He just lay there on the floor, curled up, barely speaking. On each breakfast tray there was also a plastic cup containing a clear red liquid. Stephen took a sip and was hit by a tongue-burning sugary sweetness. 'The juice is drugged,' said Steve, who spoke from the floor in a distant monotone. Stephen recoiled. He thought of his mother and the way her drugs would leave her hollowed-out and docile, so tipped the juice down the small metal sink in the corner of the cell.

Hours passed. Prison staff come in with medication for Steve, who obediently swallowed it down, and then they left. More food was presented along with cupfuls of the Day-Glo juice. It was impossible for Stephen to feel at ease. The Hole had been bad, but at least he had his own space, however small. He was allowed books and writing materials. But here? Here he was wedged between a man who seemed completely inert and another who was practically hyperactive. Stephen had spent almost his entire life stuck in close proximity to two people struggling with mental illness. And now, over 4,000 miles away, he was back doing the same. Matt quizzed Stephen about England and his crimes, before going on long, rambling, self-aggrandising anecdotes about his own criminal career. He claimed to have been a gang leader and made $10 million before finally being captured. His constant talking, probing and boasting was punctuated by violent, powdered-egg-powered bowel movements. Stephen gagged. It was a direct assault on his own heightened need for hygiene. Within twenty-four hours the claustrophobia was overpowering. He began to understand that there was a reason the other two gulped down the juice so willingly.

Stephen did his best to find out what he was doing there. When prison staff came in and out of the observation cell, he badgered them for information. They explained that he was considered a suicide risk. In order to no longer be considered a suicide risk, he must first request an appointment with one of the prison psychiatrists. But because it was now Saturday, he would just have to wait until Monday.

The next morning, Steve was carried from the cell and placed in a wheelchair by guards. He was left sitting in the corridor, attached to a drip. He was weak and his refusal to eat meant that he was forced to receive fluids, supplements and vitamins intravenously. Stephen stared at him from inside the cell.

Earlier, Stephen had tried to be encouraging, urging his depressed cellmate to just hold on, to wait until he was out of jail and could finally be back in nature, walking barefoot on the grass and listening to the sound of birds. Just talking about it gave Stephen a lump in his throat, but the man had simply looked at him. 'I couldn't give a shit about birds or grass,' he'd said, levelly.

After that, Stephen stopped talking to him. He requested some paper and a pen, which he was granted, and informed the guards that he was going to write a letter of complaint to the British embassy in Washington DC, informing them of Steve's plight and demanding that somebody come down to Strafford County Department of Corrections, New Hampshire, to see for themselves. 'I said, right, I'm writing to my embassy about this. And I said it in such a serious way that the guards just laughed and said, OK, you do what you want. They couldn't have cared less,' he says. 'I actually did write it. I don't know if they ever responded.'

Extracting yourself from suicide watch is a Kafkaesque process. The more desperate you appear to leave, the less likely it is that you will be allowed to do so. It took Stephen time to work this out. Over the next few days, meetings with psychiatrists were held in which they seemed to indicate that Stephen should be transferred. He returned to his cell only to be told by guards that, no, he couldn't leave. When he responded to this with anger, they looked at him as though he'd just proved their point. Matt told him that this was common, that they liked to see how you reacted. Another day passed under twenty-four hour fluorescent lighting and constant observation. Matt left, which came as a relief, but he was swiftly replaced by an equally young inmate who alternated between non-stop singing and what appeared to be shaking seizures. The first time this happened, Stephen rushed to the observation window and banged on it hard in an attempt to attract the attention of a guard. When one finally came, though, the inmate appeared to be perfectly well and was guzzling a carton of milk. The inmate grinned at him, finished the milk and then carried on singing.

At the University of Worcester, Stephen continued to shrink into himself as 2007 edged into winter. He couldn't break into the social group which had coalesced around Wyvern Hall and he struggled to connect with his course mates. He found the strobing lights and constant noise of student bars and night-clubs impossible to process, so in the evenings he isolated himself in his room. Sometimes he would emerge to complain about other Wyvern Hall residents playing music too loud or making too much noise late at night, before retreating back behind his door.

Seeing members of the outdoor pursuits club laughing about a homeless man had only confirmed to him that these people simply did not see how unjust the world was and how precarious its existence. Or perhaps deep down they did see it, but were already too invested in the Western capitalist system to admit it to themselves. They rushed into town to buy new outfits before a big night out, never stopping to consider why those clothes were so cheap or who was making them. They showed up to lectures and sat there bleary-eyed and listless, because they took no real pleasure or excitement in learning. All they really wanted was the piece of paper you get at the end which shows you've been to university and can therefore command a higher salary. They already knew the companies they would like to work for and the kinds of cars they would like to drive when they did. Egged on by their families – egged on by society as a whole – their ambitions were to simply earn and consume. To take what they could from the world while doing everything in their power to make sure they were never the ones being laughed at by strangers for not having a roof over their heads or stuck stitching clothes for less than a pound a day.

It was easy for Stephen to reach this conclusion because, unlike the people he was observing, he was not invested. Just as with his parents, his stake in this society was virtually non-existent. He had not drunk the capitalist Kool-Aid. Nobody had even offered it to him. He thought of all those failed job interviews and the embarrassment and frustration of not knowing why it was that nobody wanted him. He thought of the cautious excitement and optimism he had felt upon arriving at university, only to find himself unable to feel part of anything. At Worcester, he signed up to a recruitment agency who sent him to do some work as a waiter at a function centre. After his second shift, though, he was told not to come back by a manager whom he suspected he upset by being 'too direct'. As a child in Sidmouth he would sometimes walk up the hill to the observatory long after it had shut for the night and just gaze at the heavens. 'I remember looking up to the stars and wanting to be "rescued". I had this feeling like Earth was not really my home.' At university, this feeling only intensified.

When not studying, he went off on long cycle rides. He followed the River Severn, exploring woodland and swimming from its banks. One October morning he travelled to the nearby Malvern Hills. Hiking to their summit, he stood amongst the ancient earthworks of an Iron Age hill fort and looked down at the English countryside below. There were miles and miles of patchwork fields, forests, rivers and streams. It was bright, but there was an autumn chill on the wind. Alone, he walked along ancient tracks. He spotted little purple harebells and meadow saffron to either side of him. He saw sheep grazing on moorland. A pair of herons near the shore of a reservoir.

Ever since he was a boy, being surrounded by nature had helped Stephen to feel calm. This day though, he remained agitated. He couldn't enjoy the landscape around him because he knew it could not last. The fields and the reservoir, the grazing sheep and the grass-covered earthworks of the ancient stronghold: they were pretty but they were not natural. Humans had done this. And they would not stop. For years he had understood, intuitively, that the planet's resources were finite, and that if we continued to exploit these resources, then it was logical to assume that we would eventually run out. That we would mine and burn and build our way to ecological apocalypse. Stephen's fears for the environment did not run concurrently with his fears about global income inequality. Rather, they were one and the same. Our dependency on and addiction to fossil fuels, our obsession with growth over sustainability, our pathological eagerness to jump into a hamster wheel of consume and dispose. They were interwoven so tightly as to be indistinguishable.

These were not paranoid anxieties. Everything Stephen read reinforced his belief that humanity was sleepwalking to a point of no return. Ice caps were melting. Rainforests were shrinking. The planet's population was booming unsustainably. Biodiversity was falling off a cliff. In May 2007, four months before he arrived at Worcester, the United Nations' Intergovernmental Panel on Climate Change published a report which stated that unrestrained greenhouse gas emissions could drive global temperatures up as much as 6°C by 2100, triggering a surge in ocean levels, the destruction of a vast number of species, economic devastation and mass human migrations. These scientists believed that global emissions had to peak by 2015 for the world to have any chance of limiting the expected temperature rise to just 2°C, a rise which would still see billions of people forced to live without adequate water by 2050. In the event, humanity would sail past this 2015 deadline. The year 2018 would represent a record high for greenhouse gas emissions.

Stephen found the lack of urgency within mainstream society about all this incredibly confusing. None of it was secret knowledge. It was public and peer-reviewed. These were not conspiracy theories, murky stuff about the world being run by lizards or the Illuminati. Stephen had never been drawn to those ideas simply because, when scrutinised rationally, they never came close to standing up. But impending ecological catastrophe? When you analysed all the different factors, it was just the logical consequence of an entire system geared to reward and encourage consumption. In December 2007, just 10,000 people would turn up to the Campaign Against Climate Change's annual protest march through central London and past the Houses of Parliament. That same day, over 75,000 people watched Manchester United play Derby County in the English Premier League. This did not make any sense. Why wasn't everybody as worried as he was? Why was nobody really doing anything? The sense that he was from another planet never really left him.

On the bus journey back to Worcester from the Malvern Hills, Stephen told himself that he needed to do more than carry out hopeful raids on bookmakers. He needed to get inside a bank. From his room, he continued to obsessively research and read about the different methods used by successful bank robbers. He checked his email. There was nothing from Rebecca. He says her correspondence had become increasingly terse and distant. He went back to reading about bank robbers. He drank a glass of whiskey. He smoked a joint. He thought about the Organisation and what it needed to do. Scholarships for children working in sweatshops. Hospitals. Schools. Funds for conservation work. Colonies for human habitation under the sea. Or on the moon. Later, outside his door, the laughs and giggles and crashes and bangs of students coming home from a night out reverberated. They did not wake him. He had passed out on his single bed, curled up in a ball.

Stephen woke with a start. His bedroom was pitch black and the alarm on his mobile phone was ringing. It was 2 a.m. on Thursday, 29 November 2007 and several weeks had passed since his trip to the Malvern Hills. He quickly climbed out of bed, dressed himself in dark clothes, picked up his backpack and quietly slipped out of Wyvern Hall. He took his bicycle and rode away from the university campus, following the River Severn. It was cold. On the horizon, church spires rose into the darkness. Further down the river, the medieval cathedral was illuminated by soft yellow light, the reflection of its tower shimmering on the black water like a candle flame.

He got off his bike, pulled on his balaclava and walked towards a branch of Barclays bank. There were security cameras attached to the building, and while the front doors were sealed tight behind heavy security shutters, there was a ground floor window that was only protected by iron bars. Stephen already knew this. He had walked past this bank several times in an attempt to scope out any weak points. And in this window, he believed he had found one. Moving quickly, he opened his backpack and pulled out an angle-grinder. Clenching his teeth against the high-pitched *SCREEEEE*, he began to cut through the bars.

The plan was straightforward. Using the battery-powered angle-grinder he had ordered online, Stephen would force his way in through the small window. Once inside the bank, he would wait, concealed, with his knife, replica gun and balaclava. As the bank's employees arrived for the day, he would spring into action and force them to take him to the safe, whereupon he would take what he needed before escaping in his usual manner. Stephen kept looking behind him as the blade whirred, anticipating the outline of a figure passing down the empty street or the sound of urgent police footfalls approaching. It didn't take long, though, before he was more concerned with what was happening in front of him. Which was . . . not much. Ten minutes had passed and his angle-grinder barely seemed to have made a groove in the bar. He pressed the whirring blade with as much force as he dared, but there was little improvement. After twenty minutes he was still there, shivering, his arms beginning to cramp. After almost half an hour, his angle-grinder ran out of battery. He had managed to cut exactly halfway through the first bar. 'It must have been really cheap,' he says with a weary chuckle.

Cold and frustrated, Stephen jumped back on his bike and returned to Wyvern Hall. He recharged the battery then headed back to the bank with dawn still a few hours away. He pedalled fast but with the Barclays coming into view, he spotted something ahead of him that made him suddenly swerve into a side street. It was a police car, moving slowly along the road with its headlights off. Stephen's front wheel slammed into a kerb and he was almost thrown from his saddle. He peered around the corner and saw the car still creeping. Did someone hear the noise of his angle-grinder and report it? Or was it just a patrol car doing its job? He couldn't be sure. All he knew was that this mission must be aborted.

He could have punched the wall. He'd had it all so perfectly planned. He cursed himself for buying such a cheap angle-grinder. He picked up his bicycle and tried to push off, at which point he realised that his front tyre had been punctured. Tired and angry, he was forced to push his bike the mile or so back to his halls of residence, his tools, replica gun and knife in a bag slung over his shoulders. On his way back, he was passed by a police car. It did not slow down. If the officers inside the car had seen him then he would simply have been a skinny student returning to campus after a big night out. Which, in a sense, was true. Later, he wrote about the debacle in his diary: 'They say patrolling police officers don't prevent crime. But they do.'

Three days later Stephen burst into a branch of Coral bookmakers in Worcester city centre. It was 11 a.m. and he was wearing the contorted ghost mask worn by the killer in the *Scream* horror movies and holding his fake gun and a knife. He bellowed as loud as he could. Rushing towards the terrified manager, he told her from behind his long, eerie white face that he would slit her throat if she did not open the safe immediately. He recalls all this in a steady, quiet voice. 'This is one I am not keen on remembering.'

In advance of this robbery, Stephen had come to the conclusion that he was not being sufficiently intimidating. Had the manager during the Ladbrokes robbery stopped dead in her tracks when Stephen had commanded her to, rather than fleeing the building and alerting the police, he may have had enough time to force her to open the safe. Had Raymond Beer genuinely feared for his life during the Lloyds TSB attempt in Exeter, then even if he couldn't let Stephen into the bank itself, he definitely wouldn't have wrestled the replica pistol from him and smacked him in the face with it. Carl Gugasian had inspired terror – and thus compliance – by modifying already frightening Halloween masks into even more macabre visions. So Stephen decided it was time to try something similar.

That he was targeting another bookmakers should not come
as a surprise. Whenever an attempt to rob a bank went wrong,
he would often quickly follow up with a raid on a bookies. It
was a kind of reflex, born of a need to maintain momentum:
to remind himself that he was a criminal and that he wouldn't
use a failed bank heist as an excuse to back out of the whole
endeavour. Because for all his belief, Stephen still found the
act of carrying out his crimes incredibly difficult. Just because
he understood that walking into a bank or a bookies with a
weapon and walking out with money was physically possible
did not mean it came naturally to him.

'I do think that if I didn't have Asperger's I wouldn't have
been able to do it,' he tells me one night. 'I was so obsessive.
It was the sole thing on my mind. The Lloyds TSB one, the
failed one, every day I was going to the library and looking at
this guy going in and out. I was timing it and I was obsessed
by it. Without that obsession and fixation, I would have been
too freaked out. I would have been too scared.'

This was why he forced himself to keep going. 'Imagine you
were given a job, a very responsible job or a mission that you
were tasked with accomplishing, and which is much greater
than yourself or anyone else. I felt that I was going through
life with this responsibility,' he says. 'I got it in my mind that
you have this obligation to do it. If you are not going to make
a difference, then who is going to make a difference? And I
felt that if I don't do this, then I am just going to disintegrate.
That I might as well die.'

To help him carry out the *Scream* mask raid, Stephen took
cocaine. He had remembered taking the drug with Julian and
how it seemed to numb his anxiety and reduce his inhibitions.
He considered it a 'tool', a logical means to an end and something, unlike marijuana, he never used for its own sake. Inside

the Worcester branch of Coral, Stephen thrust his knife towards the manager's face while demanding she open the safe. She was terrified and tried to comply. The problem was that the safe was secured by a time lock, which means that once it has been opened and shut, it cannot be opened again for a set interval of time. Not enough time had elapsed since the safe was last opened for her to open it now. She was on her knees looking at the safe and shaking with fear. Stephen knew he had to leave quickly so opened a cash register and yanked on the tray, pulling it free before emptying the contents into his bag. As he backed out of the small shop, a customer who was walking in saw what was happening and moved to grab Stephen. The two men spilled out into the street.

Worcester is an old city. It was a Sunday, and the peals of church bells echoed above its streets, many of which are narrow and labyrinthine. Directly opposite the Coral was a ramshackle Tudor townhouse. Outside this building, a grappling contest ensued. In the process Stephen dropped his replica pistol. His mask was ripped from his face and his watch snapped from his wrist. He managed to pull himself away and with the hood of his coat still obscuring most of his face, drew his knife a second time and screamed at the man to back away. Stephen could see his assailant hesitate, so turned and sprinted down a long, tight passageway and towards the centre of town. A few passers-by saw him hurtle past. And then he was gone.

The local police couldn't work out what was happening in Worcester. In the space of five weeks, there had been two armed robberies on bookmakers and an attempted break-in at the Barclays bank. Detective Inspector Jim Fox of the West Mercia Police was one of the officers charged with investigating these crimes. He says that while violent robberies are rare enough in a region made of up largely rural areas and small towns, when they do happen, they don't happen like this. 'Usually when it does happen we either get cash in transit robberies, which are carried out by organised crime groups, or we get rubbishy, low-level robberies of convenience stores by idiots who had been in before and the proprietors know who they are,' he says. Stephen's crimes were neither. 'It was quite unusual. Not the kind of offences you get from a lone robber.'

To begin with, the West Mercia police had very little to go on. Appeals for witnesses were made in local papers, but nothing came of it. 'We had some CCTV footage of him, it had been in the media, but we were drawing a blank,' says DI Fox. What they didn't know was that, 200 miles to the south, DC Alex Bingham and Devon and Cornwall Police were stuck in a similar rut. Neither force knew that the other was looking for the same criminal. How could they? They didn't even know who he was.

Then, a few days after Stephen's Coral robbery in Worcester, the two forces suddenly found themselves working together. The *Scream* mask which had been torn from Stephen's face during his tussle with a customer was sent for forensic testing at a police lab. They took a DNA sample from spittle around the mask's mouthpiece. When they added this information to the police database, they were told that there was an existing DNA match on the system. It didn't match to an individual, but rather, to a crime: an attempted bank robbery in Exeter, three months earlier. Somebody had tried to force a courier to let them into a Lloyds TSB and when they were foiled, somehow managed to dissolve into thin air and evade the police.

Both police forces were alerted and began the process of trying to work out what could possibly connect an armed and evidently proficient criminal with a pair of small cathedral cities in the west of England. 'We had the DNA link from Devon, so we knew that there was a series of offences down there that were linked to the ones in Worcester,' says DI Fox. 'Which flummoxed us a bit really, because you are sitting there thinking . . . what's the link? It was not your run-of-the-mill thing. Everyone was racking their brains but nobody was getting anywhere with it. It was unusual.'

Many of the officers involved believed the perpetrator had to be from overseas, most likely Eastern Europe. They assumed that because he was an armed robber, he would have committed crimes before. Nobody began their criminal career with armed robbery. They always built up to it. If this guy were British then there would almost certainly be DNA links to his earlier, smaller crimes on the database. It therefore followed that he cut his teeth abroad before coming to the UK to target banks and bookmakers. Was he working alone? Did he have links to wider criminal networks and organisations domestically or abroad? How long would it be before he was responsible for someone getting badly hurt or worse? These were the kind of questions the investigating detectives were asking.

What they were not doing was asking whether their man could be a university student, dividing his crimes between his hometown and his place of study. To do so would seem bizarre. 'We just didn't get to "student", but it was right in front of us,' says DI Fox, shaking his head. 'How would you have ever predicted from his background that he would decide, in between his lectures, to go out and rob banks? We would go into every single pub in the vicinity to see if anyone matched the description. But we certainly wouldn't be going onto a college campus. It just wouldn't happen,' he says. 'So from that point of view? He had us.'

14

After four days and nights of continual observation and constant overhead light, Stephen was allowed to leave suicide watch. Further psychiatric assessments had deemed him stable enough to join the general prison population. Exhausted, he swapped his blue paper jumpsuit for the rough-cut tan uniform of Strafford County Jail. For the first time since his capture, arrest and incarceration in the United States, he found himself in and around a mass of other human beings. There was a time when Stephen's Asperger's and social anxiety would have made this overwhelming and unmanageable. Instead, he felt almost giddy with excitement. Here, inmates were not confined to their cells. There were open, communal areas. There were books and chess sets. There were televisions. There was even an indoor basketball court.

For the first few days at Strafford County he mostly slept. Then he cautiously began to feel his way into life in a New Hampshire county jail. There were three television sets in the communal area. He immediately noticed that the inmates who gathered around each set were divided by race. The Hispanic inmates all watched TV together. So did the black inmates. So did the whites. Exposed to the media for the first time in months, Stephen began to piece together a picture of what had been happening in the world. And what he learned was that the world was teetering on the brink of economic disaster.

On 15 September 2008, while Stephen was still in the Hole, the American investment bank Lehman Brothers had filed for bankruptcy. Over the previous decade, the Wall Street firm had become increasingly involved in mortgages as the US housing market seemed to just grow and grow. They had acquired a number of companies that specialised in lending to home buyers and, as a result, had become one of the key players in subprimes. By 2006, Lehman Brothers were effectively lending $50 billion a month. And in order to fund this lending they borrowed heavily, riding the housing boom to record financial returns. By 2007 the bank was, to all intents and purposes, operating as a property hedge fund.

Over-leveraged in real estate and with their books full of subprime mortgages, when the US housing bubble burst, America's fourth largest investment bank found itself trapped in a death spiral. The value of their real estate holdings fell like a stone. Nobody in their right mind would buy their toxic subprime mortgages in exchange for cash. And nobody in their right mind would lend them the cash to claw their way back from the brink. Not even the US government. Confidence had vanished. Lehman Brothers went bust. Some 25,000 jobs were lost almost overnight. The news showed employees filing out of their glass and steel Wall Street office with cardboard boxes containing their personal effects, all looking dazed. Going down with some $700 billion in liabilities, it was the biggest bankruptcy in history.

Global financial markets plummeted in response, the Dow Jones dropped 4.5 per cent overnight. A cold terror took hold. Nobody would lend to anybody. 'Credit crunch' was no longer an appropriate term for what was unfolding. Instead, analysts began to talk of a 'Financial Crisis' or 'Global Crash'. Because banks were not simply nervous about lending – they did not have the money to lend even if they wanted to.

The subprime mortgage scandal that had just brought down Lehman Brothers and Northern Rock was merely a symptom of a much deeper problem. For years, banks and bankers had been burning through the protective layer of capital – of actual, real, liquid cash – that was supposed to be held in reserve for just such a circumstance. Why had they been doing this? Because if they ploughed as much of that rainy-day money as they possibly could into the international money market, buying up mortgage debts, CDOs and other similar complex financial products, then they were guaranteed to make a return on that investment. The whole system had been set up to ensure that. By doing this, they were able to make their balance sheets look sensational and win themselves sensational bonuses year after year as a result. If you were a banker, you were riding an endless boom of your own clever creation.

Only, they had undone themselves. They had left the entire Western banking system cataclysmically under-capitalised. Where was the real money? Nobody could say for sure. Everything had been bound together by promises and projections and sleight-of-hand tricks that turned slithers in debt into bundles of profit come the next financial year. But at this rate it seemed there might not be another financial year. A domino effect looked set to commence. First banks fail. Then businesses fail. Then families fail. Then nations, eventually, fail. Governments began to panic. The dreams of national leaders were haunted by visions of the ATMs in their country no longer issuing cash. Of trust in banks evaporating as citizens began to understand that the notes in their wallets were simply broken promises. And even if people allowed themselves to believe that this money still had some value, they would hoard it jealously. Entire economies would turn to dust. Social stability would teeter. Within a few weeks of Lehman Brothers going down, US Treasury Secretary Hank Paulson told Congress they might be facing the collapse of the world economy 'within twenty-four hours'.

The only hope of averting a situation in which Western society was slowly bled white of money was massive public bailouts and stimulus packages. In a desperate transfusion, governments and central banks pumped billions into keeping alive many of the institutions whose actions helped cause this crisis. Popular anger began to manifest towards the banking executives whose attempts at financial alchemy had threatened to throw millions of lives into chaos and uncertainty. In the first week of November 2008, while Stephen played chess against Nigerian fraudsters and Scrabble with small-time drug dealers in Strafford County, it was announced that 500,000 jobs had been lost in the US over the previous two months. Car sales in the UK and US fell precipitously, threatening the automotive industries in both countries. The Chinese government announced a $586 billion domestic stimulus package to help defend against the deep global recession that was now inevitable.

Stephen viewed these unfolding events with little emotion. He did not feel vindicated, because he had always known that this was a system capable of destroying itself. What was happening was logical. Inevitable. If anything, he was surprised that people were surprised. The most vulnerable would suffer the most and those responsible would not. A loud buzzer sounded at Strafford County, which meant it was time for the inmates to return to their cells. Stephen thanked the Nigerian man for the game of chess and drifted back behind bars.

At Strafford County, Stephen experienced something new. He looked at the men he was incarcerated with and he felt a sense of comradeship. For the first time in his life, he had something in common with the people around him. They were all prisoners, all in matching tan uniforms and they were all sharing the same fate. He was not on the outside looking in. He was now on the inside. Literally. All of them were. That was the point. It was not that he enjoyed being there, but he felt there was a shared experience which bound them together.

He made connections in a way he was never able to in Sidmouth or at university. He played board games with a large, gentle African-American who was known as 'Muffin Man' on account of his overhanging belly. He did press-ups with an inmate everyone called 'Red Giant' due to his size and habit of blushing. Stephen was invited to play in basketball games. Everyone, as always, wanted to know what the hell he was doing there. And when he quietly explained, they puffed their cheeks out in disbelief and then called over to their friends, jabbing their fingers at Stephen and saying that the English kid was a fucking *bank robber*.

He shared a bunk with a skinny, sour-faced man in his mid-forties covered in rough tattoos of lightning bolts and blotchy crests. As the weeks passed, Stephen noticed that his cellmate would make angry, muttered observations about Muffin Man and other black prisoners. One evening, in their cell, the skinny man finally exploded, pacing the floor and cursing at Stephen for fraternising with 'niggers' and insisting that from now on he must only play basketball, watch TV and even eat alongside fellow 'Aryan' inmates. The inmate leaned close into Stephen, who had been reading a book on his bunk, and spat out a long, racial-epithet-filled diatribe, the overall gist of which was that whites were superior to all other races. But particularly the blacks.

Stephen blinked. He put down his book. He was shocked that the man he had been sharing his cell with held these views. He was also irritated that he was espousing something so obviously wrong. Not just morally wrong, but objectively wrong. The idea that there was some kind of hierarchy of different human races just didn't make any sense to Stephen. It didn't remotely stand up to scrutiny. He began to explain this to the man in front of him, to point out that racism is born of ignorance and only leads to destruction and division. We are all humans, he continued, speaking calmly and levelly, and the ecological and economic catastrophes which were about to be visited upon the planet would eventually affect all of us, regardless of the colour of our skin.

For some reason, this only seemed to make his cellmate more irate. He yelled that he was proud to be a white man and a member of the white race. The man tugged down hard on his prison vest and pointed to a faded tattoo on his chest which he said showed that he was a member of the Aryan Brotherhood, a white supremacist organisation. Stephen nodded patiently and said that, well, be that as it may, he surely had to accept that racism was born of prejudice and that prejudice was in turn born of feelings and emotions rather than any observable, demonstrable facts. The man frowned. No, he said. He did not accept that. He believed there was a clear, ordained hierarchy of races, crowned by the pure-blooded white man. That was, he said, the whole point of being in the Ayran Brotherhood.

But Stephen did not relent. He never would. Over the coming days and weeks, he would do his very best to bring his cellmate to reason. This debate would run for whole evenings, the pair of them lying on their bunks at the end of the day, repeating the same circular arguments for and against the existence of a white master race. Time passed and the anger seemed

to seep from Stephen's cellmate, annoyance turning to resigna-
tion turning, eventually, to curiosity about this strange, skinny,
obsessive English kid who was like a dog with a bone. Stephen
meditated and did yoga routines he had learned at Dechen
Chöling on the floor, and rather than deride him, his cellmate
asked cautious questions. As the two of them talked late into
the night, snippets of information about their respective lives
emerged. And Stephen started to see something he had already
noticed when speaking to other inmates, which was that despite
having grown up thousands of miles away, there was much in
his past that he shared with the other men. A lack of money.
A lack of opportunity. Mental health issues within families.

'Some of the stuff about his background I related to,' says
Stephen of his cellmate. 'Not the racist stuff. But I felt sorry
for him in some ways. In fact, most of the people I got to know
in any shape or form, I related to their experience and understood where they came from.'

Running parallel to Stephen's new-found feeling of belonging
and sense of bonhomie was the absolute conviction that he
must nevertheless escape. Since his arrest in the US five months
earlier, the belief that it remained possible to break free of his
confines had existed as a low whisper in the back of his mind.
Upon delivering him to Northwest State Correctional Facility,
the US Marshals who had escorted him there had made it
absolutely clear to prison staff that Stephen was likely to
attempt this. In solitary confinement, even Stephen accepted
that escape would be virtually impossible. But now he was at
Strafford County, he began to formulate possible plans of
action. 'Escape was like a constant,' he says. 'I was constantly
thinking about how I could do it.'

From his narrow cell window, Stephen could see that the
jail was surrounded by a chain-link perimeter fence topped

with a single coil of barbed wire. And beyond that? As far as he could see it was about 125 metres of green field and then thick treeline. Taking into account the wire, Stephen estimated there was probably about ten feet of fence to clear. But Stephen thought he had spotted something which meant that, if he were somehow able to get through an exit and outside, he wouldn't even need to climb over it. 'It sounds crazy, but I could see a little gap underneath the fence,' he tells me, chuckling softly. 'I thought that if I could just get outside then I could get underneath that and then I'd be away.'

With hindsight, he says that he had not even considered what his plan would be should he somehow pull this off. He was just obsessed with the idea of getting out. Everything else would have to fall into place. 'I just had this mentality of, where there's a will, there's a way.' As with his robberies, Stephen maintained this belief that anything was possible. 'I felt that the world would take care of me, as it were. The reason being that I was acting in the name of justice.'

Stephen never told any of the other inmates that he planned to escape. After his experience of being ratted out at Northwest State, he knew that directly disclosing his thoughts to others would be naive. But what he did do was muse openly about the *possibility* of it. About the potential practical requirements that would, theoretically, need to be met if a jailbreak were to happen. He was, he believed, being subtle. He wanted to know what other prisoners, particularly those serving longer sentences, felt about the subject of escape. Was it something they had thought about? he idly wondered over games of Scrabble. Was it something that they'd known people do successfully in the past? he asked as they watched other inmates playing basketball. Nobody seemed to want to talk about it. Stephen shrugged inwardly and resolved to keep scanning the doors, windows and air vents of Strafford County, constantly triangulating the different possibilities of escape. After one day of doing just that, he returned to his cell and drifted into sleep, imagining himself running free, gleeful and laughing, through the thick, moonlit forests of New Hampshire.

Stephen was woken by two guards, who entered his cell and ordered him to stand up. As he did so, strong hands reached out to twist his arms behind his back and he felt the squeeze and click of handcuffs being locked around his wrists. He was taken from his cell and marched through the long sterile corridors of the jail. He asked where he was being taken but the two men ignored him. Deep down, Stephen already knew the answer. Deep down, he already knew why. They turned a corner and the sign on the wall simply read 'SEGREGATION'. He was being placed back in solitary confinement. Another inmate had told the prison authorities about his obsessive talk of escape and now he was in a familiar six-by-nine cell. The guards ordered him to strip down to his underpants then left him alone. He began to shiver.

There was a time when Stephen would have despaired. He would have curled up on his cold slab of a bunk and wept. But the past five months had made him stronger, more resilient. Instead, he stood in the middle of his cell and took three deep breaths. Then, still in his underpants, he calmly began a yoga routine. A guard pressed his face to the small window in the cell door. He saw Stephen with his eyes clenched shut and arms outstretched, as pale and still as a statue under the dim cell light.

15

I n early December 2007, twelve months before Stephen found himself doing yoga in solitary confinement at Strafford County, he was in his room at Wyvern Hall, smoking a joint and reviewing the crimes he had carried out so far. Since his attempt to enter the Lloyds TSB in Exeter – the attempt that finished with the bomb scare and evacuation – he had only succeeded in holding up two bookmakers, making away with less than a thousand pounds in cash. He covered his face with his hands and rubbed his eyes. His plan had never been to reach the sum of £100,000 in tiny increments. Instead, he hoped to steal it all in one fell swoop. One big job, a getaway, and then he could begin the process of working out how to use this cash as seed money for the Organisation.

'Each robbery I saw as a failure,' he tells me one afternoon, sitting in a small meeting room at *The Times*' offices. 'There were one or two that I saw as partial successes. But my idea was to walk into a bank and get access to the safe, because I had done research on this and once you had access to the safe, you could more or less hit a hundred k straight away, if not more.'

Stephen knew what the problem was. The replica pistols he had used so far had not done the job intended. Not everyone was as intimidated by them as he had hoped. Raymond Beer,

the courier who gave him a bloody cheek. The punter at the
Worcester Coral who tried to grab him as he was leaving. The
William Hill manager who disobeyed his command to remain
where she was, thus escaping and alerting the police.

But having a real gun? That would change everything. Simply
being able to fire a live round into the air upon entering a bank
would show everyone that he was not brandishing a toy. A
gun, he gradually convinced himself, was the answer. He
imagined the different ways he might use one to best effect.
He could make an appointment with a bank manager, arrive
in a smart suit but with a pistol concealed on his person. Once
he was alone with the manager, he could draw the gun and
instruct them to take him 'discreetly to the safe'. The problem
with this plan was that it did not allow him to disguise his
features, unless he was willing to chance it with fake facial hair
and sunglasses. Which would most likely arouse suspicion. He
had already ordered some stick-on beards from the internet,
though it turned out that they were only fancy dress standard
at best, adequate for hiding his features from CCTV but not
for fooling a bank manager.

Another option was simply to stick to the Carl Gugasian
approach. 'Fire the gun in the air, jump over the counter, get
access to the safe room,' he says. 'If it was timed right, I could
have got in. If you look on the internet, there are plenty of
examples of people managing to do that.'

When I contacted the Crown Prosecution Service to ask if any
of Stephen's diaries from around the period of his crimes were
still in existence, I was told that whatever notebooks had been
seized by the police as evidence would have been held for a time
but would by now most likely have been destroyed. Later, though,
DI Jim Fox of the West Mercia Police says that this is not the

case. He has boxes and boxes of evidence relating to Stephen's crimes, including notebooks and journals from 2007 and 2008. In the run up to Stephen's eventual trial in the UK, these journals were scoured for evidence which could be used against him. As a result, many of these diary entries were photocopied and presented in court. Stephen provided dozens of these police photocopies to me himself. What is not accessible are the physical diaries themselves, which contain writings which were never presented in court and which therefore remain Stephen's private possessions, albeit possessions held by the West Mercia Police.

The practical upshot of all this is that there is information in these diaries which the West Mercia Police can describe in a general sense – for example, the kind of stuff Stephen was writing about and the kind of schemes he was making – but which they cannot show or publish. Some of this information relates to his plans to move beyond the Gugasian method. 'He talks about "tiger takeovers",' says DI Fox, who describes the process by which Stephen would hope to break into a bank at night then pounce on the staff as they entered, forcing them to take him to the vault. 'He was going to take them all hostage, basically, and keep them there until the vault had been opened.'

Stephen says that DI Fox is correct. He was constantly researching new ways to pull off that one big heist. 'He is absolutely right. I had plans to escalate because the whole idea was to net as much as possible. And I had realised with these note jobs, I was only netting a few thousand at once.' But just because he wrote down how he might ambush a cash-in-transit delivery vehicle doesn't mean that he ever seriously planned to do it. 'I wrote all the different techniques, which doesn't necessarily mean I would do every one. It was a mental exercise to see what I would be able to do and what the best way of doing it would be,' he says. 'I had a whole folder of it.'

But to do any of this, Stephen needed a real gun. His problem was that acquiring a gun in the UK is incredibly difficult. The regulation of firearms is so tight that the number of reliable guns on the British black market is very small which, in turn, makes the cost of acquiring one very high. Not only did Stephen lack the kind of money needed to buy a gun, he also had no underworld connections who could arrange this kind of a deal even if he did. Geography students from Devon with Asperger's syndrome do not tend to have underworld connections.

On the other hand, Stephen discovered that as a geography student, he had other surprisingly useful resources available to him. At one point during his first term, a lecturer on his geography course asked if anyone would be interested in learning how to use a new version of a three-dimensional city-mapping software, a sort of subject-specific Google Maps. All the other students remained silent, bored and impassive, but Stephen's hand immediately shot up. He used this software, which was called ArcGIS, to scope out the streets of Worcester from a bird's-eye perspective, to identify the location of banks and then envision the different escape routes he could use. Once he had familiarised himself with the programme, he spent hours toying with it. 'I found that extremely useful. It was like a tool. I could plan exactly where I was going afterwards and where the changeover locations for the clothes would be and stuff.'

One December afternoon, during a reconnaissance trip to Worcester town centre, Stephen spotted something that made his heart skip. He was walking down a pedestrianised shopping street with Christmas lights suspended overhead when he passed an HSBC bank. It was on the ground floor of a four-storey building, and while the branch itself had all the usual shutters and security doors, the bank's admin offices on the floors above seemed practically unguarded. There were no bars over the rows of large windows on the first, second and third floors. He jammed his hands in his pockets and kept his head down as he hurried past. The building was part of a large, slightly ramshackle four-sided block of street-facing businesses which included pubs, a Starbucks, a discount shoe shop and a Mexican restaurant. Some of the buildings dated back to the eighteenth century. Some, like the bank, were modern. Running through the middle of this block, though, was a series of alleyways to allow access to the rear of the businesses. Stephen quickly worked out that he could reach the back of the bank via this alley network.

Stephen returned to his room knowing that, gun or no gun, this was his best chance of breaking into a bank and executing what he called a 'tiger takeover'. Wearing a balaclava, he would force his way into one of the top floors at night, move down through the building to the ground floor and then crouch in wait for the first employees to arrive. Then, exploding into action, he would use his knife and replica pistol to intimidate them into taking him to the safe, where he would fill his backpack before fleeing.

Two nights later, early on the morning of 18 December, he slipped into the alleyway. There was a fire escape leading up to the upper storeys of the building, but it was locked from the outside. So he scaled up drainpipes and window ledges in order to reach a balcony. He smashed a window and stepped into the bank's offices. Cautiously, he cast a dim torchlight across the room. There were rows of desks, computers, photocopiers: the usual trappings of corporate life. His eyes cast about for an exit which would take him downstairs, into the branch itself. Minutes passed as he searched and searched, stumbling about, until finally he found what he calculated was the way down. But there was a problem.

'It was a massive metal door,' he says flatly. Stephen knew that there was no way he was going to be able to force it open. Perhaps he should have expected that there might have been massive metal doors – or at least something similar – preventing easy access to the bank. He shouted with anger and frustration, smacking his fist against the door with a dull clang. In a pique, he began to ransack the bank's office, pulling computer monitors to the floor and snatching a camcorder he spotted on a desk. He shoved it into his bag before fleeing back the way he had come before the noise alerted anyone.

A few days later, Stephen was skimming the local news online when he read about a crime that had been committed in Worcester. The regional office of the National Society for the Prevention of Cruelty to Children (NSPCC) had been broken into and vandalised, causing several thousand pounds worth of damage. He frowned. Who would go out of their way to vandalise and set back the work of a charity that helped to safeguard some of Britain's most vulnerable children? As he scanned the story with increasing speed, nausea began to swell in the depths of his stomach. The NSPCC offices were at the same address as the HSBC bank – indeed, they were in fact above the HSBC bank. He began to tremor as he realised that the answer to his question – who would do such a thing? – was, simply, him. He had done it. He had assumed the office space he'd broken into belonged to the bank and that his vandalism, though petulant, was still a form of legitimate retribution. A small act of defiance against a corrupt financial system. Instead, he realised he had done something incredibly wrong. 'It was the complete opposite of what I had intended.'

Stephen ran to his toilet and vomited. He cried. It's hard to overstate how much of an impact this episode had on him. He had spent at least two years methodically constructing a moral universe in which his crimes were justified and righteous. But underpinning everything was the unshakable conviction that he was doing far more good than harm. His actions in the NSPCC offices seemed to undermine this completely and he struggled to cope with the realisation. Even today, discussing the episode is a struggle. Of all his actions, it is this, along with the *Scream* mask robbery, that causes him to scrunch his body inwards, break eye contact and lose his train of thought. He says that in the aftermath of this realisation, he took his knife and cut his arm several times before pledging to repay the NSPCC £25,000, despite the fact that news reports estimated the total cost of damage to be less than £6,000. It was, he told himself, a promise 'sealed in blood'.

A few months later, an NSPCC employee sorted through the morning's post and found an envelope that made them pause. Immediately, they knew what was inside. Carefully opening it, they pulled out a large wad of cash, approximately £650 in banknotes. This was not the first time they had received this kind of post. Somebody had been putting these envelopes through the charity letterbox for a while now. As well as cash, the first envelope contained a note apologising for the damage which had been caused during the break-in and the promise of more money to come. The police had assured the NSPCC that they were looking into it, but the identity of the culprit – if that was even the right word – remained a mystery. The only clue were two letters that were always written on the envelopes. RH.

Stephen returned to Sidmouth for the Christmas holidays a few days after the NSPCC fiasco. He had bought an old red Rover for £500 and drove south. He was tense and uneasy. He felt no nostalgia for the house on Manstone Avenue. If the consultant psychiatrist who evaluated Stephen at nineteen was right and he was 'inadvertently traumatised' as a child, then this small, increasingly shabby council house is where most of the trauma happened. It was a cold, grey day, with wind and rain rolling in off the sea. He lugged his bags to the house and knocked. A few moments passed, then his mother opened the door. She looked at him for a moment, then smiled. 'Hello, Stephen,' she said.

Stephen smiled back. 'Hello, Mum.'

Peter Jackley no longer lived at Manstone Avenue. The prostate cancer he had been diagnosed with years earlier had become terminal. By late 2007, Stephen's mother was no longer able to care for her husband so he was moved into hospice care in the nearby town of Exmouth. Stephen and his mother visited Peter, though all he can remember is the oppressive stuffy heat of the place, the old people drifting about the corridors and the locks on the outside of every bedroom door. At one point his father, diminished and frail, grabbed Stephen's arm and said 'get me out'. He told him that he couldn't. When he and his mother left the building, one of the residents attempted to escape with them.

Back at Manstone Avenue, Stephen struggled to communicate with his mother. 'She was like someone that was drugged,' he says. Which is exactly what she was. Whichever different cocktails of medications she had been prescribed over the years, they all ended up having the same numbing effect on her. She sat quietly on the old brown sofa in her motley living room, her own sketches and paintings of plants and animals hanging from walls painted a combination of yellow and green. Wearing a thick, pink turtleneck jumper and brown embroidered waistcoat, Jenny Jackley quietly read and drank tea and talked to Stephen in an absent, passing sort of way. She never asked him questions. And when she responded to questions he asked, her answers were short and often inconclusive, though delivered with a smile.

Seeing her like this was painful. It was also frustrating, because Stephen knew that she was creative and warm, but that these traits were being erased, collateral damage in the constant struggle between her illness and her medication. He didn't like to admit it, but Stephen knew he had characteristics in common with his father, particularly when it came to being stubborn and single-minded. But he had even more in common with his mother. They both loved nature. They both seemed to ask searching questions about the world and reality. When Stephen was just a child, Jenny Jackley had written a poem called 'Money'.

Just pieces of crumpled paper
Small round coins
Marked with the face of 'Her Majesty'
What majesty?
So small and insignificant
Yet why should it be so important?
What is money?
What is life?
Life is the sun . . . the wind . . . the sea
People who feel love and happiness
People who feel sorrow and pain
Money is . . . ? . . . nothing
Why must it be so important in our lives?
~~~

Someday . . . one day
We'll find a way . . .
. . . Follow the sun . . .
. . . Everyone run . . .
. . . Leave the world alone . . .
. . . Live . . .

A few days after arriving home for Christmas, Stephen successfully robbed his first bank. It was the Lloyds TSB in Seaton,
where the cashier asked him if he wanted a bigger bag when
handing him the money, and when Stephen escaped along the
clifftop path back to Sidmouth before depositing £4,830 in the
nook of a tree in some woodland not far from Manstone
Avenue. 'Trees, for some reason, I thought were secure,' he says.
'It was an old oak up the top of a hill and it was really hard to
climb. I thought that nobody else would have climbed it.'

In his diaries, Stephen wrote that despite the fact he had
not hit the £100,000 jackpot, the Lloyds TSB qualified as a
'semi-success' rather than a failure. For one thing, he had
escaped. More importantly, though, it demonstrated what he
had always believed: that it was possible to walk into a bank,
slip a note under a counter, and walk out with thousands of
pounds. Now that he had done it, he had no excuse not to do
it again.

His obsession with reaching his target was deepening by the
day. On top of the 'mission' he believed it was his responsibility
to carry out, he now had an additional obligation to the
NSPCC, to repay them for the harm he had done. 'It was just
more motivation for me to get to that hundred k. I had that
extra pressure on me to do a proper heist. I had to pay them
back tens of thousands of pounds, and I couldn't do that just
by going into a bookmaker and getting a few hundred.'

After returning to Manstone Avenue following the Lloyds
TSB robbery in Seaton, Stephen couldn't sleep. He was too
keyed-up. He sat on the edge of his single bed and looked around
his tiny childhood bedroom: at his collections of fossils and
minerals, the piles of reference books stacked up in the corner,
the paintings of trees and flowers on his wall, done by his mother.
Eventually, he made a decision. He would carry out another

bank robbery. The very next day. 'I remember thinking, whilst I am in this mindset, I might as well do another one.'

At 4.50 p.m. the following day, Thursday 20 December 2007, Stephen walked into the Britannia building society in Exeter city centre. It was less than 100 yards away from the Lloyds TSB he had attempted to gain access to three months earlier, on a bustling high street of shops, cafes and offices. He was wearing a black beanie hat and had a black scarf covering all of his face apart from his eyes. As he strode towards the counter, he hurled one of his defaced pound coins, which had by now became a trademark of his robberies. In Stephen's mind, this gesture was not so much a flourish as a necessity. 'I saw it as something to get out of the way.'

Stephen accepts that announcing his crimes by throwing a coin towards the people he was about to rob was, from a practical perspective, probably not a good idea. For one thing, it gave them a split second to look up and register what was going on. Secondly, while it was strange and confusing behaviour, it was not necessarily intimidating. Thirdly, it was evidence. Even if the police already had a pretty good idea that the mini-crime-wave breaking around South Devon and Worcestershire was the work of one person, these pound coin calling cards only proved it.

'I wasn't stupid,' he tells me. 'I didn't do these things not realising they would be able to connect them. But I felt I had a duty, and as part of the mission, it was my obligation to leave these things behind. It was out of principle.' He smiles awkwardly. 'Which sounds strange, I know.'

In the Britannia, he strode towards the middle-aged woman behind the cashier's desk, tossed her a backpack and demanded she fill it with cash. Only, she refused. Detective Inspector Fox describes what happened next. 'She stood up to him. He has come in and has pointed a gun at her and she said that she felt so angry that she throws the bag back at him and says, "Go on, take that and fuck off!"' He chuckles. 'She sounds like quite a character to be honest.'

At this point the bank manager, another middle-aged woman, stormed out of a back office and also started yelling at the startled figure of Stephen, ordering him to 'get out of my branch'. And so he did, turning and running out the door before making for the leafy cover of Rougemont Gardens, the same public park he had used for a change of clothes after the Lloyds TSB attempt. He walked back through town as police sirens blared, his eyes tracking the pavement ahead of him, hands wedged deep into his pockets. He caught a bus back to his house in Sidmouth, where he sat at the small dinner table with his mother, trying and failing to make conversation with the gentle figure he loved but couldn't know.

Later, in his room, he analysed the failure of the Britannia job. Why didn't they take him seriously? 'I think there were a few reasons,' he reflects today. 'I was just one person, and most successful robberies – with the exception of "note jobs" – are undertaken by groups, not individuals. Also on top of that it is well known that, in the UK, firearms are practically impossible to get hold of. So an individual who is probably quite young coming into the bank branch by themselves and acting bizarrely by throwing this coin? All of that probably didn't encourage cooperation.'

Devon and Cornwall Police immediately knew that the enigmatic figure at the centre of Operation Gandalf had returned to the south coast. He had robbed a bank in Seaton and then, the following day, attempted to rob the Britannia in Exeter. And yet again, on both occasions he had managed to just . . . vanish. They had his DNA, they knew he had been operating up in Worcester, but beyond that they were no closer to catching him than they had been three months earlier. Detective Alex Bingham says that the department was by this point beginning to feel the weight of institutional expectation that they unmask whoever was doing this.

'There was a lot of pressure on the boss at the time,' he says. 'You have had a number of armed robberies on your patch, you know, and the bosses above him want to know what's going on.'

In January 2008, Devon and Cornwall Police arrested a twenty-nine-year-old local man in connection with the crimes, a fact which made the local news. When Stephen learned of this, he wrote an anonymous letter to the Exeter *Express and Echo* to announce that the police had the wrong man and that he was in fact the person responsible.

'I will continue to take from the rich and give to the poor,' he concluded in his letter. 'I am the modern day Robin Hood.'

Again, this letter did not help Stephen in any practical way. Quite the opposite. But Stephen felt that it was part of his duty to let the authorities know he was still at large. 'I just didn't like the thought that someone else had been arrested for an offence that I committed.'

There was also a part of Stephen that enjoyed taunting the police. On more than one occasion during his childhood, he watched as officers removed his mother from their home either during or in the aftermath of psychotic episodes brought on by her schizophrenia. Also, as far as Stephen could see, the police just didn't seem to be any good at their jobs. With some sensible forward-planning, Stephen had been able to evade them more or less at will. 'I had this sense that they were totally incompetent, which didn't help the situation either,' he says. 'I kept doing it and there weren't any repercussions. They seemed to be going in the wrong directions and arresting the wrong people.'

Detective Bingham says that Devon and Cornwall Police viewed Stephen's letter to the *Express and Echo* with a professional scepticism. 'There are always suspects who want to try and wind you up or send you down different tracks and different avenues. You have to look at it and wonder if this is the actual person doing it? Or is it a hoax?'

Just because somebody contacts a newspaper claiming to be the perpetrator does not necessarily mean they are. During the Yorkshire Ripper investigations, continues Bingham, the police spent valuable time and resources pursuing leads provided to them by hoax calls. 'It can lead you down a line of inquiry that stops you doing the actual inquiry.'

While the pressure Stephen felt to successfully pull off that one big heist grew by the day, he was also enjoying the double life he had created. Having spent so many years feeling thwarted and anonymous, he had created a world in which fantasy regularly became real.

'Why have I turned to crime?' he asked himself in his diary during his first term at university.

Many reasons. Anger at the establishment; the status quo, the rich getting richer and the poor getting poorer. The forgotten millions of southern lands who live in acute poverty, with just a grain of opportunity which Westerners ignore. And even the knowledge of being sought by the law is a draw in itself. It brings self-importance, you can make elaborate storylines out of every stroll, plotting and spotting the weaknesses of businesses. Always looking for opportunities, possibilities.

As a new year began, the lure of this new identity meant that Stephen drifted further and further away from the insecure young man he had been. 'I wanted to escape the child I had grown up as, and I wanted to put what I had experienced behind me and become someone else,' he says as we talk late one night on the phone. 'Whether that was the Robin Hood persona that I embraced or someone pioneering a new future for humanity.'

He had blonde highlights put in his hair. He swapped his glasses for contact lenses. He fell behind on his university studies. He smoked cannabis alone in his bedroom. The irony was that, taken in isolation, these were things that many under-graduates do during their first year of university. Reinventing yourself in this way is completely normal. What is not completely normal is coupling this reinvention with a compulsion for drawing detailed maps of city streets and bank locations, plotting escape routes and creating whole folders of minutely plotted heists.

'Crime is so damn appealing,' he wrote to himself. 'The money, the planning, the power, and the dubious fame of it draws me like a magnet.'

Stephen's obsession was complete. The line between fantasy and reality was no longer clear. It was no longer an obstacle. 'I am a bank robber, an armed raider and bloody proud of it,' he scrawled in his journal. Anything, he told himself, was possible.

16

Within a week of returning to Worcester to begin his second term at university, Stephen was contacted by an aunt. She informed him that his father had died. Stephen frowned. His response was just a soft 'Oh . . .' He waited for a wave of grief to wash over him but it did not come. He had known for a long time that the logical conclusion of his father's cancer was that it would eventually kill him. When he first learned of the diagnosis, years earlier, he spent a whole night crying while Ben Weaver, round for a sleepover, snored on the floor of his bedroom. But in his halls of residence bedroom, at the age of twenty-one, Stephen did not seem sure how to respond. 'Although I had my issues with my father, I still considered him someone quite close,' he remembers. 'I have a strange way of processing things.'

Peter Jackley remains an enigmatic, unresolved presence in his son's life. Stephen still does not seem to understand the man his father was. He is somebody whose character was clearly marked by his own issues with mental health, but these were not issues he fully accepted or addressed. He appears to have been stubborn, secretive, controlling, obsessive and quick to anger. His attempts at charm seemed only to repel people. Stephen believes that his 'heart was in the right place', but from the outside looking in, it is impossible to decide whether it was

Peter Jackley who kept his small, dysfunctional family together, or whether it was he who dragged them down, compounding their isolation and creating an atmosphere of conflict and tension.

That said, it is also clear that Peter Jackley faced many challenges beyond his control. He could not help that he suffered from manic depression. He could not help that Stephen never received an Asperger's diagnosis which would have at least given him the chance to understand aspects of his son's behaviour and perhaps even begin to support him more effectively. He could not help that his wife was schizophrenic. Unless, like Ben Weaver and even Stephen up to a point, you believe that there was something about her condition that he liked – the vulnerability or malleability – and which may have attracted him in the first place.

The day after he received the news about his father, Stephen flew to Amsterdam for the weekend. He had booked the trip when he had returned to Worcester to discover the 'unreliable' campus drug dealer was nowhere to be found, and resolved to fly out and smuggle some cannabis back himself. Looking back, Stephen thinks that his fixation on his mission may have meant that there wasn't space in his head to accept and process his father's death. 'Plus I saw myself as someone else, in effect. It kind of got pushed out of my mind that he had died.'

Returning to Amsterdam was a huge risk. It was still less than a year since Stephen pulled a knife on the Dutch hostel employee he felt was trying to fleece him before making off with a fistful of euros. But as he boarded his flight he reassured himself that everything would be fine. Nobody seemed to have connected him with the crime, which seems strange. The hostel had made a photocopy of his driver's licence when he first checked in, so the Dutch police knew his name. Yet for some reason they never contacted British authorities to let them know that a Stephen Jackley was wanted in connection with an armed robbery.

Or perhaps they did, but nobody was able to work out exactly who he was. Because, by chance, Stephen's driver's licence contained a misprint. His date of birth was wrong. He could no longer remember exactly how wrong, but he told himself that it was evidently wrong enough to make tracking him down very difficult. After his plane landed, he stood in line at Schiphol airport passport control until he was beckoned forward. He handed his passport to the Dutch border control officer, who scanned it before waving him through.

Stephen spent two days smoking and drinking in Amsterdam. He sat in the corner of cannabis cafes with his notebook, getting increasingly stoned, writing down plans for robberies and the Organisation as well as long, meandering poems and stream-of-consciousness treatises on the nature of reality. Looking back, he wondered if the real reason he returned to Amsterdam was because, subconsciously, he wanted to get caught: that however much he was relishing his new identity as Robin Hood there was still a part of him that remained an insecure boy from Sidmouth who wanted this all to end.

After two days in Amsterdam, Stephen began to descend to earth and the reality of his father's death started to seep into his psyche. He realised the simple finality of it, and the fact that it was now just him and his mother. He looked around him and saw strange faces speaking strange languages and felt an overwhelming need to return to Sidmouth. He abandoned his plan to smuggle a supply of weed back with him. Pale, pink-eyed and exhausted, he returned to Schiphol. He went to the check-in desk, presented his passport and was handed his boarding pass. Then, passing back through airport security, he was stopped by a member of staff, who politely asked if he by any chance had a driver's licence with him.

Tired and foggy-headed, Stephen thought this was a strange question. But he 'gormlessly' handed it over. What happened next is jumbled in Stephen's recollection, but he was told that he was going to be arrested. If he did have a subconscious desire to be captured, then in the moments that followed he did not act like it. He dropped his bag and turned to run, bolting towards a quiet-looking corridor leading away from security. He pumped his arms but it felt like running from something in a dream, horribly slow and uncoordinated. Strong hands grabbed him from behind and though he tried to prise himself free, it was useless. Stephen was placed in an arm lock as travellers and airport staff stared at him impassively. His head was throbbing. His mouth was dry. All he could hear was the distant sound of departure announcements and the two large men who had him by the arms, chuckling and talking in Dutch. 'They were just laughing and joking about it,' says Stephen. 'I thought, shit. This is it. This is the end.'

He was taken to a small, bare holding room in the bowels of Schiphol. Every hour or so, a member of the cheerful security staff popped their head in and asked if he would like a pack of cigarettes. 'They were massively into smoking. I remember thinking I don't want to say no, because that would seem kind of rude. So eventually I just accepted.'

Dutch police came and explained to Stephen that he was being charged with 'robbery or theft or something'. He was put in handcuffs, escorted to a van and transported to Rotterdam where he was placed in a holding facility. He had his fingerprints taken before sitting through a court hearing in which a judge and other legal officials sat down with Stephen and explained that he would be held in a Dutch prison until a date for his trial was set.

It was Stephen's first experience of incarceration and the shock of it was overwhelming. Knowing that he was no longer free, he felt a wave of nauseous horror flush through his body. His pulse raced and he breathed in short, shallow bursts as he was processed and taken to his cell. At the time, he could have cried, though he admits that looking back, this Dutch prison cell was incredibly comfortable by the standards of what he would later endure. 'You walk into this massive room with an en suite bathroom. There are cakes on the table and loads of croissants and food everywhere. It was really unusual,' he says. 'They have a different perspective on imprisonment there, I think.'

There was plenty of recreation time, prisoners were free to wander their wings of the jail and Stephen dutifully smoked the cigarettes the guards kept giving him. When he finished a pack, they brought him more, so he felt obliged to smoke even more. They made him light-headed and giddy. Inside his comfortable cell, he tapped his foot. He was convinced that it was just a matter of time before everything came crashing down. The Dutch police would contact their British counterparts to let them know of his arrest which would somehow result in him finally being connected to the robberies. He chewed on a croissant and despaired.

Then, just like that, he was able to walk away. After a week or so in the Dutch prison, he was informed that he was being allowed to leave on compassionate grounds. Stephen had told them about his father's recent death and impending funeral, and while this had not appeared to sway the authorities initially, it seemed that they had a change of heart. He was told that he would be contacted in due course, when a court date had been set, and that he must then return to the Netherlands to stand trial when instructed. He agreed. And so they let him go.

Stephen arrived at his father's small funeral in Exeter to be greeted with a flurry of hushed but urgent questions from his relatives. Where had he been? Nobody had been able to get in touch with him for the past week. Stephen looked at these people blankly. He was not close to any of them. He told everybody that the reason he had been uncontactable was that he had been arrested over some 'drugs issue' in Amsterdam but that it was all sorted now. He was chided by some, but he didn't care. He sat beside his mother during the service and then stood at her side during the wake. Lisa Watson, Peter's daughter and Stephen's half-sister, remembers watching him and feeling uneasy, though not being able to say exactly why.

'I didn't really understand everything that was going on because obviously you couldn't really get much information from Jenny. I don't know whether she was oblivious or just didn't understand,' she says. 'You only really heard snippets from other members of the family. But Stephen was being very mysterious at the funeral. I found him . . . he was mysterious over what he had done.'

Lisa describes how Stephen didn't just appear unmoved at the funeral, but that there was something else about him: an air of slyness and superiority. 'I just thought it was strange that he didn't seem to be upset. He just seemed to be . . . he had a smug expression on his face for half of the time, like a grin if you like. And I just found that really strange.'

She says that knowing about his Asperger's may help her understand why he didn't appear as upset as she had thought he would be. But his expression was unsettling. Later, after the funeral, Stephen walked with Lisa and her husband near the seafront. 'He was talking about money,' she says. 'And he said, "I can give you a thousand pounds today." My husband and I said, how can you do that? And he said, "I've got money hidden around Exeter." I think he said he had some money hidden in a tree by Exeter Cathedral. Three grand in a tree by Exeter Cathedral.'

Lisa and her husband looked at each other. Neither believed what Stephen was telling them. 'We just thought it was fantasy.' Later, as the three of them passed a quayside, Stephen pointed at one of the boats. 'He was saying to my husband, "I bet you I could jump down there onto that boat", or something like that. My husband was like, "We're at your dad's funeral here, why would you be doing stuff like that? I don't even know you and you are making bets with me."'

Stephen wandered off, but both Lisa and her husband were left unnerved. They discussed what happened later that evening. 'My husband said, "He's dead behind the eyes, he's quite scary to look at." There was just no emotion there. He didn't seem upset. There was just nothing behind the eyes.' She sighs. 'He just seemed so separate.'

After his father's funeral, Stephen returned to Worcester in early February 2008. Late one stormy night, alone in his room, he says that he called Rebecca. He described how, immediately upon hearing her voice down the line, he knew what was coming. In his heart he had known since they parted at Dechen Chöling that a future together was only a faint hope and that their long-distance relationship was never going to be sustainable. But it still cut jagged and deep when she quietly told him that she had met somebody else at her university.

She said that she never meant to hurt him and that she was sorry. She had tried calling him the previous week but he never answered. Stephen told her that was because he'd been in a

Dutch jail, and when she exclaimed in shock and asked what had happened, he simply brushed her off, ignoring the question. Instead, angry and on the verge of tears, he hung up on her. Immediately, he regretted it, so tried to call her back. She did not answer. He would never speak to her again. Stephen felt his throat contract and he clenched his eyes tight to stem the tears he could already feel forming. He stormed out of his room and into the cold, wet night, making for one of the playing fields just behind Wyvern Hall. He broke into a run and began to do lap after lap around the football pitch. Letting himself go as he ran, he gasped for breath between deep, ugly sobs, hot tears and cold raindrops streaming down his face. After twenty laps, he dragged himself back indoors and fell asleep on his single bed, exhausted and despondent.

Stephen finds talking about Rebecca difficult. He believes that had they physically been together during this period, she would have been the only person able to talk him out of continuing with his crimes. That's not to say that she would definitely have been able to – 'it could well have been that I had committed to this thing and nothing whatsoever would have deviated me from that path' – but rather, she would have represented his last best chance at breaking the obsession and pulling away. 'She is the only thing that could have stopped me.'

With Rebecca now gone, Stephen committed the very last wavering vestiges of himself to his mission. He had nothing else to commit to, nothing else to live for.

Stephen explains to me that he would rather not provide any details which might allow Rebecca to be tracked down and approached for interview. He says that he does not want to intrude or impact on her life in any way, or run the risk of landing her in trouble because, while he is never entirely clear about the exact extent to which he revealed his plans and actions to her, he worries he may have said enough to incriminate her in some way or other. He also admits that there is an aspect of psychological self-preservation to all this. He does not particularly want to discover that she is now married, or that she has children, because it would only emphasise what he'd once had and what he has lost. 'Rebecca,' he writes to me in one email, 'was like a beacon of light in a very cold cave, at a stage in my life when I was starting to lose hope and direction.'

Nobody from Dechen Chöling is able to recall her. Ralph Williams, Lisa Steckler, Maizza Waser . . . they all remember Stephen very well, having spent weeks working and living alongside him. But none of them remember him having a relationship with a tall girl from Colorado who enjoyed playing Scrabble and going on long bike rides and who had a gentle but infectious laugh. Waser, the older German woman whose tent was opposite Stephen's and who has autism herself, admits that she is probably not the best person to ask about these things. 'I am sorry, there are many romantic relationships that completely bypassed me. I just don't have a sense for that. It has never developed in me all my life.'

Williams shared a tent with Stephen for six weeks. Under the canvas they had their long late-night conversations about global income inequality. But Williams said that they never talked about love or relationships. 'He wasn't dating anyone at the time, there were no romantic interactions and I got the feeling that I was his only kind of friend there. That I was his safe place.'

Williams left Dechen Chöling in late June or early July of 2007, while Stephen stayed until the start of September, developing his obsession with the likes of Carl Gugasian and André Streckler. So it is quite possible that Rebecca arrived after

Williams had gone. And his account of Stephen's lack of a love life doesn't mean that it was impossible for him to form a relationship. In Stephen's telling, the fact that Rebecca was able to see past his awkward exterior is what made her so special. That was the whole point.

Lisa Steckler, the chatty, outgoing head of human resources at Dechen Chöling, tells me that she has a good memory for people and simply cannot remember a Rebecca from Colorado matching Stephen's description. Her brow furrows and she puts a finger to her cheek. 'There is a part of me – and I hope this is not mean – that thinks . . . did he make her up?'

This is what Detective Inspector Jim Fox thinks. He says that the whole thing is 'bullshit'. He has Stephen's journals from Dechen Chöling and reviewed them after they were seized. 'A girlfriend in France, 2007? That didn't happen,' he says brusquely. 'I have got diary entries from every day when he was in France and it's all about how lonely he is and how nobody likes him and he has got no mates. There is no girlfriend. That is a fairly consistent theme through his stuff, that he is lonely. I am sure Rebecca or whoever exists and was there. But he certainly has not referred to any relationship or some sort of holiday romance or anything like that.'

Stephen laughs when he hears this. 'Maybe he thinks I'm too ugly for a girlfriend,' he says, before saying that DI Fox is simply wrong. 'I did write about her many times in the diaries. It just goes to show that he didn't pay much attention.' Stephen thinks that Fox is subconsciously reinforcing his own view of Stephen as a dysfunctional loner. 'It's a phenomena. People see what they are looking for. He has probably constructed this image of me in his mind, a stereotype of a guy who was totally outside society.'

He says that he had thought that, in amongst the various

materials he has given me, there are police photocopies of diary entries which contained references to Rebecca. There are not. Within the material I have from the period and subsequent months the name 'Rebecca' does not appear once, though this material is by no means complete. There are a number of romantic and somewhat sensuous poems written later, after he had returned from France. In one of these Stephen describes cycling from Dechen Chöling with a nameless young woman – 'her auburn hair streaking behind in the wind as she cycles before me' – passing fields and chateaus as they travel through the countryside.

Dr Sajid Suleman says that it is not uncommon for people with Asperger's to invent imaginary or 'fantasy' friends. But, he continues, when Stephen told him about his relationship with Rebecca during the compilation of his psychiatric report in late 2012, he absolutely believed it to have been real. He still does. 'I clearly remember the discussion,' he says, smiling. 'At the time I didn't have any impression of him making it up. The way he described it was, in my experience, quite typical of the way people with autism spectrum disorder form romantic relationships.'

Their shared deep interest in Buddhism was the common ground that first enabled Stephen to begin and then maintain a rapport with her. Then, as the relationship developed, Stephen found that he was more comfortable in group situations when she was with him, that he was able to take certain cues from her. This, says Dr Suleman, is what he sees all the time in relationships in which one person has Asperger's and the other does not. And if, as DI Fox maintains, the relationship was 'bullshit', then it means Stephen has contrived to concoct a fantasy account which somehow lines up exactly with what an expert in Asperger Syndrome would expect to see. Dr Suleman adds, 'It didn't come across like that. She pushed him to do social things with others. I felt it was a real relationship.'

And Stephen has always maintained it was. His cycling poem, which is charged with emotion, describes an idyll. It may be a memory. It may be a daydream. A wish. The poem finishes with him and the auburn-haired girl arriving at a lake.

We both plunge into the sparkling water, washing away the sweat of the ride. And then, reaching the other side, we make love in the tall grass. A moment of heaven. There, in France.

17

On a drizzly evening in March 2008, Stephen was sitting in the corner of a small pub on a housing estate not far from Birmingham city centre. It was dimly lit and smelt of stale smoke. He sat on his own, nursing a pint of lager. The pub was quiet but the handful of regulars watched Stephen with a mix of amusement and suspicion. Across the room, at another table, two tall Afro-Caribbean men talked quietly into the ears of an older man who looked at Stephen with heavy, impassive eyes. Eventually, all three stood up. Two of them, including the older man, left the pub and climbed into a car parked just outside. The third man walked over to Stephen and peered down at the blinking figure in an anorak, a hiker's backpack between his legs.

'Come with us,' the man said.

Stephen got to his feet, clutching his bag. He followed the man outside and climbed into the back of the waiting car. The older man was behind the wheel. He turned around to look at Stephen again. Then, slowly, the car pulled away into the inner-city night. Stephen looked out the tinted passenger window and saw street lights, raindrops and darkness. Nobody spoke. He was on his way to do something he knew he must. He was on his way to buy a real gun.

Birmingham is forty-five minutes from Worcester by train,

but the two cities could not be more different. Worcester is small, compact and old. Birmingham is the second largest city in the UK after London, a sprawling conurbation replete with sparkling high-rises and modern shopping centres. But like all large cities it has areas of poverty, deprivation and crime. Birmingham, in particular, has a problem with gangs and guns. Stephen knew this. Or at least he did by the time he had carried out some online research in Worcester, which told him that one of the most likely places to acquire a firearm in the UK was, so to speak, just down the road.

He'd signed up to a website called couchsurfing.com, a sort of hippyish precursor to Airbnb which allowed users to find hosts willing to offer free accommodation. Stephen created a profile in the hope that he would find somebody in Birmingham to put him up for the night. Stephen's couchsurfing.com profile page still exists, although he listed himself as 'Stephen Mason'. It includes a photograph of himself half-smiling at the camera as well as some basic biographical information. In the 'About me' section, Stephen created his own subheadings, which he then answered as follows:

CURRENT MISSION
To defy the odds
ABOUT ME
A traveller and seeker of truth
PHILOSOPHY
'It is your mind that creates the world' – Buddha

A couchsurfing.com host read his profile and thought that he sounded like a nice guy and offered him a place to stay for the night.

When Stephen arrived he began, 'very discreetly', to ask his host about guns. He explained that he was a university student and that part of his degree required him to conduct a study into crime in Birmingham, and he wanted to know the kind of areas where somebody might go and buy an illegal firearm. His host, who Stephen remembers as being Greek, wasn't quite sure what to say. People who sign up to karma economy websites in order to offer Buddha-quoting strangers free accommodation do not generally know about where to purchase illegal firearms. Nevertheless, there were certain areas of north Birmingham that did have reputations. Lozells. Ladywood. Balsall Heath. Stephen nodded as he jotted these down. Then thanked his host and left.

Stephen spent the next few hours traipsing these areas of inner-city Birmingham. As evening fell, he spotted what he judged to be the most disreputable-looking pub he'd seen all day and entered. 'It was a Jamaican-type pub,' he remembers, meaning the drinkers were predominantly black Britons of West Indian origin, a large community within the city. He ordered a pint and loitered at the bar. Something about his manner seemed to invite an approach, and a pair of tall men moved beside him and asked, in friendly tones, if he needed anything. Was he looking for drugs? Weed? Coke? Stephen, still in his anorak, shook his head. 'I said, "Look, I am looking for a firearm."' Upon hearing Stephen say this with his matter-of-fact directness, they instantly became far more circumspect, almost concerned. They told Stephen to go sit in the corner, then quietly conferred before one of them made a phone call. Some time later, the older man arrived and then, some time after that, they all piled into his car to begin the process of finding Stephen a gun.

Stephen felt anxious. Not for his safety, but because he was worried that they might not succeed in getting the gun. The three men told him that for £2,000 they could get him a shotgun. 'Which I thought was ridiculous,' he tells me, frowning. As they drove, Stephen and the men negotiated until they finally settled on £750 for a pistol.

Over the next hour, the men in the car made a number of stops, with one of them leaving the car to enter a building for a while, before returning. None of this was explained to Stephen. Eventually, though, he was told that the next stop would be where they got the gun for him, so he needed to produce the cash and stay in the car while they went to retrieve it. Stephen hesitated. He wasn't stupid and didn't feel comfortable just giving £750 to a group of criminals in a dark corner of a city he didn't know. But then, he really wanted that gun. It felt so close. He gave them the cash. They pulled up in a quiet street and the two younger men stepped out of the car. Stephen could see them dividing the money between them, which made him frown, and he began to say something when, suddenly, they ran. In opposite directions. 'They just . . . ran off with the money.'

Stephen pulled open the car door and chased after one of the two men. Behind him, he heard the car accelerate and speed off into the night. Stephen didn't even turn to look. He had one of the men in his sights and was gaining on him, pacing past street lights, parked cars and dark, high-rise council blocks. Then, suddenly, up ahead, Stephen saw what he thought was a police car. This made him hesitate and break his stride. If the police saw Stephen chasing after somebody through inner-city Birmingham in the middle of the night, they would probably have questions. Questions he couldn't exactly answer honestly. Rational thought began to whirr into gear. Because even if it wasn't a police car and he did succeed in catching the man who had half his money, what then? 'I reasoned with myself that, even if I did catch up with him, he would probably have beaten me in a fight,' he says. 'Probably beaten me senseless.'

He returned to Worcester deflated. But in a pattern that was now established, any setback was simply interpreted as a reason to keep going with even more conviction. Inadvertently commit armed robbery at an Amsterdam youth hostel? Just a reason to keep going. Accidently vandalise a children's charity? Just a reason to keep going. Ripped off by gangsters in Birmingham? Just a reason to keep going. Even his arrest in Holland was a reason to burrow deeper and deeper into his obsessive world. In his mind, it was just a matter of time before Dutch police shared his forensic information with British police, at which point both the Devon and Cornwall and West Mercia forces would receive an alert informing them that their man was named Stephen George Dennis Jackley and that he was a twenty-one-year-old student from Sidmouth.

As a result, Stephen developed a sense that he did not have much time to hit his target. 'I had this increasing sense of a giant clock over me,' he says. He imagined that once he'd hit his £100,000 goal he would have to assume a new identity and leave the UK forever. On some level, he hoped this was what he would have to do. But doing this would likely require even more money. So just another reason to keep going.

By February 2008, something else was happening too. For the first time in his life, Stephen was beginning to know what it felt like to have access to money. Not loads of money, but still, several thousand pounds stashed in trees around Worcestershire and Devon. The exact status of this cash was ambiguous. Stephen says his plan was not, and never had been, to reach his £100,000 in increments. Instead, everything depended on him pulling off one big heist: forcing his way into a bank, cleaning out a safe and vanishing forever. So the money he had already stolen served as a kind of expense account. Yes, he had given a percentage of what he had stolen to the homeless, possibly something in the region of £600. And he was also anonymously paying back the NSPCC in instalments, a sum which would stand at £1,255 by the time he was finally captured. He spent much of the rest on materials relating to his mission: disguises, fake beards, battery powered angle-grinders, half a dozen different replica pistols. He had just lost £750 on the Birmingham debacle. These things started to add up.

But he was also spending money on himself. Of the eventual £100,000 he hoped to steal and use as seed money for the Organisation, he earmarked a percentage which would serve, effectively, as a salary. 'I think it was either 30 or 40 per cent,' he says. 'I don't think it was as high as forty. It might have been one quarter. But there was a bit that I designated for me, for travelling and seeing the world.'

He told himself that travelling back to East Asia, to Thailand or Cambodia, would tie in with his overall philanthropic mission anyway. It would be like fieldwork. Going to Amsterdam to spend two days smoking cannabis, on the other hand, cannot be rationalised away. Stephen accepts this. 'It would be wrong to say that "he did this exclusively for the greater good and not for himself", because I did write that there would be a percentage that I would keep personally.'

West Mercia Police – the force who would ultimately prosecute Stephen – made much of the fact that he had planned to spend some of his stolen money on himself. DI Fox says that in the diaries they hold, there were lists of the things Stephen planned to acquire for himself, from laser eye surgery to round-the-world travel to his own flat. He does not believe Stephen's plans for the Organisation were genuine. 'He talks about setting up a company to look at living on the moon.' DI

Fox also describes how strange he finds much of Stephen's writing. 'I think sometimes it's almost like a brain fart. It comes out and appears on the page and then that's that. It might not ever appear again.'

The question of how to interpret Stephen's diaries is important. Because they are preserved in black and white, in his own handwriting, the temptation is to view everything on the page as Stephen's considered final word. So if he writes that he would like to pay for laser eye surgery with some of the money he has stolen then this must mean he is absolutely committed to doing so. Likewise, if he writes that he wants to start moon colonies, then this must mean he is completely delusional if not mad.

But Stephen did not chisel his diaries in stone. They are not his final word on anything so much as a written record of a mind in motion: snapshots of thoughts and ideas as they passed through his head. If he imagined buying his own flat with some of the money he would steal, then there was a good chance he would write about it. If he imagined moon colonisation or underwater cities as a solution to global overpopulation, then there was also a good chance he would write about it. It didn't mean that either of these things were driving his actions the following day, or crossed his mind for the weeks or months to come. They were just things that occurred to him and which he wrote down. Like DI Fox says, brain farts. Everybody has them. Stephen just spent a lot of time committing them to paper. We also have to keep in mind that he went through periods of smoking a lot of cannabis. 'That's another thing to be aware of. Just because I wrote something doesn't mean it is exactly what I think. It might have been clouded by my weed smoking.'

On the flipside, what you do see in his diaries is Stephen's inability to lie to himself about himself. Even though he had created a world in which he was heroic, a new Robin Hood, he nevertheless confessed that one of his motivations was 'power and wealth'. A fan of *The Lord of the Rings*, in one diary entry he compared the corrupting effect of crime and money to the dark lord Sauron's ring of power. Frodo Baggins, a naive hobbit from the countryside, sets off with the intention of destroying this evil only to find that the longer he is exposed to it, the more the evil whispers seductively. Stephen wrote how 'the allure' of wealth is doing the same thing to him. 'Like the "One Ring" it is subtle, so small – yet there is a draw in money – one which accompanies the feeling of getting momentary control.'

Then there was his mother to think about. In the spring of 2008, Stephen returned to Manstone Avenue for her birthday. He told her that he was going to take her out for dinner to celebrate, and drove her down to Sidmouth seafront where he had made a reservation at the Hotel Riviera. A posh hotel which seemed to pride itself in belonging to another era, it had an imposing cod-Georgian facade and an atmosphere of hushed propriety. It was popular with the kind of affluent retirees Sidmouth had always attracted, either as residents or visitors, and was used to serving them. It was not used to serving schizophrenic women from local council estates and their socially awkward sons. But Stephen felt an overwhelming desire to do something special for his mother. So a waiter walked them to their table and left them there, facing one another, as the sea rolled and broke on the beach outside.

Earlier that day, Stephen had returned to the quiet woodland outside of Sidmouth where he had hidden £1,000 in cash. He located the old oak tree and hoisted himself up, climbing its branches until he could see the nook where he had hidden the money. But after fishing it out and lowering himself back to the ground, he found that the plastic bag he had wrapped it in had done nothing to stop rain and damp reaching the now soaked banknotes. It was a warm morning, so he decided to dry them out in the sunshine, laying a long row of notes out on the grass. He sat beneath the tree, waiting contentedly. At one point, a pair of dog walkers passed within ten yards or so of him, but didn't spot the money. They waved at Stephen. He waved back.

He used £70 of this money to pay for his mother's birthday dinner. Back at the Hotel Riviera restaurant, the two of them looked at one another and smiled a little awkwardly. 'This is nice,' his mother said after a while. Yes, Stephen nodded. It was nice. He ordered his mother a series of desserts knowing that she was unlikely to eat anything else. He quietly asked the waiter if he could put a candle in one of the slices of cake, but when it arrived his mother was not quite sure what to say or do. People, Stephen noticed, were looking at them. His mother's hair was frizzy and wild, her clothes bright and mismatched. 'She didn't know,' he says. 'She always saw people in a very positive way, even when they were clearly not that, which used to frustrate me sometimes. But I didn't say anything. I just tried to ignore them.'

As he entered his teens, Stephen had tried to understand why his mother was like this. Was she born with schizophrenia? Or did she develop it somehow? His mother had grown up in Paignton, a town thirty miles down the Devon coast from Sidmouth. Her father had worked in telecommunications and her mother had been a Labour councillor. Stephen's mother had been considered a 'rebellious' teenager by the standards of 1950s Devon, and ended up spending time in some kind of 'care home' where she suffered abuse, the exact nature of which Stephen does not know. He remembers his father still being angry that Jenny's parents had allowed her to be taken away. In the 1960s, she became involved with CND and Devon's hippie scene. It is possible, says Stephen, that a combination of abuse and exposure to psychedelic drugs exacerbated an underlying psychological issue.

Equally, though, she may have simply inherited her schizophrenia. Her uncle Noel also had the condition. He once made the news for canoeing around the fountains in Trafalgar Square. 'He was a really eccentric person apparently,' Stephen brightly tells me. 'He ended getting lost at sea. That was the demise of Uncle Noel.'

At the Hotel Riviera, Stephen and his mother shared ice cream. Because of her medication, normal conversation was impossible, but there was still a sense that they were both trying their best. 'It was an effort on both our parts,' says Stephen. Perhaps they came close to feeling some kind of connection and intimacy, the kind which Stephen only had the faintest memories of but had craved his whole adult life. He enjoyed the act of paying for her dinner. He told himself that, with his father dead, he had an obligation to support his mother financially. At that moment in time he couldn't really do that. But once the Organisation was up and running? Then he would. It was just another reason to keep going. Everything was.

18

In his room at Wyvern Hall, Stephen took a cardboard folder from a pile under his desk. It had the word 'LEDBURY' written on it in block capitals. He opened it and removed several print-outs of maps and photographs which showed a picturesque old market town surrounded by fields and woodland and located some twenty miles south-west of Worcester. Circled, on a market square, was the Ledbury branch of HSBC. Elsewhere, he had marked the locations of potential changeover spots and drawn getaway routes that would see him quickly vanish into the trees. He had many of these folders, each with the name of a different location in and around Worcester – 'HEREFORD' or 'PERSHORE' – carefully researched and prepared and ready for whenever he needed them. 'They were like a pack of cards,' Stephen remembers. 'Do I do this one or that one?' And on a crisp bright morning in early March, he chose Ledbury.

He made the thirty-minute drive down into Herefordshire, rattling down narrow country lanes in his old Rover. He felt anxious. It had now been over two months since his last successful heist, the Lloyds TSB in Seaton. There was a part of him that wondered if he had been shying away from his mission ever since his arrest and confinement in Holland, his first real exposure to consequence. It made sense. The easiest thing in the world would be to simply . . . stop. To forget the heists and dreams of the Organisation, to keep his head down, focus on his degree and see the Holland arrest for the urgent reality check it was.

But then, what was reality anyway? He had made his own and he was not going to turn away now when there was so much at stake, so many lives that could be lifted out of poverty and exploitation if only he could see his task through. Stephen gripped the steering wheel tightly, pressed his foot down and overtook a tractor. He wound his window down, and the air was cold and fresh with just a faint tang of manure. It reminded him of Devon.

About a mile outside of Ledbury, Stephen parked on a quiet road adjacent to some woods. He slipped into the trees and after walking for ten minutes or so, spotted what he was looking for: a tall tree with branches that made it possible, though not easy, to climb. Checking that nobody was around, he took off his backpack and produced a disguise. He put on a shaggy auburn wig, styled in the manner of a 1960s pop singer, plus a stick-on goatee beard and a pair of mirrored aviator sunglasses, before hiding his bag. Then he hiked through the woodland until he reached a large grassy common. He knew from his maps that this was Ledbury Park. All he needed to do was cross it, then follow the high street north, passing rows of crooked Tudor and Stuart buildings until he came to the HSBC.

He strode across Ledbury Park, trying to visualise what was about to happen, when he heard something behind him. It sounded like a laugh, hard and pointed. He ignored it, but then came a shout.

'I like your hair!'

Stephen turned round. Sitting underneath a tree about ten

yards away was a group of teenagers, about four or five boys
and girls. They were wearing baseball caps and smirking. Some
of them were whispering to one another and laughing, keeping
their eyes on Stephen the whole time. The boy who had spoken
repeated himself.

'I said, I like your hair. Is it real?'

'Can I touch it?' shouted one of the girls.

'Nice beard!' said another.

Stephen stood there on the common, paralysed by the
sudden scrutiny. He tried to concentrate on what they were
saying. As they continued to call out to him, sarcasm slowly
giving way to outright insults, he understood what was
happening. 'I was basically being taunted by a group of kids.
I'm surprised, in hindsight, that I didn't realise that such an
overt disguise was going to be detrimental. At the time I
thought it had been a good disguise. Now I can see that it was
overkill. But there you go. We get absorbed in stuff.'

He made his way into the town. As he walked, he burned
with self-consciousness. Those teenagers in the park had left
him rattled and jumpy. Did his disguise look obvious? He
glanced at the people he passed on the street, mostly older
couples, and wondered if they considered him suspicious or
unusual-looking. From their expressions, he couldn't tell. He
couldn't really see too well through the sunglasses anyway.

The HSBC was now in sight. He walked into the branch
and it was quiet, with just one elderly man being served at a
cashier's desk. This, Stephen tried to reassure himself, was good.
He walked to the second cashier's desk and slipped her a piece
of paper under the perspex screen. It had been written on a
paying-in slip, the kind you filled out with your name and
account number when depositing cheques or cash at your local
branch. Only Stephen had altered this slip. Instead of 'Paying

In' he had amended it to read 'Paying Out'. The sum he had written was £8,500 and the name he had provided was 'ROBIN HOOD'. The woman on the other side of the screen looked at the note and then up at him. He then placed his imitation pistol on the counter. The woman took the slip and quietly said that she would be back shortly.

So Stephen stood there, at the empty cashier's desk, in his wig, goatee and sunglasses, waiting for the woman to return with the cash. Later, the police would release stills of CCTV footage from inside the branch. With his wig, reflective sunglasses and soul-patch goatee beard, he looked like a Las Vegas street magician, albeit one in baggy blue jeans and black waterproof jacket. He says that the 'paying out' slip made out to 'Robin Hood' was not just a whim or conceived to be funny. It was, he says, a very serious part of his methodology and designed to underline the ideological cause behind the heist. 'I felt I had to adhere to this kind of modus operandi,' he says. 'Maybe it derives from the Asperger's, but I had to follow this very defined methodology I couldn't deviate from. It was the same with the coins I would leave and the way I would mark the banknotes with "RH". I felt that if I went outside of that, I would just become a normal robber, I guess.'

Because the Ledbury branch was small and out of the way, he had already decided against trying to force his way to the safe on the grounds that it was less likely to contain a large amount of money, making the potential risk greater than the potential reward. Which was why he used the note. He frowns and says he cannot remember why he specifically asked for £8,500, although it may have had something to do with the maximum amount of money he believed would be kept in the cashier's registers. A minute passed. Then another, and Stephen was still standing at the empty desk. The quiet sounds of a rural bank branch drifted around him: a low, unhurried conversation between a clerk and an elderly customer, the tap of computer keys, the soft clack and thud of cheques being stamped. It felt airless and stuffy. His goatee seemed to be coming unstuck with perspiration. Where was the woman with his money?

He knew, already, that he had failed. He had not been forceful enough. His confidence had been terminally ruptured by the teenagers in the park. Simply handing over a note asking the bank to pay Robin Hood £8,500 and then displaying a replica pistol had not been enough. Maybe the cashier thought it had been a joke? Or a drill? Where had she gone? He had just allowed her to walk off. Had she been afraid? Panicked? Compliant? Stephen couldn't tell. He could not read her emotions at all.

She had probably already hit a button that alerted the police, he told himself. Armed response units were probably already being scrambled. He needed to move. Now. And so Stephen turned on his heel and walked out the door, back onto the main street.

He didn't run. During the getaways from almost all his robberies, successful or otherwise, Stephen resisted the very urgent human instinct to flee as fast as he could. He knew from his hours of online research that running out of a bank would, quite logically, only attract attention. During his escape from the very first attempted robbery, the Lloyds TSB in Exeter, he felt an overwhelming compulsion to sprint and he very nearly did. Ever since then, though, he had trusted in a steady, even pace away from the bank towards a changeover location and then a steady, even pace away. Stephen walked back through Ledbury and then vanished into the woodland. He found the tree with his bag of clothes, quickly changed, then emerged on the other side of the woods to find his car. He got in, started the engine, and then turned around and drove back to Worcester. A few days later, images of Stephen in the HSBC would be printed in local newspapers along with a call for witnesses. 'We would like to speak to anyone who saw this man that day,' said Detective Inspector Rich Rees of Herefordshire CID in the appeal. 'He would have made quite a distinctive sight.'

The following day, Wednesday, 5 March 2008, Stephen attempted another heist. He cannot remember whether he had always planned to carry out consecutive raids, or whether his failure in Ledbury prompted him to act quickly, to chase his loss like a gambler trying to break a losing streak. The target was the same branch of Barclays bank in Worcester he had tried and failed to break into late one night the previous November using his battery-powered angle-grinder.

Located only a mile away from Wyvern Hall, Stephen had spent hours studying and surveying this particular bank since he began university. He had been inside many times, pretending to browse through leaflets about personal loans while scanning the interior and memorising the layout. He had walked the streets around it over and over again, plotting escape routes, changeover locations, everything. The bank itself is a solid, unremarkable Georgian building beside a run-down launderette and opposite a Citroën garage. But Stephen knew it was more than that. It was many different things. It was a substation helping to power a global grid of income inequality. It was a small temple to an economic system that demanded constant growth and constant expansion, even at the cost of the planet's finite and diminishing resources. It was, above all else, a repository of stolen wealth. And he was going to steal it back.

At 12.40 p.m. he walked into the branch wearing the same wig, sunglasses and clothes he had worn the previous day. A few minutes later, he left, walking briskly but not so quickly as to attract attention. About fifty yards behind the bank was the St John's sports centre – a council-run gym with squash courts, a weights room and football pitches. He entered the shower rooms, used a key to open a locker and quickly slipped into a change of clothes. He then left and collected his bicycle, which he had left locked nearby. As he unchained it, he saw police officers approaching the leisure centre and his heart skipped.

He pushed off, rounding a corner, and then began pedalling as fast as he possibly could. Swerving into a junction, he missed a moving car by a few inches. A horn blared behind him and he almost fell off his saddle with shock. He didn't look back, but just kept pumping his legs until he was back on the University of Worcester campus. Knees shaking, he managed to dismount and then hurried into one of the buildings. Moments later he arrived, breathing heavily, in a lecture theatre. He took a seat at the back. As the lecturer began to speak, he attempted to review what he had just done.

The heist had not gone how he had hoped. In his backpack, between his feet on the lecture room floor, he had £4,100, handed over to him by a nervous clerk. But again, this was not what he had wanted. He had wanted the bank staff to open a door behind their cashier's desks which he felt sure would lead him to a safe or a vault or at least somewhere he would find the thick stacks of banknotes he had always envisioned accessing. 'I tried to get them to open it,' he remembers. 'But they wouldn't do it.'

During the robbery, Stephen became angry. He cannot remember why. It could have been because the staff would not or could not open the door he wanted them to open. It could be that they were taking too long to bring him the cash register money he had then demanded instead. It is also possible that he was simply trying to assert himself in the way he felt he had failed to do the previous day in the Ledbury HSBC. Inside the Barclays, he took out his replica pistol and pointed it at the cashier. After Stephen left with the money, the cashier collapsed on the floor and had to be taken by ambulance to hospital where she was treated for severe shock. 'I think I laid it on a bit too aggressively. I didn't swear or anything. But I was speaking angrily,' he says. 'It didn't feel good.'

An hour later, he filed out of the lecture hall. There were no police officers swarming the campus. One thing was now absolutely clear in his mind. He needed a real gun if his mission was ever going to succeed. Forget scrabbling round inner-city Birmingham at night, getting ripped off by third-rate gangsters. He was going to go to where he knew he could find one.

First, though, he had something he needed to clear up. A few weeks after the Barclays heist, Stephen was in his halls of residence room. He had his mobile phone in his hand and was pacing the three or so strides between his bed and his desk. His room was bare and functional: no posters, no pictures, just a calendar with various dates circled, the significance of which only Stephen knew related to heists both past and planned. On the wall by his desk he had scratched the initials 'RH'. He looked at the letters and took a long, slow breath. Then he dialled a number and put the phone to his ear. On the other end of the line, a police officer answered.

'Hello,' said Stephen calmly. 'My name is Stephen Jackley. I'm a geography and sociology student at the University of Worcester. I was wondering if you could help me.'

Since returning from Holland, Stephen had been waiting for everything to collapse around him. The Dutch police had his name and fingerprints. They had allowed him to return to the UK for the time being, but expected him to travel back to the Netherlands to answer for his crime when summoned. It was inconceivable, therefore, that they had not alerted the British police to this fact. And when the Dutch police sent the British police their file on Stephen, his fingerprints were sure to match fingerprints associated with evidence recovered from the scenes of his crimes. And that would be that.

Only, three months had now passed and there had been no midnight police raids on his room. He had not been collared coming out of a lecture and hauled in for questioning. As the weeks went by, Stephen's curiosity gradually got the better of him. He felt a sharp, insistent need to know what was going to happen. Or at least, why nothing had happened yet. Logically, he reasoned, the best people to ask were the police. So from his university email account, he contacted the police and explained that he was an undergraduate and that, as part of a sociology module in his course, he was doing a study into criminality and law enforcement. If it was not too much trouble, he wrote, he was hoping to speak to somebody involved in police forensics? After some polite back and forth it was agreed that, yes, this would be fine. So one day in April 2008, he called the number he had been given and had a fifteen-minute conversation with a very helpful officer.

'I spoke to a woman in the forensics department and said I was doing a study, blah blah blah,' says Stephen. The one piece of information he was desperate to find out was whether police forces in different European Union countries automatically exchange the forensic information they hold on individuals. 'I phrased it in a way so as not to raise any suspicion that I had done anything. I think I threw in a few extra sideline questions that had no relevance, stupid questions like "what happens when someone gets arrested", stuff like that.'

Stephen couldn't quite believe what he was told. 'I was shocked to find out that there was no automatic database or exchange of forensic detail. So someone can commit a crime in France and then in the UK, and the French might have previously arrested them and have their forensics, but the British police won't.'

In fact, it turns out that police forces in the EU will only share this kind of forensic information if there has been a specific request to do so. Later that night, he summarised his findings in his diary. 'Learned that there is no <u>automatic</u> exchange of criminal information between EU countries unless a country issues a "match/no match" search'.

But rather than experiencing an intense rush of relief at this news, Stephen felt almost upset. It just made so little sense. Having maintained an innocuous, dispassionate tone on the phone with the forensics officer, he now couldn't help sounding incredulous. Why *wasn't* there an automatic exchange? There really should be. Think of the criminals who could be getting away with all sorts in one EU country while the police just across the border have all the forensic information needed to identify and capture them. 'It dawned on me that there could be rapists or dangerous people committing offences and getting away with it because they haven't exchanged the details,' he says. 'I remember writing to the police from prison in America saying, look, this is an issue. You need to sort it out. This is how I managed to continue. Because if these details were exchanged automatically, I would have been found out in Holland and there would have been no further crimes after that.'

Throughout the spring term of 2008, in between planning and executing his crimes, Stephen continued to read, study and pass long days wandering the countryside. His diary entries from the time show a young man whose life might seem, to those who even noticed him, to be solitary and mundane. But his inner conviction that the world was on the brink of disaster burns on every page. In one journal entry from early March, he describes a day which included a trip to check that some of his stolen money was still safely hidden in a tree.

Today got up at 10:30 (went to bed at 2.15 with the usual sleep 'wake up') – took a cold shower and went cycling into town. Got a chicken roll + 'steak bake' (£2.75) before heading to 'the tree on the hill'. Ate then walked the windy hills. Returned in time for SOC61006 lecture . . . interesting, but all the atrocities of the bourgeoisie were spoken in the past tense, when really they are still happening!!!

In February 2018, it was announced that British computer hacker Lauri Love would not face extradition to the United States despite being wanted by the FBI. The thirty-two-year-old former engineering student was alleged to have breached the security networks of several federal agencies and stolen massive amounts of confidential data. In a successful High Court appeal, Love's lawyers argued that their client's Asperger Syndrome would make life inside the Metropolitan Detention Center Brooklyn, the federal prison in which he was to be held, virtually impossible. They described the conditions at MDC Brooklyn as 'unconscionable' and 'medieval'. This is a facility which has housed everyone from Al-Qaeda operatives to Mafia killers. This is a prison where eleven guards were charged with abusing inmates, beating them with such ferocity that bloody pieces of scalp were later found on cell floors. Cameron Lindsay, the former warden of MDC Brooklyn, would later describe the prison as 'one of the most, if not the most, troubled facilities in the Bureau of Prisons'. A young man with Asperger's, Love's lawyers stated, would simply not be able to survive in such a place.

This was where Stephen was taken in late 2008. Along with a dozen or so other manacled and shackled inmates, he was escorted from his cell at Strafford County, placed on a prisoner transport bus and driven 300 miles south to New York City. Guards with shotguns resting on their laps sat facing them throughout the journey, silent and impassive. As the bus crept into the city, snow began to fall. MDC Brooklyn is a solid, utilitarian, multi-storey building wedged between a raised expressway and commercial freight docks. From inside the cold bus, Stephen peered up and shivered. The prison seemed to rise up out of the ground like some vast igneous rock formation. He did not know if he had the strength to withstand any more time in solitary confinement. He thought back to his father, dying, and pleading with desperate eyes to just get him out of his small hospice room. Now he understood.

Stephen was processed. He was given a baggy brown jumpsuit, taken to a small room and asked a series of box-tick questions by two disinterested members of prison staff. He was asked if he'd ever felt suicidal. 'Definitely not,' he responded emphatically. Had he ever attempted to escape prison? He shook his head. One of the two men looked at the paperwork in front of him, frowned, and then seemed to regard Stephen properly for the first time. 'Says here that you tried to escape the US Marshals after you were arrested,' he said cautiously. Stephen sighed. It was, he said, a simple misunderstanding. And besides, he had never been charged with attempted escape. The prison staff made a few final notes and then Stephen was led away with a group of other new inmates. One of them deliberately barged into Stephen as they entered a large service elevator, then glowered at him and demanded he watch where he was going. Stephen did not know how to respond. He just opened his mouth and blinked a few times.

Glancing around him as he and the other inmates were marched along corridors and into further elevators, Stephen tried to take in his surroundings. It was unusually cold. The air tasted foul, stale and almost greasy. There was, he would soon discover, no outside space whatsoever, just cage-like areas with metal grates to allow for some breeze. There were hardly any diversions for inmates and nothing that could be classed as rehabilitative. As he was led up and along, along and up, it began to dawn on Stephen that he was simply inside a vast human warehouse. Cell after cell stacked on floor after floor. He already knew enough about prison to understand what this would cause in inmates. Tedium. Resentment. Anger. Violence.

But to his surprise and silent euphoria, he was not taken to the segregation unit he had fully expected. Instead, he was shoved into a cell which contained a double bunk and a small, neat-looking middle-aged white man with glasses. The man welcomed him with a smile and, once he learned that Stephen was British, proceeded to pepper him with the usual questions which Stephen, cold and weary, answered distractedly as he made up his top bunk before hauling himself up and in. His cellmate breezily explained that he had arrived a few days earlier and said he was serving time for the unauthorised possession of biochemical compounds. What, he asked, was Stephen in for? Lying on his back with his eyes shut, he said that he robbed some banks in the UK. The small neat man on the bunk below chuckled and shook his head.

'Then what are you doing here?'

Stephen yawned. 'It's a long story,' he said, already drifting towards the oblivion of sleep.

Stephen woke up feeling cold. From his cell's narrow window, he could see fine snowflakes blow past on the wind, dancing lightly over the expressway and neat, rectangular residential blocks of Brooklyn. His cellmate explained that they were only in a holding wing. When they had been properly processed and undergone medicals, they would be moved. Of the 2,000 or so inmates at MDC Brooklyn, many were awaiting trial or sentencing, which was one reason why such an atmosphere of tension and fear seemed to permeate.

A few days later, Stephen was taken from the holding wing, marched back into a service elevator and then deposited into the general population of a wing on the floor above. There was a cramped communal area where men sat at round tables screwed to the floor. The majority of them, it seemed to Stephen, were large and tattooed. Only a thin, bald inmate with a pale and sunken face turned to smile at Stephen. As he did so, he bared his teeth, which Stephen saw had been filed down into sharp points. It was only after he was deposited inside his new cell that Stephen heard the sound of low conversation in the communal area start back up.

As the guards called for 'lock up!' and the inmates drifted back to their cells for the night, Stephen discovered that his cellmate was now a morbidly obese African-American. Tattooed and shaven-headed, he seemed constantly breathless. There was no physical possibility of him taking the top bunk, so Stephen climbed up, pulled the thin bedding over himself and tried to sleep. But it was very quickly clear that there was a problem. Every time the man below him moved to get comfortable in his bunk, the entire bed frame seemed to shake. For five minutes, Stephen was tossed about, unsure whether to say anything to the giant figure below him. Then, for a few moments, there was silence and stillness. Just as Stephen began

to drift off, he was startled by a noise: a deep rumble followed
by a long, shrill hiss. It happened a second time. With mounting
horror, Stephen realised what it was. Snoring. The loudest
snoring he had ever heard. When the cell doors were buzzed
open come morning, Stephen dragged himself to the communal
area, hollowed-out and spent.

He told a guard he wanted to move cells. The guard directed
his attention to a large sign saying that on no account would
there be any cell moves, so don't bother asking. Later, as Stephen
sat at a round metal table trying to read a Stephen King paperback, the skinny bald man with the devil teeth took a seat
beside him. He whispered in Stephen's ear. 'If you really want
to move cells, you need to get into a fight with your cellmate,'
he said, nodding towards the huge, groggy figure across the
room. His voice dropped even lower. 'And if you can do him
any lasting damage, you'd be doing me a favour.'

He smiled and then drifted back to a group of inmates
gathered around a table. Stephen rubbed his eyes. Less than
twenty-four hours at MDC Brooklyn and he was already being
pushed towards violence by other inmates. But he would sooner
be strapped inside a blueberry suit than spend another night
with his snoring cellmate. So he came up with a plan. He
approached the same guard he spoke to earlier and told him
that he needed to move cells because he felt threatened. When
asked to elaborate – to provide the name of the inmate threatening him – Stephen shook his head and said he couldn't. A
circular conversation ensued until the guard, exasperated,
manacled Stephen and led him from the wing.

Finally, Stephen was taken to an office marked
'ADMINISTRATION'. He was placed in a chair facing a desk,
behind which a debonair-looking man with dark hair and a
suit sat at a computer. Leaning on the desk was a middle-aged

African-American man in a senior prison officer's uniform, replete with gold-braided epaulettes. They both regarded Stephen levelly. Who, they asked, had been making threats against him?

Hesitantly, he began to spin a story about how he had reason to believe that some of his former criminal associates from the UK wanted him silenced. Or at least, he was pretty sure that they did. As he talked, the man in the suit punched the computer keyboard and brought up Stephen's file. The two men peered at the screen, then back at Stephen, in his baggy brown prison uniform, talking vaguely about underworld deals gone bad.

'You're wanted for armed robberies and firearms offences in the UK?' the man in the suit said, cutting Stephen off mid-mumble.

'That is correct, yes.'

'And you're a college student?'

'Yes.'

The prison officer with the epaulettes leaned forward.

'Then why did you get into crime?'

The question caught Stephen off guard. Almost everyone he had met in prison over the past seven months had asked him *how* he ended up here. He was used to that and he would sometimes take a deep breath and describe the actions that ultimately led him there. But *why* was a different question altogether.

But to explain what he had actually wanted to achieve and what had driven him to achieve it? Where would he even begin? By talking about a small squinting boy, standing with his mother in the kitchen of a council house, listening to her having desperate conversations with an invisible stranger and not quite knowing what was real and what was not? Or by describing the Shoemaker–Levy comet impacting Jupiter before his eyes, and the equal measures of fear and love for Earth that the sight instilled? Or of a night spent shivering in an Asian jungle? Or of barefoot children rooting through dunes of rubbish? Of the need – the absolutely terrifying need – of capitalism to focus the minds of everyone on selfish, short-term gains while widening the gap between the wealthy and the destitute? Of the esoteric delusion that is money? Or of the time a wise old Buddhist monk once told him that it was right to take this money and return it to those whose lives and resources had been sacrificed so that it might exist?

Stephen shifted in his hard plastic chair. He looked up at the two men watching him from across the desk, waiting for an answer. If he told them, would they believe him? Would anybody? He shrugged. 'I met the wrong people,' he said. 'Made stupid mistakes. Wanted the fast route to riches.'

The two men nodded. The prison guard was then instructed to take Stephen to a new unit. Stephen knew that they did not believe a word of his story about his underworld connections wanting him dead. Eventually, he reached a new wing where he was placed in a new cell. Inside, a thin, deeply tanned Hispanic man with a bald head but a long grey ponytail and moustache stood up to greet him. His face was wrinkled, his eyes were dark and alert, and he moved with an unusual fluidity. Around his bunk Stephen could see small Roman Catholic icons as well as other less familiar symbols and patterns: florid, stem-like lines intersected with crosses, hearts, stars and tridents.

The door buzzed shut behind them and the two men looked at one another. They each did their best to be polite. The man with the grey ponytail explained, in halting English, that he was a witch doctor from Haiti and that he could read fortunes.

Stephen smiled and nodded, then explained that he was a geography and sociology student from Devon. The witch doctor nodded in return. Then they each climbed into their bunks. Later, Stephen would notice with weary pleasure that his new cellmate did not snore at all.

19

Eight months earlier, in late March 2008, a security official sat behind an X-ray machine at Istanbul's Atatürk Airport and carefully scanned the skeletal images that drifted across his screen. Deaf to the departure terminal loudspeaker announcements and the rolling, heaving chatter of a thousand people speaking a dozen different languages, he registered one familiar shape after another. A hardback book. A digital camera. A pair of sunglasses. Some lipstick. A laptop computer, its wiring as complex and intricate as the veins of a dried leaf.

A sports bag passed before his eyes. Before he even knew why, he moved his hand to stop the conveyor belt. There was something inside the bag that was wrong. He blinked to focus his eyes and then peered closely at his monitor. What was it? Or, more to the point, what were *they*? There was a jumble of things, dense pieces of metal machinery and thick wires and . . . were those *bullets*? Or were they batteries? He snapped back to the world around him and immediately called for a colleague. Pointing to the screen, they both squinted at the odd but increasingly ominous series of shapes in the bag. Without discussing it, one of them hit an alarm, and a bright yellow siren began to flash and wail. Within seconds, there was the hard clack of boots as half a dozen armed policeman arrived.

After very carefully removing the bag from inside the X-ray

machine, one of the security officials pointed to it and demanded to know who it belonged to. He barked this first in Turkish and then, after being greeted by silence, in English. At this point, a slim, shy-looking young man with short dark hair and glasses raised a tentative hand and obeyed the order to come to where the bag was without hesitation. The other security officer had already gingerly opened the bag and, wearing a pair of latex gloves, was sifting through the contents. He found and removed a series of shiny, irregular objects. It was immediately obvious that they were bundles of something which had been wrapped in tinfoil.

One of the officers demanded to know what they were – 'What is this? What is this? What is this?' he kept repeating – and the young man beside him quietly explained that they were simply parts of a digital camera. The officer took one. Using tweezers, the tinfoil was slowly peeled back. Finally, the officer with the tweezers found himself staring at something long and metallic and unmistakable. It was the barrel of an automatic pistol. His eyes widened. 'You have pistol!' he cried. The armed police suddenly turned to try and quickly make sense of what was happening.

'They looked at me and I looked at them and then they looked at the security officer,' says Stephen, describing the seconds before a scrum of men fell upon him. 'I remember they had initially thought it was a bomb and that's what had panicked them. They were on the verge of evacuating the place.'

It was not a bomb. Instead, Stephen had a Browning Hi-Power semi-automatic pistol in his luggage. He had stripped it, mixed the various component parts with assorted electrical items, including bits of camera and power cables, taped them together and then wrapped these bundles in tinfoil in the belief that this would somehow scramble the airport security X-rays and allow him to smuggle it back to the United Kingdom. The tinfoil did not, in fact, scramble the airport security X-rays. 'I had this weird idea that wrapping something in foil would deflect the rays. But a twenty-two-year-old should know how X-rays work.' He frowns to himself when he tells me this. 'There were times where I could do some really stupid stuff.'

A week earlier, on 16 March 2008, Stephen arrived in Istanbul with a plan to buy the gun – the real gun – he had been obsessed with acquiring for so long. He had not come direct from the UK. Instead, within a few days of the Ledbury HSBC attempt and the Worcester Barclays robbery, Stephen went on holiday to Europe. First, he returned to Dechen Chöling, where he stayed as a guest in the old chateau. It was misty and quiet in the French countryside. On 7 March, shortly after arriving, he wrote about how different it felt now compared to the previous year: empty, overcast, almost eerie somehow. 'Of DCL, perhaps there is too much to write tonight. Disappointing? Yes. Weird? Even more. Disturbing? To a degree! Why? The people, the lack of people, the flickering lights . . . ' he wrote. A sense of belonging that existed the previous summer now seemed to be gone.

By the following day, though, he seemed to be easing into things. At the Buddhist retreat where he first committed to his course of action, he now plotted its endgame. 'It's so relaxing here. And it has given me time to review my plans. We will go to Turkey and get the tool, after visiting Cadaqués and Barcelona.' He then noted that the total cost of this trip would amount to some £1,500, not including the £350 or so he had budgeted for a gun.

'Looked on the web,' he continued, 'and it seems the Worcester newspaper has published 2 CCTV pictures of the robberies, both clear. We will need to be careful.' On a new line he finished the day's entry: 'BTW, a brilliant sleep.'

On 10 March, he made another short note.

Second day in a row relaxing, mediating and reading. Weather has turned wet and cold so mostly indoors. Two mini workout sessions. You need to think how you're going to conceal a handgun from Turkey.

From France, Stephen travelled south to Spain as planned and then flew from Barcelona to Istanbul. Stephen's research had led him to conclude that this represented his best chance of finding a real pistol. With gun ownership laws in Turkey considerably less stringent than across most of Europe, the supply of firearms – both new and used – was high. Guns, he read, could be found in one of every three Turkish households, and the vast majority of these weapons were unlicensed and unregistered. As he made his way from Atatürk Airport to the cheap hotel he had booked for seven nights, he looked out the window of the transfer bus at the sprawling metropolis around him: at the traffic, the high-rise towers, the minarets and domes, the wide, palm-lined boulevards and the occasional glimpse of cargo ships moving across the Sea of Marmara looming hazily on the horizon. Why had he not come here sooner, he wondered. He unfolded a piece of paper on which he had scribbled an address. He stared at it for a while, then carefully placed it back in his pocket.

He visited the tourist sites. The Topkapi Palace. The Blue Mosque. Roman and Byzantine ruins. Ancient catacombs. Wandering the city alone, he visited street markets and souks. He visited the Grand Bazaar, a sprawling labyrinth of indoor streets home to hundreds and hundreds of shops, stalls and merchants hawking everything from jewellery to carpets, antiques to clothes, plates, confectionary, pastries, shoes and handbags. It was packed with people, a mix of tourists and locals, and the colours were kaleidoscopic. The sound of music and of fast, fluent sales patter bounced off the high, vaulted ceilings, pushing Stephen's tolerance for noise to its limit as he drifted through the crowded streets and alleys. Eventually, he came out the other side of the bazaar and into the open. Moving away from the huge structure he walked through tight winding streets which were still packed with shops but seemed shabbier, quieter and free from gawping holidaymakers.

Eventually, he found what he was looking for. A shopfront on a quiet street. There was no mistaking what it sold. On display in the window were dozens of handguns, hunting rifles, knives and binoculars. Stephen's heart trilled. He stepped inside the shop and made his way to the counter, where a middle-aged Turkish man was watching him.

What happened next is a little confused. Stephen had memorised a few Turkish words and phrases to help him try and explain that he wanted to buy a handgun, but communication with the shopkeeper was stop-start and unclear. 'I remember having to answer lots of questions. He wouldn't just give it to me,' says Stephen. 'It didn't help that he didn't speak English that well, it was "what do you want it for?", that kind of thing. I remember I said clay pigeon shooting.'

The idea that it might be a little unorthodox to turn up to a clay pigeon shooting event with a semi-automatic pistol, given that you typically use shotguns for the sport, did not occur to Stephen. Nor did it seem to bother the shopkeeper. In an otherwise empty shop in a small, quiet street, he eventually agreed to sell Stephen a used Browning pistol and a box of ammunition. Stephen paid him about 560 Turkish lira – some £225 – before quickly returning to his hotel room, his mind already racing with the different possibilities now finally open to him. He could begin a heist with a bullet fired into the air to demonstrate his seriousness and thus ensure compliance when demanding access to the safe. He could conduct his version of a tiger takeover, springing out when bank staff arrived and forcing them to take him to the vault. He could target large cash-in-transit deliveries. He floated back through the Grand Bazaar half in a dream. The noise did not even bother him.

When Stephen returned to his hotel room and unpacked the pistol from its box, he sat on his bed to examine it. On one side of the barrel, it had the word 'BROWNING' stamped in black steel. On the other side, it said 'UMAREX – Lizenzfertigung', which made Stephen frown. He had thought Browning was an American make of gun, so why the German? He unwrapped the box of ammunition and then, with a sinking sensation, immediately understood how he had been able to acquire the pistol so easily. The store owner had not sold him a fully functional gun. The ammo was blank. The box said so. He picked one out and immediately saw that they were just cartridges – small, copper-coloured tubes – with no bullet at the end. He went online and searched for 'UMAREX' and found that it was a German company who made replica, blank-firing versions of real firearms.

DI Jim Fox says Stephen's diaries from this period describe how he had bought a replica by mistake. 'He thought he had bought a real gun and then he got it back to his hotel and realised it is just a blank firer and is wondering if it can be converted or not,' says Fox. Blank-firing guns can sometimes be 'converted' into live-firing guns by altering some of the internal mechanisms and replacing parts of the barrel. 'He thinks he might be able to do so, so he decides he is going to bring it back.'

Stephen says he quickly got over the disappointment of not securing a real gun. 'I wasn't too bothered to be honest. The only reason I wanted a live one was because in the case of imminent arrest, I would have used it on myself,' he tells me matter-of-factly. 'That was the only negative to getting a blank-firing one. But I thought, why not think positively? That is not going to happen and I just need this one to cause a noise.'

He sat on his hotel bed and stared at the gun. He had a very strong urge to load and fire it, there and then. 'But I didn't think it was a good idea and I remember restraining myself. But I did sit there for a long time thinking, *I really want to see what it does.*' In the end, he decided to wait until his return to the UK. There was a small, remote valley in some woodland outside of Worcester. That, he told himself, was where he would test it. Suddenly, he felt very impatient to fly home.

Which is why, two days later, Stephen was at the departure terminal in Atatürk Airport, surrounded by armed police as a security officer accused him of trying to smuggle a pistol onto a plane. Which was more or less true. He was marched to an interview room where he faced an incredulous security officer who spoke through a translator, a middle-aged Turkish woman who sat between the two of them. Just because the gun was blank-firing did not mean it was harmless. It was not an inert replica or even a BB gun. The cartridges it 'fires' still contained gunpowder, this powder just didn't project a bullet down the barrel. Instead, it discharged the wood or plastic wadding used to keep the powder in the cartridge. At short ranges, this discharge could still be harmful, sometimes even fatal. If the cartridges themselves were damaged or imperfect, they could jam, and when the trigger was pulled again, the jammed metal cartridge casings could be fired from the barrel. Stuntmen have been killed by faulty blank-firing guns on movie sets. They were, under British law, considered a firearm. And nowhere in the world can you simply take one onto a commercial airliner. So what, the Turkish security officer demanded to know, did Stephen think he was doing trying to sneak one onto a plane?

He had a story ready for them. He told them that he was a student who was just on his way back after a sightseeing holiday in Istanbul. He had the blank-firing gun, he continued, because a friend at university bet him £100 that he wouldn't be able to get one back into the UK. Is this the kind of bet that university students make with their friends? Stephen didn't really know. He didn't have any friends. But this was the story he gave. He watched the face of the stern security officer while the translator relayed this in Turkish. He absorbed it impassively. A pair of police officers were summoned and Stephen was escorted to a small holding cell within the airport.

At this point, Stephen knew that he had reached the end. Even with all his faith that the universe would take care of him, he understood that he couldn't expect the same kind of reprieve he'd experienced after being arrested at Schiphol. 'I thought, this is it. There is no way they won't be able to join the dots now.'

There was already another man inside the holding cell. He was Turkish, heavy-set and probably in his sixties. He glowered at Stephen, who felt intimidated but nevertheless continued to pace the cell, remonstrating with himself. Eventually, the Turkish man addressed him in a deep voice.

'You bring drugs?'

Stephen stopped and looked at him. He shook his head and

began to explain everything. The man stared at him from beneath heavy eyes and then, once Stephen had finished, simply said, 'You go to jail for a long time.'

Stephen squeezed his eyes shut. 'I remember asking him, "What are Turkish jails like?" He looked at me for a long time. And then he just started to laugh.'

But after a few hours, something unexpected happened. He was collected and taken back to the security officer who first interrogated him. Speaking through the translator, he explained that after very, *very* careful consideration, they would release him. They would keep his firearm and he was to never – never – attempt anything like this again. Stephen nodded vigorously. As he was escorted back to the departure terminal, he felt like laughing. He turned to the translator who was walking beside him, and though he can no longer remember exactly what he said, he made some passing reference to Amsterdam and the fact that he had experienced something similar there. 'I mentioned something about Holland. Not that I was wanted there, but she must have figured out there was some issue. I think I kind of asked her if I would be blocked again at customs because of the Holland thing, and then she marched back to this place where all the police officers were and she told them what I had told her.'

So Stephen was returned to the holding cell. 'I was ready to punch myself for being so stupid.' But after another long wait, he was released a second time. It helped, he thinks, that aside from parts of a firearm wrapped in tinfoil, his bag contained all the things you might expect a young tourist to have, including guidebooks and souvenirs. If they found his diary, they either did not read it or did not pay it close enough attention to spot the references to bank heists and his need for a real gun. It also helped that Stephen was young, nervous and bookish. He says that the attitude of the Turkish police changed markedly when he produced his University of Worcester ID card, almost as though they were relieved he really was the out-of-his-depth student he was presenting himself as. 'After showing them the card, they just waved their hands and said "get him out".'

The Turkish authorities never contacted the British police about what Stephen had tried to do. He could have stopped at this point, forgotten about the Organisation, and it is very likely that he could have just got on with his life as a geography and sociology undergraduate. Instead, Stephen sat on the plane back to the UK trying to work out what to do next. He tried to think positively. That blank-firing Browning wasn't really what he was after anyway, he told himself. But it had felt so close – '€270 wasted', he wrote as the plane approached London. 'The whole Turkey trip cost around £800. I need to stop wasting money.'

At MDC Brooklyn, Stephen described all this to the witch doctor. The two of them were sitting in their cell, eating bowls of rice and beans. Stephen had discovered that his Haitian cellmate not only boasted supernatural abilities, but that he was also a gourmand. A contraband cache of spices and seasonings meant that he was able to transform the bland prison meals into something altogether more exotic. 'He had some very strange ways, although he was a great cook. He could turn some really shitty food into something decent.'

'I can read futures and help sickness,' he told Stephen one evening after lockdown. 'In my country I am very well known.' Every so often Stephen would return to his cell to find the witch doctor dealing with another inmate. He quickly came to realise that they were having private consultations and that the man was telling their fortunes, making them grasp hold of a special charm while he chanted and entered trance-states. He seemed to command a high level of respect across the unit and amongst Hispanic inmates in particular.

One man, though, was universally acknowledged as untouchable, a de facto figurehead for all prisoners regardless of race. He was a bald, thick-set Hispanic man from New York who simply went by the nickname 'Monsoon'. He was fortyish, amiable, heavily tattooed and had a direct, appraising gaze. A former drug dealer and gang member, he was waiting to stand trial for murder. He was also an evangelical Christian who led a popular though informal church service on the wing every Sunday at 2 p.m. He would announce the commencement of the service by slowly walking up and down the unit and, in a deep, resounding voice, crying out, 'IG-LE-SIA! IG-LE-SIA!' Stephen attended these services and was blown away by Monsoon's intense charisma. 'It is no overstatement to say that he literally burned with evangelical faith,' says Stephen. Monsoon was often called upon to mediate disputes between prisoners. On several occasions, Stephen saw him physically intervene in order to prevent violence.

One night, after lockdown, the witch doctor offered to read Stephen's fortune. Not wishing to seem rude, he agreed. The witch doctor chanted while making Stephen grasp a charm, and then, after appearing to lie down and fall asleep on his bunk, he opened his eyes suddenly, then sat up and presented his findings.

'You have led an interesting life. Done many good things. Many bad things.'

Stephen nodded. He just about resisted the temptation to speak out and say, well, yes, that's a pretty safe assumption to make about anyone in jail. Instead, he asked whether the witch doctor could tell him anything else.

'People look for you,' he said quietly. 'Be careful.'

Stephen had to bite his lip. This would have been really helpful information eight months ago. It was altogether less helpful now that he was being held in a large federal prison. He asked the witch doctor what the coming years held. The tanned, leathery face of the man before him creased into a deep frown. He shook his head and could only offer vagaries. The only thing he seemed certain of was that the year 2014 would be a particularly dark one. Though even then, he would not say why.

Stephen said he wanted to know about the future. But as the weeks passed at MDC Brooklyn, he found that he was spending more and more time thinking about the recent past. Instead of fantasising about escape, he kept returning to that unexpected question posed by the prison warden. Why did he turn to crime when he had other opportunities ahead of him? Had it been the right thing to do? Would he do it again if he had the chance? If reality really is malleable, as he believed, then how come he was eating rice and beans with a witch doctor in a Brooklyn jail? How much good had he actually achieved? How much harm had he done? And to whom?

This shift towards introspection was slow but sure. During the months of solitary confinement, his primary focus had been survival. Free from the distraction of other people and perspectives, he allowed himself to brood over the injustice of it all. Thinking about his own personal accountability did not figure in his thoughts. Since coming out of solitary, first at Strafford County and now here, he had met more and more other inmates. They all had their own stories, their own reasons and their own feelings about whether or not they had done something wrong. Often, they acknowledged that they had. 'Many of the prisoners I encountered in America came across as normal, grounded, intelligent and remorseful,' Stephen explains. 'American drug laws meant that what would be a relatively minor offence in the UK could equate to many years in prison in the US. It meant many people had lived next to normal lives before they came to prison.'

Stephen was befriended by an inmate called Michael. A short, fit man in his late thirties with pale blonde hair, he had been handed a nine-year sentence for counterfeiting money and for the supply of amphetamines. Michael read paperback books of philosophy. He followed world events and had a serious-minded, almost teacherly way of talking. The two of them spent hours discussing what was happening in the world around them, the economic catastrophe that by then, in late December 2008, had unleashed the worst global recession since 1929. As a counterfeiter, Michael knew first-hand just how much value ordinary people placed in the pieces of paper the banks handed them, and he knew that the modern, human desire for more money – at the expense of all else – would never be cured. At that very moment, just across town at the Metropolitan Correctional Center in Manhattan, a conman named Bernie Madoff was in the same brown federal prison uniform as Stephen and Michael. He was waiting to stand trial for orchestrating a Ponzi scheme which prosecutors alleged resulted in investors being defrauded of $65 billion. Michael predicted, correctly, that Madoff would spend the rest of his life behind bars. But, he continued, while jails would continue to fill with ordinary people who had turned to crime in the face of recession and foreclosures, most of those responsible would simply walk away from the crisis they helped to create with multimillion-dollar payouts.

Even Stephen expressed some doubt at this. But it was proved true. Lehman Brothers CEO Dick Fuld – 'The Gorilla of Wall Street' – would amass almost $500 million in compensation during his tenure as head of the bank, a tenure which only ended when the bank itself did. Stephen asked Michael why he turned to crime in the first place. 'I wanted what was best for my son,' he said.

New Year's Eve came a week or so later. All the inmates in MDC Brooklyn had been in their cells for hours by the time midnight came, but they cheered and shouted and smacked the bars as they welcomed in 2009. From his dark cell, Stephen put his hands to the narrow window and looked out. Across the water he could see the Manhattan skyline suddenly lit up by a million different flashing colours. The last time he'd seen a fireworks display had been years ago, as a little boy on Sidmouth seafront. He had been with his father and they had walked back home together, through their little seaside town nestled between the sea, cliffs and countryside. He had gone back to his cramped little bedroom filled with books and fossils and posters of planets, and he had fallen asleep in his bed wondering if his mum might be back home the next day.

Standing there, shivering in his prison uniform, watching the Empire State Building turn from red to white to blue, the reality of it all finally seemed to snap into focus. This was not an adventure. He was not Robin Hood. 'I just remember thinking . . . what am I doing here?'

20

S tephen came back from Istanbul undaunted. He returned to Worcester, attended his lectures, wrote his essays and passed long days alone walking the countryside, making pencil sketches of hills and rivers and writing paeans to the natural world around him. He continued to develop his vision for the Organisation. While other students competed for the attention and approval of tutors during seminars, Stephen remained almost silent, the same secret half-smile Lisa Jackley remembered from their father's funeral sometimes hovering on his lips.

While others talked, he allowed himself to imagine the stories they would tell of him in the future, of how a hero rose up from nowhere and fought back against the injustices of capitalism. His Robin Hood identity – the 'RH' he left scrawled on his stolen banknotes, in his journals, on his bedroom walls, in letters to newspapers – was everything to Stephen. It had been for almost eight months, ever since he resolved to take this course of action at Dechen Chöling. Neither the Devon and Cornwall nor the West Mercia police forces were any closer to working out who the mysterious bank robber in the wig and sunglasses was, the Dutch authorities had not yet summoned Stephen back to Amsterdam and, as the weeks passed, it was clear that there would be no long-term consequence to the Istanbul airport incident. So, like a record needle slipping back into the same scratched groove, Stephen sat at his computer and tried to work out the best way of getting the real gun he needed.

The answer was Vermont. The small New England state had, in 2008, some of the loosest gun laws in the US. In fact, Stephen discovered that they were practically non-existent. From the age of sixteen you could buy scoped sniper rifles, sawn-off shotguns, armour-piercing bullets, assault weapons with no maximum magazine capacity, pretty much whatever you liked. All you needed was a valid form of ID. There were no background checks and no waiting periods. It was a very, very easy place to buy a gun.

So Stephen spent £50 on a high quality fake Vermont state driver's licence, which he sourced from the internet and which showed his name as 'Stephen Mason'. Continuing to search online, he saw that there was a large gun show scheduled to take place near the state capital of Montpelier on 16 May. Here, anyone could show up and buy or sell weapons, new or second-hand. Stephen reasoned that it would be even easier to buy a pistol at this gun show because there would be A) less scrutiny and B) more options if the first vendor he approached wasn't convinced by his ID. Then he paid for a British Airways flight from London to Boston.

A few months after giving me the bulk of his notepads, journals and papers, Stephen posts me an A4 envelope. He has found some photocopied diary entries from this trip to America and thinks they may be interesting. The only thing he asks is that, once I've read them, would I mind returning them to him? They are a record of his final days of freedom, he says. His last connection with the young man he had been.

* * *

The evening before his flight, Stephen sat in Trafalgar Square as the sun began to set over London. He nestled at the base of Nelson's Column, beside one of the four elevated ornamental lions, overlooking the very fountains where Uncle Noel once caused a scene by paddling a canoe. From there, he could see the Houses of Parliament and the start of the Mall leading down towards Buckingham Palace. He was happy. Everything was golden and there was still warmth in the stone beneath him. As the shadow of the column lengthened he pictured the Earth orbiting the Sun, the vastness of space, the mystery of existence. London was heaving, but Stephen felt invisible. He watched as thousands of people flowed and swirled around him, moving in every direction, like strange particles, the true nature of which he knew he would never understand. With a penknife, he spent five minutes carving 'RH' into the stone lion's leg. On his journey to London, he wrote in his diary, and his mind returned to a possibility that he had entertained since childhood. 'On the train here, I reconsidered it . . . Perhaps I am from another planet.'

The diary entry continued,

Tomorrow – if the pigs don't pounce – it's the USA; the US of A, 'land of opportunity', centre of so much past changes, most powerful nation on the planet. To Vermont, Green Mountain State, to buy that one item I need and need badly.

He had by now attempted ten robberies. Half of these had ended in failure. He had failed in his effort to force his way into the Lloyds TSB in Exeter city centre. He had failed to cut his way through the metal bars and slip into the Barclays bank in Worcester. He had accidentally ransacked the offices of a children's charity, had his nerve desert him at the HSBC in Ledbury and been hounded out of a Britannia building society by an indignant manager. Even his successes had been failures, because he'd never made it to the safe or the vault or wherever he thought the jackpot would be found. But having a gun would change everything.

The next day, Stephen almost missed his flight, but made it on board with just two minutes to spare. Arriving in Boston, he cleared customs and travelled by bus to Dartmouth College in New Hampshire, before taking a taxi to the small, rural town of Barnet. Here, he had arranged to stay at the Blue Skies Guesthouse, a cosy timber building run by a welcoming Buddhist couple with interests in Tibetan art and gardening. About a fifteen-minute walk away there was a Shambhala Buddhist retreat, Karmê Chöling, a sister centre to Dechen Chöling, replete with kyūdō archery courses, vegetable gardens and meditation classes. Sitting in his room, on a single bed covered with a bright patchwork quilt, he wrote about what he had seen so far.

> What can I say about the USA? So huge – so spacious – so wealthy and Vermont is unbelievably forested, trees that go off over green hills to a woodland horizon. It's beautiful. I watched a documentary about black bears on the plane, how friendly they can be, and wonder if I will also see them – here in America.

The next morning, Stephen's whole plan depended on him hiring a car and then driving to the scheduled gun show. He travelled to the nearby town of St Johnsbury, where he used his fake ID to hire a car, a silver Dodge Charger saloon. But he never made it to the gun show. When he'd woken, he'd looked out of his bedroom window and the sun was shining so brightly over the thickly forested hills that he found himself caught in a long, happy reverie. He thought about the black bears and how fascinating they were, curious and somehow sweet despite their teeth and claws. Suddenly, he felt a very strong urge to try and find some. It was a beautiful day. The gun show wasn't vital anyway, he told himself. He had already established email contact with a private gun dealer in St Johnsbury, to have as a backup option. He would pay him a visit later in the day, writing that evening:

> Today was sunny so I went on a black-bear spotting mission,. Drove up the wide roads through St Johnsbury, where I got some (delicious!) snack food and free maps from the tourist office. The people here are so friendly! Always smiling, greeting and wishing you a 'nice day'. I drove to a lake with two granite mountains on each side. As I ascended the views were fantastic. Like out of a dream. I walked for about four hours – man I'm unfit! – before returning and heading to St Johnsbury to 'complete' the main reason I'm here – to get a gun. And yet the scenery – the FREEDOM OF TRAVEL – alone is enough reason to be in this beautiful place.

After his hike he drove to the home of a private gun dealer named Steve. 'He was overweight and he was in his forties. He had a moustache and a balding head, I remember that he had food stains on his clothes,' says Stephen. 'He lived with his mother. This little old lady offering us tea while he was talking about guns.'

The chubby gun dealer glanced at Stephen's fake ID but nothing more. Stephen explained that he was half-American, half-British. The dealer didn't seem to care. As his mother fussed around them in her chintzy living room, he asked what he could do for Stephen, who explained that he wanted a Glock 26 semi-automatic pistol. He had done his research and concluded that this compact, reliable gun was the weapon he needed. The dealer produced a heavy-looking revolver and said that, if Stephen wanted to leave with a gun today, he could buy this. Otherwise, he would have to source the Glock for Stephen, which would take a few days. Stephen's mind was set on the Glock. He paid the dealer $500, who said that he would be in touch when the gun was ready for collection. Upon exchange of the weapon, the remaining balance of $75 would be paid. They shook hands and Stephen left.

After Istanbul, Stephen was not going to try and smuggle the gun back to the UK in his luggage. Instead, his plan involved parcelling up the pistol and ammunition in a box along with BB guns and children's toys to serve as camouflage, and then posting it back home under a different name. He knew it was not guaranteed to work – the surest method would be to import a car and hide the gun parts about the vehicle – but it was worth trying. 'I subsequently found out that this was a common method of receiving firearms in the UK,' he says. He reflected on all of this back at the Blue Skies Guesthouse, on the evening of 17 May 2008. 'So far I've done really well – got a car with a fake licence, almost got a gun – hoping! Seen so much beauty. Freedom flies along with this ship of solitude.'

The next day, Sunday 18 May, Stephen made the short drive to Canada. He visited the Coaticook Gorge in Quebec, found a quiet river to bathe in and marvelled at the fact that everything was written in French. On the drive back to Barnet, he wondered whether it might be worth buying a stun gun too.

It could be a useful accessory. He decided in favour of it. Back at Blue Skies Guesthouse, he hunched over his diary and reviewed his thoughts and actions.

> The gun mission's still green . . . haven't got it yet. Tuesday will post it, with electronic toy, in Canada, separating out the ammo. The idea is to get an electronic toy, strap the gun to the toy or inside it, put a few bullets in the battery compartment, box it up, package it and label it 'kids toys + paintballing'. It might even be worth getting some paint- balling items. Also consider posting stun gun.

The writing then stopped. No more entries followed. The rest of the page – the rest of the book – is blank.

The following morning, Stephen rose early and drove to the Groton State Forest. There, he hiked to the top of Owl's Head Mountain, a rocky peak rising high above the endless green below. It was an overcast day, but as he broke the treeline and reached the summit, the view revealed itself. Standing on rocks, catching his breath, Stephen looked out and saw nothing but woodland, lakes and hills, stretching off into the horizon. The sky felt huge above him. As he breathed the cold, mossy air and surveyed the landscape below, an odd sensation overcame him. It was a feeling that this moment was significant in some way. And while the reason was not yet entirely clear, Stephen seemed to understand that it marked some kind of culmination. 'It was very strange,' he tells me, frowning. 'On the top of this peak I had this sense that I needed to remember this. That it was the end. Of course, I didn't have any idea what was going to happen next.'

After eating a packed lunch, Stephen descended Owl's Head

Mountain. He drove to Montpelier, where he found a public library. He wanted to go online and check what upcoming university assignments he had. He also wanted to search for more gun stores. He had plenty of cash with him, so decided that there would be no harm in buying another pistol, just as a backup option. He found that in the nearby town of Waterbury there was a large and reputable store known as 'Parro's Gun Shop and Police Supplies'. He made a note of the address and left the library. By now, it was raining heavily. He started his rental car, flicked on the wipers and headed north towards Waterbury.

The rain was now coming down in torrents, reverberating against the roof of his Dodge like a mad drumroll. He knew that the chubby private gun dealer had believed his story about being a dual national because he had wanted to make the sale. At a proper gun store, though, he told himself that he couldn't show up speaking like someone from England. Even if they accepted his dual national story, they would most likely ask for additional documentary evidence which Stephen did not have. So as he cruised towards his destination, Stephen practised speaking in an American accent.

'Got any Glocks?' he said to nobody, affecting a slow, steady, confident drawl.

'Got any Glocks?' he asked again.

Did that sound convincing? He gripped the steering wheel and tried to decide. It was hard to tell. He tried again.

'Gimme a Glock,' he said, but immediately shook his head. It sounded wrong. Also, he knew, that's not how gun shops work anyway. He cleared his throat and tried again.

'Got any Glocks?'

That actually sounded pretty good. He smiled and kept repeating it as the rain came down.

'Got any Glocks?'

'Got any Glocks?'

'Got any Glocks?'

As he approached Waterbury, he spotted what he was looking for through the driving rain: a large, long, single-storey lodge with an American flag flying over the front door. Outside, a wooden sign said 'Parro's'. He had come within a split second of driving past it. Instead, he hit the brakes then pulled into the forecourt, parking beside a pickup truck. He checked he had his wallet with him. And then he ducked into the store.

Inside, Parro's was large and brightly lit. There were stag heads mounted on the walls. There were black bears, mouths open, teeth bared, glassy eyes staring ahead into nothing. Down the central aisle there were racks of shotguns and hunting rifles, while black assault weapons were mounted on a wall beside a long, wooden front desk. There were boxes and boxes of ammunition and hundreds of pistols in a long, low row of glass display cases. The place had the reassuring and familiar smell of a good hardware store, of cardboard and metal and domestic chemicals. On a stand by the entrance was a gumball machine.

It was about 2.30 p.m. when Stephen entered Parro's. There were one or two other customers browsing the aisles and a couple of staff members chatting by the front desk. Seeing the number of weapons on display, Stephen had to stop himself from gawping. He was awestruck by the sheer firepower spread out before him. One of the staff members was a middle-aged man with a grey moustache, horn-rimmed glasses and a t-shirt tucked into blue jeans secured by a large belt. This was Henry Parro, the owner of the shop.

'Hey, how are you doing?' he asked, smiling cheerfully.

'Pretty good,' replied Stephen. He was trying to talk calmly and casually, but it was a struggle. The thrill of seeing so many guns had now been replaced by a sudden anxiety – a panicky, pulsing sensation of fear cut with anticipation, like an underage teenager in an off-licence. His voice seemed as though it was being dragged out from inside him, and it did not sound American at all. Parro asked if there was anything he could help him with, and Stephen, sounding more and more English by the second, responded quietly.

'I would like to look at a Glock 26 please.'

'Not from round here?' Parro asked brightly as they walked towards the pistol display cases. Stephen mumbled something inaudible. Parro unlocked one of the cases, took a Glock 26, checked that it was empty, and then handed it to Stephen, who held it by the butt, staring at the functional black sleekness of it, enjoying its weight and the feel of the grip in his palm.

'He looked at it and said "I'll take it"', remembers Parro, who talks with a warm but measured clarity. 'And that was the first indicator that there could be something wrong. Most customers will ponder the purchase. They will try to negotiate the price or to get some accessories thrown in. But within thirty seconds of him entering my building, he was saying "I'll take it".'

While Stephen's Asperger's often made it hard for him to read the emotions of others, even he could see the flash of suspicion that passed across Parro's face. A voice in his head told him to just stop, to think up an excuse and leave. But he ignored it. He was so close. He already had the pre-paid United States Post Office parcel in the boot of his car. He could be robbing banks in Worcestershire and beyond with a real gun in a little over a week. Why turn back now, having come so far? *Are you Robin Hood?* he asked himself? *Or are you just a frightened, anxious nobody?* Under the gun store's bright lights and the unblinking, unseeing gaze of deer and black bears, a battle between fantasy and reality was playing out in Stephen's head.

Stephen followed Parro to the front desk. Parro placed the Glock beside the till and then asked an assistant to provide Stephen with the paperwork needed to complete the purchase. He then asked if Stephen could provide some ID. Stephen nodded quickly, handing over his fake licence.

What Stephen did not know was that Henry Parro had served as a police officer for over twenty-five years. In fact, on a part-time basis, he still did, working as a local patrolman. Parro examined the licence and immediately something he saw made him want to frown, though he managed to keep his expression mild and neutral. All Vermont driver's licences include a signature from the state's Commissioner of Motor Vehicles. As it happened, the commissioner of motor vehicles was a personal friend of Parro's. But the signature on Stephen's ID was not his. Parro smiled at Stephen, thanked him and told him to complete the form while he went into his office for a moment.

Minutes passed. Stephen had completed the form, filling it with false information about himself, and was almost beside himself with anxiety. He tried to hand the assistant the $500 they had agreed for the Glock plus ammunition, but he just smiled and said they just needed to wait for his boss to sign everything off. He knew he should leave. But he would not do so without his fake ID. So he took a breath and then walked towards the door to Parro's office. He pushed it open and saw the grey-haired man with a receiver tucked under one ear and Stephen's licence in his other hand. Stephen looked at him and Parro looked at Stephen. They both understood what was happening. Parro had already called the state police, asked them to run the details from Stephen's ID through their system, and established that the licence was fake. He had just finished a conversation with the local Bureau of Alcohol, Tobacco, Firearms and Explosives to let them know someone had just tried to buy a gun using false information.

'I was speaking to the ATF when Mr Jackley comes into the doorway of my office and says, "I need my licence back",' says Parro. Stephen says that the stolid figure before him responded by calmly explaining that he could not do that. At which point Stephen turned and bolted back out the door. 'He ran very quickly and jumped into his car, backed across the parking lot at a rapid pace,' says Parro. Stephen reversed into one of the trucks in the lot with a loud thunk-*crack*, but fought the urge to pump the accelerator and fishtail onto the quiet country road. Instead he did his best to leave the scene of the crime as casually as possible. He indicated, then slowly pulled onto the road and away.

Parro told the ATF agent on the line that the suspect had just made a break for it. 'I told them, "He's running!" And then I grabbed my portable radio and my gun and I ran out after him.' He jumped into his truck and accelerated, radioing the local state police barracks as he did so, describing Stephen and his car. Within sixty seconds, an alert had been passed to all state troopers on the roads within a twenty-mile radius. Parro couldn't see Stephen's car as he drove, but he knew that he had fled east, along Route 2. He was scanning every car he approached to see if it was a silver Dodge Charger. His gun was at his side, the rain driving down in torrents.

It was a Sunday afternoon at MDC Brooklyn, and Stephen was watching Monsoon preach to a large group of prisoners. The unofficial *iglesia* services he led were not just popular with inmates of all races, but with many of the prison guards too.

They attended, standing at a remove from the men they were supervising but still nodding their heads in affirmation while Monsoon spoke with white-hot conviction, murmuring their 'amens' and squeezing their eyes tight in prayer and contemplation.

Stephen was in awe of Monsoon. Not just because of his oratory and conviction, but the way he was able to bring inmates out of themselves during the services, to make even the toughest, most nihilistic men in this federal prison stand up and tell strangers about their hopes and fears and regrets. Monsoon had been a drug dealer and a gang leader, he told the assembled inmates. He had been motivated by greed and by anger. He had grown up in a world that was hard and mean, so he decided that he needed to be hard and mean too. He had never thought or cared about the consequences of his actions so long as they led to him getting what he wanted. More money. More respect. One day he learned that his sister's husband had been unfaithful to her. So he killed him.

Stephen watched entranced as the shaven-headed, tattooed man in front of him described undergoing a religious conversion in jail, about how one night he was so consumed with hatred and anger that he just collapsed in his cell. Writhing on the floor, Monsoon had finally cried out for forgiveness from God. And in a moment, he knew that forgiveness had been granted. Grace had been bestowed. A second chance provided. At Monsoon's encouragement, other inmates stood up and talked about the crimes they had committed and how deeply they regretted them – not because they got caught and ended up in jail, but because they could see that what they had done was wrong. These confessions sometimes took place in smaller groups, after the main service. Which was how, later, Stephen came to be sitting quietly with a group of inmates who, at

Monsoon's gentle encouragement, were describing the worst thing they had ever done. Some talked of stabbings and shootings. Others of gangland cruelty and betrayal. Eventually, it was Stephen's turn to speak. All eyes turned to him. He cleared his throat and spoke quietly.

'I burgled the Worcester offices of the National Society for the Prevention of Cruelty to Children,' he said. This only drew blank looks from the men listening to him, so he added that he also robbed quite a few banks. Now the inmates around the table nodded slowly. 'I thought I was Robin Hood,' he continued. One of the men sighed in sympathy and said he knew that feeling, telling yourself that you're some kind of outlaw. But Stephen just shook his head. No, he said. He genuinely thought he was Robin Hood.

Monsoon asked if he hurt anyone. Stephen thought of Raymond Beer, and how close he had come to seriously wounding somebody who had just been going about their job. He thought of the screaming, trembling bank and bookmaker employees he had threatened with guns and knives and how he had allowed himself to believe that their momentary fear would pass once he had gone. But after months in jail, he was beginning to understand that this was not how trauma worked at all. He thought of his mother, on her own at Manstone Avenue, and how during the few brief telephone conversations they had had since he was jailed, she had simply not understood where he was or why. He thought of the ice cream they had shared at the Riviera Hotel in Sidmouth and wanted to cry. Stephen looked at Monsoon and nodded. 'Yes,' he said. 'I hurt people.'

Later, after the inmates all drifted away from the service, Monsoon approached Stephen and sat beside him. He asked if was true what he had said about robbing banks. Stephen nodded. Monsoon couldn't help smiling, but saw that Stephen was troubled, so he asked how he'd ended up getting captured. Was there a shoot-out? Hostages? Betrayal? Stephen sighed.

'No,' he said. 'I just got caught.'

21

Stephen drove away from Parro's gun store, keeping to the speed limit and heading east into the small town of Waterbury. His forearms trembled as he gripped the wheel. Nevertheless, he reviewed what had just happened and looked for positives. Had he really done anything so wrong? It was not like he had snatched the gun before he ran out or made threats to anyone. Yes, the owner seemed to suggest he was on the phone to the police. But even if he was, were they likely to send officers to investigate a fake ID? And if they did, how urgently were they really going to respond? If he could just put some distance between himself and the gun store then he would be in the clear. The key was to behave normally. He drove past rows of pretty colonial-style houses, their timber walls painted white or deep russet red, with neat green lawns and American flags out front. At a roundabout, he took a left onto Route 100, which headed north out of Waterbury, over the interstate and past the factory where, he had read in a tourist leaflet, they made Ben & Jerry's ice cream.

He drove for ten seconds. Twenty seconds. Thirty seconds. Then up ahead, at a junction for cars coming off the interstate, he spotted a police cruiser with lights flashing. This did not worry him immediately. Over the last few days, he had often seen police cars waiting at roadsides, lights on, letting drivers know they were there while watching for speeders. Stephen kept driving. He passed the junction, aiming his car down the wide, quiet road and towards the thickly forested hills crowding the horizon. More seconds passed and nothing happened. He pressed the accelerator down just a fraction. Trees sped past him on either side. Something in the heavy grey sky caught his eye. He wondered if it was a bald eagle.

Sirens sliced through his thoughts. He immediately checked his mirrors and the police cruiser was about twenty yards behind him and closing, flashing him to pull over. Stephen complied, bringing the Dodge to a halt beside the metal crash barrier, beyond which there was open country. From his wing mirror, he watched the trooper approach his car, right hand on his holster, rain flowing over the edges of his broad-brimmed hat. Opening the window, Stephen saw that the state trooper was a young, clean-shaven man with a crew cut and dark, impassive eyes. He asked to see some ID, and Stephen handed him his genuine British driving licence. 'Then he said, "I would like a few words with you please"', remembers Stephen, who stepped out of the car and into the rain. 'He said, "Have you been at Henry Parro's gun store?" I denied it at first. For a fleeting second I looked at the car and thought . . . can I jump back in and drive away?'

A few moments later, a pickup truck pulled up behind the police car. Henry Parro stepped out with his gun, but deliberately kept his distance from the two men before him. 'One of the things that we do is that when a police officer is dealing with someone, I always stay back because it could be intimidating or overwhelming if two people are trying to talk to them,' Parro says. It was, he continues with a chuckle, an incredible coincidence that Stephen happened to drive right past the police car when he did. 'There was a trooper that just by luck was coming off the interstate and Mr Jackley drove straight past him. The trooper pulled out, turned his siren on and stopped him within a hundred yards of where he was passed. It was just perfect timing.'

On the roadside, the trooper briefly glanced back at Parro, who gave him a nod. Then he told Stephen he was under arrest. He said that he had reason to believe that he had been involved in a hit and run. Which was true. He had failed to stop after backing into a truck when leaving the gun store, a fact Parro had made sure to tell the police dispatcher. Stephen was hand-cuffed, placed in the trooper's car and driven to the state police barracks in the nearby village of Middlesex. There was a large German shepherd in the rear of the cruiser, impassive and still behind a wire mesh. Stephen looked out the window and saw what seemed like smoke rising from a valley below. It puzzled him. He asked the trooper what it was. Just condensation, he replied. Rising up from a creek.

As he was driven through the countryside, Stephen's mind turned. He could get out of this, he reassured himself. It might involve paying a fine. It might involve posting bail. But he could afford that. He was just an English geography student on holiday who tried to get a gun as part of a stupid bet with a friend. They had believed him in Istanbul. They would believe him here.

A very short time later, Special Agent Scott Murray of the ATF was driving to the Middlesex police barracks in order to inter-view Stephen. A former officer with the Phoenix Police Department, Murray joined the Bureau of Alcohol, Tobacco, Firearms and Explosives in 2001. He is short and was then in his mid-thirties, with close-cropped dark hair and bright, appraising eyes. The laxness of Vermont's gun laws meant that the state was a magnet for arms traffickers, and there existed a circular underground trade, as organised criminals from the big east-coast cities came there in order to obtain cheap and readily available high-powered weapons, which could then be smuggled out of the state and back to New York or Boston. But as part of the process, cheap and readily available drugs from New York or Boston were brought into Vermont and sold at a healthy mark-up. New England junkies were happy. Big-city gang members were happy. Agent Murray was busy.

'The majority of the cases that I work are related to heroin, cocaine, methamphetamine, things like that,' he says. 'A lot of gun cases that we do are using firearms in the furtherance of drug trafficking, or related to robberies and murders.'

When Murray arrived, Stephen was being held in a small interview room. He had been advised of his Miranda rights and had signed a document waiving them. He was ready to talk. Murray sat opposite him with an ATF colleague and began to ask him questions. It was not the kind of interrogation you see in movies, says Murray, where men with rolled-up sleeves lean over a suspect and try to break his will or catch him out somehow. 'For me that has never worked.' Instead, Murray spoke to him directly but with a matter-of-fact congeniality. Above all, he wanted to listen to what Stephen had to say and judge to what degree it seemed coherent. 'The general thing you are looking for is, does the story they are telling make sense to you? Do the set of facts they are telling me come easily to them? Do their answers come easily? Or are they grasping and trying to think up a story, rather than just telling you the truth, which should come out pretty naturally?'

To begin with, the story Stephen presented seemed to have elements of truth to it. He explained that he was a geography student from the United Kingdom and that he was on holiday.

He told them where he was staying. He admitted that the ID he had was fake, that he bought it online and that he had tried to buy the gun at Parro's store in order to win a £100 bet with a friend. He told Murray that had he succeeded, he would most likely have just taken a photograph of it and then tried to sell the weapon on before returning to the UK. Special Agent Murray frowned internally at this explanation. It sounded . . . well . . . *odd*, and the way Stephen presented it was vague and halting. 'He was a little elusive about what his intentions were,' says Murray. But the ATF agent did not want to rush to any conclusions. It was not impossible that this awkward young British man really was just doing all this for a strange bet. It was no more or less likely than him being a wanted criminal. 'If an average person looked at him walking down the street, they would not think of him as a bank robber, right?'

Even so, something about his story and, increasingly, his countenance did not feel right. Stephen had never been very good at lying to people. For one thing, his social isolation meant he had had very little practice. And, as is the case with many people on the autism spectrum, when Stephen did interact with others, he tended towards directness and unfil-tered honesty. It is not that he is incapable of lying, because the whole 'bet with a university friend' story was one. But rather, he struggles to lie on spec, to convincingly improvise. He was acutely aware of this, and so preferred to talk around potentially incriminating questions rather than just come up with something untrue. 'I guess it's part of the Asperger's,' he says. 'But even with the police, even with people I saw as the enemy, when they asked me difficult questions, I had to circum-vent them rather than lying directly.'

And there was something else that Special Agent Murray noticed and did not like. Stephen was not at all subtle about his desire to get out of this small, secure space. Every so often, Murray and his colleague might leave the room for a few moments, and then on their return, peer at Stephen sitting alone, looking at the window, glancing about for cameras. 'You could see his thought bubble,' says Murray. 'He was constantly looking around thinking *how do I get out of this situation that I am in?*'

After an hour or so of questioning, Murray asked Stephen if he would allow them to search his car. Stephen says that he was told they would be able to do this with a judge's permission anyway, but that securing this permission could take some time. If he just gave his consent for the search now, they could get it over with and then perhaps he'd be able to go. 'He made it seem as if they just wanted to check that there were no guns in the boot.' So with the possibility of release in sight, Stephen agreed.

The agents searched the car. They found a United States Post Office shipping box. They found a backpack. Inside the backpack, Murray found a red A5 notebook. It was Stephen's diary. To this day, Stephen does not know why he thought it would be a good idea to bring his diary – a book which absolutely implicated him in a one-man web of crime and chaos – along with him on his attempt to illegally acquire a firearm. 'I could have left it at the guest house,' he tells me ruefully, shaking his head. 'I don't know why I took it with me. It's crazy. I thought there was a chance they might flick through it. But I didn't think they would actually read the thing.'

In a separate room, Special Agent Murray actually read the thing. He scanned the handwriting and tried to get a handle on precisely what it all meant. As he worked through it, he saw that in some ways, it did seem to confirm what Stephen had already claimed: that he was a British student on a sightseeing trip to Vermont, who wanted to hike the wilderness, see black bears and also, if possible, to get a gun.

But then there was more to it than that. In amongst the pages of poetic odes to nature and thoughts on the general cheerfulness of Americans, there were references that were unambiguously about crime. 'He talked in some of these writings about prior bank robberies,' says Murray. 'He even wrote in his diaries about potential interest in committing an armed robbery here in the United States before he goes back. And so, as an investigator, you first look at that with a healthy scepticism. You think, OK, it's written down here, but is it true?'

Special Agent Murray came back into the interview room. It was now evening. He sat down opposite Stephen and told him that they had 'obtained some detailed information from your vehicle' though to begin with, he did not reveal that he had read the diary in detail. He asked about the shipping box and Stephen told him that, OK, yes, he had considered trying to smuggle the Glock back to the UK in the post, but that he doubted he would actually have gone through with it. Murray asked about the diary. And while Stephen was cautious, he was still not too concerned. He seemed to believe – or perhaps he just allowed himself to hope – that the contents weren't so incriminating. Even today, he says the diary was mostly just observations about New England. Which is true. Apart from the bits that aren't. In a signed affidavit provided to Vermont's District Court the following day, Special Agent Murray described how he found 'handwritten notes inside alluding to the commission of an intended armed robbery. Notes were made about the "multi-missioned USA trip" where Jackley listed obtaining a Glock pistol with ammunition, silencer, stun gun, stun grenades, wigs, beards and makeup.'

Did Stephen plan to commit a heist in America? He says that he'd briefly considered it prior to setting off but ultimately rejected the idea. Same with the apparent desire for 'stun grenades' and disguises. They were just thoughts that had passed through his head, which he had written down and then forgotten about or abandoned in favour of other ideas. 'There was an irony in the fact that he was an intelligent person. But he was writing down his plans and prior involvement in criminal acts on paper which could be used as evidence against him,' Murray tells me, with patient good humour. 'Some of his writing showed intelligence for sure. But it's just not stuff that most people would want to write down.'

He still did not confront Stephen directly with the specific contents of the diary. Instead, he continued to ask Stephen straightforward, general questions before then homing in on what seemed like very specific things that helped corroborate some of what he had seen written down. Agent Murray somehow got Stephen to divulge that he was wanted for armed robbery in the Netherlands, though he insisted the charges were false and that there was no warrant out for his arrest. Murray made a note and thanked Stephen for the information.

'I think he was very clever,' says Stephen. 'I don't think they ever showed their hand. Agent Murray was clever in his questioning by leading the conversation on casual things – what I studied, what university was like and so on – before suddenly firing a drilling question that I needed to answer really carefully, like why did I want that specific type of Glock or what had I been doing in London the previous week. And I would think . . . how did you know I flew from London?'

Stephen encouraged Murray to disregard the contents of the diaries, claiming most of the entries were written when he was stoned or drunk. At one point, they found a handwritten receipt for the Glock Stephen had ordered from the private dealer hidden in his sock and showing that he had paid $500 and only needed to pay a final $75 to take the gun. 'Nonetheless,' Murray noted in his affidavit. 'Jackley denied it.'

Night had fallen around the Middlesex police barracks. The ATF had by now contacted the British Consulate and explained that Stephen had been arrested and that he was going to be charged by the US Attorney's Office with knowingly providing a false statement and providing false identification intended to deceive a licensed firearms dealer in the attempted acquisition of a firearm. Stephen was told that he would be held until he could stand before a judge, who would then rule on bail terms. He was handcuffed and escorted to a waiting police car, then driven the thirty or so miles to the city of Burlington, where he would be detained at the Chittenden Regional Correctional Facility. From the back of the car, the passing hills now loomed inky black and were even more beautiful for their mystery. Stephen gazed at them and thought about black bears, and whether he might still get the chance to see some in the wild on this trip. Despite everything – despite the odd sensation he had experienced at the summit of Owl's Head Mountain – he did not feel as though his mission was now over. 'I thought, OK, I'm going to spend a couple of days in a county jail. But all I need to do is get bail, which I didn't see as an obstacle. I don't think at that stage they had indicated they had read the diaries,' he says. 'Or that they would be contacting the UK police.'

At some point over the next few days, between 20 and 22 May, detectives with the West Mercia Police were contacted by federal agents in the United States. Detective Inspector Jim Fox says it was the FBI who first got in touch by email. They explained that a University of Worcester student had been arrested in Vermont, that he had tried to buy a gun using a fake ID, but that based on the evidence they had recovered they had reason to suspect that he was connected to further, deeper, altogether more dangerous levels of criminality.

One of the things that seemed to concern the growing number of US law enforcement officials who had now seen Stephen's diaries was his habit of using the word 'we' when writing about his plans for robberies and the acquisition of firearms. *We will do this. We will do that. We must be careful.* It is not uncommon for people with Asperger's to sometimes refer to themselves in the first-person plural like this. But the agents with the ATF and FBI poring over the diaries recovered from Stephen's car did not know he had Asperger's. Nobody did. So in order to find out more about the odd young man currently held at Chittenden Regional Correctional Facility, they asked if Worcester CID would be able to search his halls of residence room. They said that of course they would.

A search warrant was quickly issued and on Friday 23 May, detectives arrived at Wyvern Hall and started to root through Stephen's small, spartan bedroom. They began to take replica pistols and real knives and place them into evidence bags, but they did not get very far. One of the officers discovered what he realised was an improvised explosive device. There were some urgent conversations between officers and, very quickly, an evacuation of the entire area was ordered. Students, teachers and small children from a nearby nursery school were ushered outside and into the spring afternoon. Army bomb disposal experts were called in. A tight police cordon was quickly established.

Louise Alice Cawood was returning to Wyvern Hall with a group of fellow residents around mid-afternoon when they spotted the heavy police presence. Approaching a uniformed officer, they asked what was happening. 'All we got told was that there was a policing incident and investigation in the top flat,' she says. Quickly, rumours began to spread amongst the students. 'We were hearing stuff about all these machine guns and knives and blades being found.' Everyone present seemed to agree that it was almost certainly something to do with the quiet guy whose room was in that flat. None of them could recall his name, but it just made a sort of sense. 'One of the rumours was that he was going to set fire to our halls. Or that he was going to go around and do that American thing when they go round and kill loads of schoolkids,' Cawood says. 'We never even got told the truth.'

Not for the first time, the bomb disposal team realised that the bomb Stephen had constructed was not really a bomb. Detective Inspector Fox was not at Wyvern Hall at the time, but grins when he describes what he later heard about the incident back at the station. 'I am told an officer came wandering down the stairs holding a bomb, and I think some advice was given to the officer on procedures when finding a device, which didn't involve carrying it down the stairs and saying, "Sarge! I've found a bomb!" We had a forensic report done and it did actually have a firework involved,' he quickly adds, a little more sombrely. 'So it would have made a bang and sparks and stuff.'

After hearing about the bomb and some of the items found in the room, DI Fox decided he wanted to visit Wyvern Hall and see for himself. Because, wildly unlikely though it sounded, the shape of a possibility was beginning to form in his mind. The fake guns. The fake bomb. The knives. 'We realised he was potentially our robber,' he says. On 27 May, Fox entered the empty room on the top floor of Wyvern Hall. He saw the letters 'RH' carved on the wall and a jolt shot through him. He opened folders and found maps of nearby towns with the locations of banks clearly marked along with escape routes and changeover locations. He picked up diaries and read them. He saw plans. Dates. Times. Amounts. Descriptions of the robberies that had succeeded and descriptions of the robberies that had failed. Descriptions of driving home to Devon and further robberies committed there. He found the clothes and backpack he recognised from the CCTV stills. He found the 'Paying Out' slip made out to Robin Hood. He found the silly blonde mop-top wig the teenagers had jeered at. He found everything, there, in a small bare room on the local university campus.

After taking the time to absorb it all, Fox stood in the centre of the small room and let out a breath.

'Christ,' he said, to nobody in particular.

A few days earlier, four thousand miles away, Stephen had been escorted to a pre-trial hearing before US Magistrate Judge Jerome J. Niedermeier. It was taking place in the Federal Building in Burlington, a large complex home to several different agencies, including the local ATF field office where Special Agent Murray was based. It was a bright, blue morning and Stephen was escorted from the Chittenden Regional Correctional Facility by a pair of US Marshals. As well as apprehending fugitives and guarding federal facilities, the responsibilities of US Marshals include the transportation of federal prisoners, and the two men who came for Stephen were businesslike but friendly. One of them was young and broad, the other much older, with neat grey hair, a pressed short-sleeve shirt and a distinctive dicky bow.

It was 22 May. In the two full days since his arrest, Stephen had been assigned a public defender, a bespectacled man with a goatee who he described as being scatty, meek and suffering from a bad case of halitosis. The two of them entered the courtroom, Stephen in handcuffs and watched over by the two marshals. The judge sat in front of a large Stars and Stripes, and displayed on a screen in large black letters was a single sentence.

THE UNITED STATES OF AMERICA VS STEPHEN JACKLEY

The hearing began. Stephen was already agitated and struggling to contain a fizzing, nervous energy when, almost immediately, it became clear that this was not going to end how he hoped it would. As soon as the prosecutor began to speak, he realised that they had read his diary from cover to cover. Nothing about Stephen's references to stun grenades, disguises, heists, evading 'the pigs' and gun smuggling made Judge Niedermeier sympathetic to the idea of allowing bail. Stephen Jackley, the prosecution continued, was an individual who had not just broken federal law, but someone who might well have committed offences in other countries too. They explained that they were already liaising with UK police forces about this strong possibility. While there was still so much about the true nature of Stephen Jackley's identity that needed to be uncovered, to allow him to walk away would not just be unwise, it would be dangerous.

'They mentioned something about Interpol saying that I was a flight risk, and they mentioned Holland as well, that I might be wanted globally, that I might be part of a terrorist cell,' Stephen recalls, sighing at the memory. 'They were really drawing it out of proportion.' Months later, when Stephen was interviewed by an FBI agent at Southern State Correctional

Facility, this concern was still present. 'He asked me some pretty far-flung questions, most of which were completely irrelevant to my case or anything I have ever done. Stuff about criminal organisations, explosives and anarchism. Perhaps some of this explains the nightly strip-searches and cell moves.'

Whatever his attorney then stood up and stammered had no effect. Stephen couldn't even hear his words. The judge would not grant bail. The two marshals escorted Stephen back to a small holding cell within the federal building. The choking panic that had already begun to slowly creep up his torso during the hearing now had him by the throat. Strange faces regarded him blankly as he was led down corridors in handcuffs. He needed to be free. Not simply for freedom's sake, but so that he could try and think of some way to dispose of all the evidence in his halls of residence bedroom before the police found it. Perhaps he could call someone – anyone – and ask them to clear his room? But he couldn't do that from inside a cell.

The marshals locked the door and left him. He began to pace agitatedly, covering his eyes with his hands and muttering in distress. Suddenly he stopped, slammed his head against the wall and fell to the ground in a heap. He lay there, twitching every few moments, spittle dribbling from his mouth. After some time, the younger of the two US Marshals came to check on him and found him prostrate. 'He was on the floor, stiff as a board, foaming at the mouth and twitching uncontrollably,' remembers the marshal, Deputy John Curtis. 'It was what you'd see if a bad actor were having a seizure on television. I opened the cell and asked him if he was OK and he looked up at me then rolled his eyes back into his head. He would stop for a while, maybe fifteen to twenty seconds, and then get right back into it.'

Curtis called for the older deputy in the dicky bow, and the two men stood over the sporadically convulsing Stephen, trying to work out what to do. Deputy Curtis did not believe Stephen was having a fit. His intuition was correct. Stephen was faking it. His hope was that he would be taken to hospital, where an opportunity to escape might present itself. Mimicking full body spasms on the floor, he ignored the two marshals' patient demands to stop. Instead, he just kept making himself shake and spray drool. 'I was twitching and shaking because when I've seen seizures, people generally move slightly,' he explains. 'So I was doing that constantly. But it was surprisingly tiring just doing this constant small movement. I was exhausted.'

Protocol demanded that the marshals provide Stephen with medical attention. An ambulance was called and, under the constant supervision of the two men, he was driven to the University of Vermont Medical Center. Upon arrival, he was placed in a wheelchair and taken to be assessed by a doctor and a team of nurses. Stephen's actions were not founded on total fantasy. Two days earlier, prison staff had observed that he had a rasping cough and fever. After completing a medical questionnaire in which Stephen truthfully answered that he had visited East Asia in the last few years, he was taken to hospital for some tests, most likely to guard against the possibility of him having avian flu. He had noticed then that, even though he was under escort, security had been relatively low-key and relaxed.

To Stephen's annoyance, things were very different on this occasion. The two marshals were taking absolutely no chances. 'I remember them being really keen that I was handcuffed to the wheelchair. They were totally obsessed about security,' he recalls, frowning, as though this were some curious personality quirk of theirs. 'I didn't expect them to be constantly watching over me.'

He continued his bouts of fake fitting. Doctors and nurses ran a plethora of tests. The room was filled with people, but Stephen's plan required that he be left alone for at least a short period of time. 'I thought that if I could get out of a window, then I could just run and outpace them,' he says, despite the fact he was in handcuffs. 'I am not a violent person, but worst case scenario, I thought I will be able to disarm one of them. My preferable option would have been just jumping out a window. From there, I would have just run into the wild.'

All the tests showed that Stephen was fine. He sat slumped in the wheelchair, pretending to be unconscious. Then the room began to empty. The voices of medical staff and the older marshal drifted away and a door shut. All Stephen could hear now was the low, steady beep of a heart-rate monitor. Finally, he was alone. He let a few moments pass to be sure. 'Then he opens his eye real quick, thinking no one else is in the room,' says Deputy Curtis, who had been standing over him in absolute silence. 'He sees me and then closes his eye immediately. I have a quick conversation with him about how I am here and I just witnessed what he did and that it's time for us to get back to the office. It wasn't too long after that he recovered from his symptoms. I think he just needed someone to say, "the jig is up, you can stop with the act, this isn't working and we have places to be."'

Deputy Curtis says that given the nature of his job, he is well-used to being around some very desperate and upset people, and the key to managing these situations is to be firm but patient and understanding. 'It's the worst day of their lives and I'm not trying to make it any harder.'

Even then, handcuffed in the back of a secure moving vehicle, the front of his orange jumpsuit drenched in his own spit,

Stephen had still not given up hope of escape. But he knew that he didn't have much time. 'I realised the doors were locked but I thought there might be a way to disarm the lock, so I was discreetly trying to reach the buttons,' he says. Deputy Curtis could see what Stephen was thinking – he could see the thought bubbles over his head – and intervened. 'He was paying way too much attention on how to exit the vehicle. I got his attention off the door and on to me and told him that it wasn't a very good idea.'

The marshals then made what seemed to be a series of long phone calls from the front of the van. They were speaking to the staff at the Northwest State Correctional Facility, where Stephen was being taken, and advising them about his behaviour. Despite his crime and despite his diaries and despite the possibility he was wanted in other countries, at the start of the day, it was not guaranteed that Stephen would be placed straight into solitary confinement. But like a panicked child trying to free themselves from a Chinese finger trap, the more he strained towards freedom, the tighter the grip around him became. 'I am sure that information was passed on to the facility about his alleged seizure and his behaviour,' says Deputy Curtis. 'And the facility is going to treat it as they see fit. He happened to act up on one day with the marshal service while he was in federal custody. That's it really.'

When Stephen arrived at Northwest State, there were eight armed guards waiting for him in an underground car park. The doors of the van swung open and he was ordered to lie on his back and large, heavy hands reached out, pinning his ankles to the floor as leg irons were clamped and locked around him. The guards surrounded him and he was half marched, half dragged through the prison intake area. He passed the marshal with the dicky bow, who was talking to a man in a suit. Both men watched Stephen as he passed, but said nothing.

Entering a corridor, the chains around his legs made a long, eerie groan as he lost his footing and was pulled along the hard, polished floor. Voices from the cells lining the corridor called out, shadowy faces pressed against doors, but Stephen's eyes were on the floor. The procession stopped outside a six foot by nine foot prison cell and he stumbled inside as the door buzzed shut behind him. Breathing short, shallow breaths, he looked around him. All he could see was solid wall. He couldn't move. He couldn't breathe. He shut his eyes and tried to wish himself free. Images flashed and dissipated. He saw the view from Owl's Head Mountain. He saw a Cambodian forest at dawn. He saw a lake in the French countryside. From high in the branches of a tree he could see a small Devon town nestled beside by a vast green sea, and it looked beautiful. He thought of Robin Hood. He thought of children searching through scrapheaps and beggars in Exeter and of cities on the moon. He opened his eyes and the walls were still there. It was the end. It was over. He sat down on his concrete bunk and cried.

The materials uncovered at Wyvern Hall proved beyond doubt that Stephen was the mysterious figure at the centre of Operation Gandalf. Prosecutors would later describe his room as being a 'treasure trove of evidence'. Detective Inspector Fox admits he has never seen anything like it. 'You start reading this stuff where he's basically confessing to the robberies in his diaries and you just think . . . he's copped it for us,' he says, puffing out his cheeks. 'I think the Americans call it a "slam dunk".'

DI Fox and Special Agent Murray liaised. Federal agents in the US provided British police with Stephen's fingerprints and

DNA, helping to make the looming case against him water-tight. The Dutch police issued a European Arrest Warrant after Stephen failed to respond to their requests to return to Amsterdam, and there was some to-and-fro between authorities in the UK, US and the Netherlands over procedure. Upon learning the full facts of the case, though, the Dutch seemed more than happy to walk away. 'I think they were pretty much like "if you have him for eight armed robberies you can keep him,"' says DI Fox. '"We don't really want him that badly."'

The British police built their case against Stephen while, at the same time, he waited to be tried for his crime in America. After a month at Northwest State Correctional Facility, Stephen was moved to Southern State, to Foxtrot Unit and the Hole, to 'Stinky' and the snapper. According to records held by the Vermont Department of Prisons, Stephen spent 134 days, 5 hours and 36 minutes at SSCF. A few weeks before he left he was visited by Special Agent Murray and an FBI agent who briefly questioned him again. In late October 2008, Stephen was escorted by US Marshals to Burlington Courthouse, where he stood trial for his attempt to buy a gun from Henry Parro using a fake ID. He was sentenced to ten months in jail, inclusive of the five he had by then already served. When asked if he wished to say anything upon being sentenced, he stood up. 'I am sorry for breaking your law,' he said quietly, before being taken away.

He was moved to Strafford County Jail, where he endured suicide watch before joining the general population. Then he was transferred to MDC Brooklyn, to the witch doctor, *iglesia* and New Year's fireworks over Manhattan. In February 2009, he was visited by a woman working for the British Embassy who explained to him that upon the completion of his US sentence, he would be deported to the UK. If he contested his deportation, she said, he would simply be extradited. He agreed not to contest it. He was then moved to New York's Orange County Correctional Facility, where he spent a further seven weeks seeing out the remainder of his sentence, before being transferred to Varick Street Detention Center, a facility in Manhattan run by US Immigration and Customs Enforcement. He spent almost two months there, guarded by ICE agents and waiting to be deported.

On 12 May 2009, Stephen was escorted back to the United Kingdom. He spent the flight from JFK to Heathrow wedged between a pair of federal agents and was arrested the moment he stepped off the plane. That night, in his cell at Worcester police station, he wrote a long, rambling poem in black biro, filling both sides of a sheet of A4 note paper.

Sitting in a jail cell, deep in the black night
back from America, one year in prisons;
back to the Isle – my home, my punishment;
no chances, no ways – nabbed off the flight,
first breaths of Freedom flew like a cloud
just like the vapour the aeroplane passed
I stole from the rich, gave to the poor,
took from gambling houses, banks and corporations –
now they've put my face on 21 cards;
but no game of Blackjack is this, no Ace and King –
it was sweet, when I ruled the world,
when every horizon was a dream and opportunity,
when the wind blew strong and fresh,
the sky so high and clear – no barriers, no
    boundaries . . .
but now these four stale walls border my world
    casting darkness deeper than the night outside

The lamentation and self-reproach went on and on and on. There was angst but also a perceptiveness and self-knowledge that seemed to bely his actions over the past two years. One line, jotted at the bottom of the first side of paper, is jarring in its clear-eyed analysis.

O learn this well and know the moral:
Chase not your obsessions without forgetting your
   dreams.

EPILOGUE

On 21 August 2009, Stephen stood trial at Worcester Crown Court. He pleaded guilty to five offences of robbery, three of attempted robbery, with seven related offences of possession of an imitation firearm as well as offences of burglary, attempted burglary and assault occasioning actual bodily harm. The presiding judge, His Honour Judge John Cavell, described the journal entries in which he wrote about kidnapping bank staff as 'chilling' and stated that Stephen 'would have carried on into more serious offences' had he not been stopped. 'I cannot begin to imagine what possessed a man of your obvious abilities to resort to this appalling series of serious crimes,' Cavell told him. He sentenced Stephen to thirteen years in jail. Had Stephen pled not guilty, which for a time had seemed a possibility, Cavell said he would have faced twenty years. Stephen did not react. He just stood there and wrung his hands.

A number of Stephen's victims were present at the trial. Luke Twisleton was there, the young William Hill employee who went several years unable to sleep without a night light after Stephen raided his branch. He remembered how Stephen would not make eye contact with him during the nine-hour trial, but how just seeing him in the light of day made him feel a bit better. DI Fox says that some of the other victims voiced

similar sentiments after seeing Stephen in the dock. 'A couple
of them after they had seen him in court were like, is that him?
Is that what I have been so upset about? This insignificant,
skinny lad? But that's not what they remember, is it? They
remember the mask and the barrel of a gun.'

Immediately after the trial, DI Fox stood outside the courthouse and addressed the assembled press. He told them that
Stephen's claims to have been motivated by a desire to rob from
the rich and give to the poor were bogus. Of the £10,686 he
stole, virtually nothing was recovered. Yes, he gave £1,255 to
the NSPCC and wrote in his diaries that he planned to give
them much more. But beyond that? Where did the money go?
On travel. On trips to Amsterdam, Istanbul, France, Spain and
America. On guns and angle-grinders and seafront hotel
dinners for his mother. If he gave any money directly to the
homeless, as he claimed, then it was impossible to trace or
prove. 'Jackley's crimes caused a great deal of distress,' DI Fox
announced to reporters. 'The reality of his behaviour is a far
cry from the self-styled character of Robin Hood that he
depicted in his deluded diaries.'

Local press in both Devon and the West Midlands followed
up on the story. Reporters knocked on the door at Manstone
Avenue only for his mother to peer around the corner and
softly tell them she did not want to speak to anybody. Quotes
from unnamed neighbours described Stephen as quiet, anonymous, never any trouble at all. Ben Weaver remembers being
at university and getting a frantic phone call from his stepmother. 'She was saying, "You'll never guess what Stephen has
done!"' he remembers. But when she explained, Weaver found
he wasn't surprised at all. 'He was always very moral, even if it
was "off" in terms of him lacking empathy. But that he had
seen an injustice in the world and tried to do something about

it? There was no surprise in that. Most people would probably donate money to charity rather than try and act like Robin Hood,' he says. 'But it wasn't shocking. "These banks are making loads of money." I could see the logic that he might have been following.'

In September 2009, Stephen made the front page of the *Worcester News*. There was a colour photograph of his face and a headline in large, heavy type. 'I'M SORRY', it read, 'Armed robber's letter of remorse from jail'. In a handwritten letter sent to the paper he tried to explain how he now comprehended the lasting, long-term psychological pain he had caused.

> Reading the witness statements in the robberies has given me great shame and remorse. Innocent people were hurt through my actions. This was never what I intended. I am aware of the mental hurt and fear experienced by clerks and tellers in the robberies – which is totally unforgivable and totally unintended. To these people I can only express my deepest regrets and apologies. I am willing to see these people to say this to their faces and, if it would make them any happier, see the pain and depression I've gone through. If I'm able to repay the damage I did, I will do it.

Alex Bingham of Devon and Cornwall Police later spoke to the local *Express and Echo* newspaper in an article headlined 'Detectives believe "Robin Hood" thief apology is genuine'.

'Jackley has written a very articulate letter,' he told a reporter. 'He is clearly an intelligent individual. He could have thought about his actions and how his victims would have felt at the time, but he chose to go on and commit those offences – and there were numerous offences.'

Nevertheless, he continued, 'He doesn't appear to be trying

to gain anything in writing this letter, but is reflecting on what has happened. He's trying to say he has done wrong and is sorry.'

Like the sentencing judge – like so many people involved in the case – he said that he still could not begin to imagine what possessed Stephen to do it.

The possibility that Stephen might have some form of autism was raised before he stood trial. On 30 July 2009 Stephen was assessed by a psychiatrist at HMP Hewell following a period, he says, of 'what they classed as "odd behaviour"'. The psychiatrist concluded that Stephen may well have Asperger Syndrome, and Stephen says told his defence team that he would benefit from a full psychiatric report in advance of his trial. No request for such a report was ever made by his legal advisors. 'I told my solicitor that the prison psychiatrist had said, "Look, I think you might have Asperger Syndrome,"' says Stephen. 'And the solicitor said, "Oh no, we can't disclose this. This might risk you getting an IPP."'

An IPP is a type of indeterminate sentence known as 'Imprisonment for Public Protection'. They came into effect in England and Wales in 2005 and were conceived as a means of protecting the public against criminals whose crimes were not serious enough to warrant a life sentence. The idea was that upon completing an initial sentence, a parole board then judged whether the inmate was safe enough for release. If the inmate was refused parole, they must wait another year and try again. And there was no limit to the number of times an inmate could be refused. Between 2005 and their abolition in 2012, IPPs were widely handed down but inconsistently and unpredictably applied. They became a source of controversy. You could, in theory, come up for parole after serving five years in jail for armed robbery, but then spend the rest of your life trying to prove you are no longer a danger to society.

So you can understand why some defence lawyers may have been spooked by the idea of presenting a direct link between armed robberies and a mental health condition, such as Asperger's, that cannot be cured or treated. The possibility of being caught in a catch-22 situation was real. Better to downplay or simply not mention it and take the certainty of a fixed-tariff sentence. In any case, Stephen did not question his defence's decision. 'I just said, OK, whatever you think is best.'

He began his thirteen-year sentence. He struggled badly. While his time in the US prison system had been hard, something about the surrealness of it – the sense that the experience still formed part of the grand sweep of his adventure – made it easier to manage. In the UK, this illusion was shattered. He couldn't settle. His directness and social naivety was not indulged by inmates and prison staff who did not find his Englishness a novelty. He was bullied for his obsessive need for routine and his urgent insistence that certain things be done in certain ways at certain times. He continued to chide himself for what he had done and the hurt he had caused. On sheets of official Prison Service notepaper, he sat in a cell and wrote to himself.

My dreams were to be a modern Robin Hood, lifting the worldwide poor up from the oppression of banks and corporations. Steal from the rich and give to the poor, the voice of Justice resounded. Caught in a cycle of drugs, righteous indignation, social angst and an obsessive vendetta against capitalist foundations I followed the road of good intentions and ended up falling down into a pit of hell.

If people got hurt (mentally) through my actions it was never what I intended. And some did get hurt . . . casualties of my war against banks and bookies. There's no justification for that. If there is one reason I should be imprisoned, that's it.

Years passed. Stephen moved from prison to prison. In 2011 he consulted another solicitor who advised that the possibility of autism was worth exploring. Eventually, in February 2013, Dr Suleman met Stephen and compiled a full psychiatric report in which he concluded that 'there is little doubt that Mr Jackley suffers from Asperger Syndrome'.

The following month, Stephen launched an appeal against his thirteen-year sentence. In a skeleton argument submitted to the Court of Appeal, Stephen's new solicitor argued that his Asperger's should be considered a mitigating factor for three key reasons:

(i)   As can be seen from Dr Suleman's report, the Appellant's condition has been present for some considerable time and has impaired his ability to relate properly to the world around him. Typically, his social interactions have suffered significantly; he displays some paranoid traits and he has an obsessive personality. All are consistent with his diagnosis.

(ii) The combination of these traits are bound to have affected his culpability in that, once the idea entered his head to commit the robberies, he became obsessive about them and was unable to 'reason' with himself, despite knowing that it was wrong.

(iii) He was unable to evaluate the harm he was causing to the people caught up in his wrongful actions as a result of his condition.

Against the advice of his solicitor, Stephen also presented the judge with his typed seven-page essay titled 'Desperate Times'. Within it, he attempted to explain what it was he had been trying to achieve and why. The central chunk of it runs thus:

For every so-called progression, for every monetary fortune, there is usually a cost. As Mario Puzo said, 'behind all riches lies a crime'. This is true just as much for humanity as for the natural world. In a finite world there is one cruel but insurmountable inevitability: when one has more, the other must have less . . . I made a promise, perhaps more accurately termed a vow, to change things. To make a difference. And I knew time was running out.

Even five years ago the awareness of an ecological crisis was strong. Drastic, unprecedented courageous actions were required. But for every goal and dream there is one crucial ingredient to bring it to fruition. It is the same ingredient that all human endeavours now require, regardless of effort or need. Yes, money was what I required.

I decided on a drastic, almost revolutionary course of action. There were two points, A and B. And all I could think about was getting to B. The end of global inequality, the survival of humanity, the exploration of space . . . all this I aimed for. It would take time. It would mean many sacrifices. But – and this was the idea I clung to most – it was possible.

Banks, bookmakers and building societies are icons of the current socio-economic system, presided over by the global oligarchy. They are more than just exchanges of money and legalised loan sharks. They were, to me, a legitimate target – not for the money they controlled but rather for what they represented. This was a time when banking

CEOs were paying themselves millions in bonuses, when the City's top echelons were buying new yachts and prestige cars. Why should they care that 'the economy' was struggling; that unemployment and financial uncertainty was spreading like a plague? . . . History's greatest injustice was being repeated: the poor and the vulnerable suffer, whilst the rich and powerful escape unscathed.

The appeal was not a success. In hindsight, Stephen admits it was probably a bad idea to include the essay. The judge, Lord Justice Treacy, dismissed the arguments put forward by Stephen's solicitor about the mitigating effect of his Asperger's. Stephen, he said, was intelligent enough to complete his A levels and secure a place at university. He had previously lived a law-abiding life and so he knew the difference between right and wrong. He must have known his actions would have terrified his victims and, he continues, 'his modus operandi was to strike such fear into his victims so that they would comply with his demands'.

Lord Justice Treacy did make two small concessions. He accepted that once Stephen had freely chosen to begin his crimes, his Asperger's made it more likely that he would become obsessed with doing so and continue to offend. He also acknowledged that his 'rigid thinking and aversion to change' made life in custody more challenging for him than most prisoners. So because of his Asperger's, Stephen's sentence was reduced by twelve months. From thirteen years to twelve.

Dr Suleman tells me he had hoped his report would have helped Stephen secure a much greater reduction in sentence. The problem was that it was much harder to do this on appeal. The courts don't have the same kind of leeway second time around, he explains. He believes Stephen's Asperger's should have been part of his original 2009 defence. He holds his hands up, smiles and sighs. 'I personally feel that if the report was done and the diagnosis was made the first time, he would have got much less of a sentence.'

During his time in British prisons, Stephen studied for a degree in sociology with the Open University, which he achieved with first class honours. He wrote poems and short stories for *Inside Times*, the UK prison newspaper. He won an arts charity award for creative writing. He embarked on a series of lengthy one-man legal battles against his sentence, all of which came to nothing. He moved prison eighteen times. He envisaged the creation of a social enterprise which would publish the writing of ex-offenders and other vulnerable members of society, which he created upon his release and which he called Arkbound. He began to write two books. The first, *Good Intentions*, is a novella about a young couple named John and Sarah who live a Bonnie and Clyde-like existence, conducting casino heists and using the takings to help those in need. The second, *Just Sky*, is a slim autobiography. Both books would later be published through Arkbound. From prison, he sent a letter to Dechen Chöling and explained everything. 'I was leading a multiple life of traveller, student and bank robber,' he wrote matter-of-factly. 'Most people I tell my story to don't believe it.'

He asked if anybody at Dechen Chöling would like to write to him. Maizza Waser, the autistic German woman, said she would. The two of them corresponded for a while, making observations about the weather, about the changing seasons at Dechen Chöling, about his crimes and about Buddhism. Sometimes his mother would come and see him, brought to whichever jail he was in by Ken and Judy, her born-again Christian friends, though her condition made these visits rare.

He made her small decorative items in the prison workshops.
She sent him a harmonica.

Stephen was released on parole in May 2015, almost exactly
seven years after being pulled over by a state trooper on a rainy
afternoon in Vermont. He was twenty-nine years old. The world
he re-entered was very different to the one he had left behind.
The Global Financial Crisis had changed everything. Popular
protest movements like Occupy and Extinction Rebellion had
seen millions of ordinary people march against Wall Street, the
One Per Cent and capitalism's banzai charge towards ecological
oblivion. Inequality had only grown. America needed to be
made great again. Brexit Britain wrestled with itself as nativism
spread across Europe and the far right muscled into the mainstream, pointing fingers, screaming at scapegoats. Around 2,000
migrants drowned each year crossing the Mediterranean in an
attempt to escape war, poverty and the impact of climate
change. Globally, the last five years had been the hottest ever
recorded. Sea levels continued to rise. In 2019, the Greenland
ice sheet lost 11 billion tonnes in a single day.

Re-reading Stephen's teenage diaries from what is now almost
twenty years ago, it's hard not to feel that he really was a canary
in the mine: that from his little bedroom in his cramped council
house in Sidmouth, he was able to see the threats facing
humanity and predict their damage with more clarity than
world leaders or so many professional prognosticators. The
economic, ecological, political and social problems facing the
world, he concluded, cannot be tackled one by one because
they have become so interlinked that they are, effectively, one
and the same. And the only way of saving humanity is by taking
urgent, radical action. Today, there are millions of people who
not only hold these same convictions, but for whom these

convictions form the basis of their very identities. They believe what Stephen believed.

Did Stephen's own radical course of action – his righteous, self-appointed, Robin Hood mission – become warped? He admits that yes, in many ways it did. There were times when he enjoyed the power that came with being an armed robber. There were times he enjoyed the notoriety and the ego-stroking fantasies of playing some pivotal role in the salvation of humanity and of going from anonymity to folkloric renown. There were times he enjoyed the money he stole, predominantly for travelling. The idea of escaping, whether into a world of fantasy or just away from his life in England, underpins so much of what Stephen did.

Does this mean that there eventually came a point when he was simply in it for himself? That the Organisation was just some fantasy fig leaf that allowed him to continue a fundamentally selfish lifestyle of smash-and-grab raids while telling himself he was more than just an ordinary criminal? This is, essentially, the interpretation presented by his prosecutors. That Stephen's crimes were cynical, calculated and not at all what he presented them as.

But Stephen never lost sight of his driving motivation. He remained convinced that the world was hurtling towards ecological and economic catastrophe. If he simply wanted money for his own personal use, then he was daring and resourceful enough to just put a brick through a jeweller's window. But he was fixated on robbing banks not because banks are easy to rob, but because banks have stolen from ordinary people and are engines of inequality. The defaced pound coin calling cards, the apologetic repayments to the NSPCC, the letter to the police saying they've got the wrong man . . . these all form part of Stephen's moral landscape during this period.

Looking back, he describes the Robin Hood identity he had adopted as an 'invisible uniform' he was incapable of taking off. It wasn't simply that this identity provided him with a sense of purpose or that it allowed him to indulge in private delusions of grandeur but, more than anything, what Stephen's secret new persona provided him with was a clear set of rules for behaving within the world. Stephen did not know he was on the autism spectrum, but he knew that he found negotiating life challenging, sometimes overwhelming. If, as Dr Suleman says, having Asperger's can feel like living in a foreign country without knowing the rules, then what if you could give yourself a set of rules to live by? It may involve robbing from the rich to give to the poor. But at least you would know where you stood. This was partly the reason why Stephen persisted with robbing banks. If he just wanted £100,000 to start the Organisation, there were many safer – and perfectly legal – ways of doing this. But Robin Hood robs. From the rich. This does not make it the right thing to do. But it's what he did.

It is this sense of absolute belief that characterises his crimes more than anything. Why, for example, did Stephen believe that tinfoil would scramble the airport security X-rays? Ostensibly, it makes no sense at all. His journals were packed with page after page after page of handwritten notes and diagrams relating to cosmology, string theory, space–time and quantum physics. If you knew about this kind of stuff, it seems almost inconceivable that you did not also know that X-rays detect metal. And even if the tinfoil did repel the X-rays, all that would mean is that the security officers would see a load of strange, X-ray repellent items in his bag. Which would be suspicious.

For someone who approached his crimes and escapes so methodically and so rationally – a trait that every police officer involved in his case readily acknowledges – Stephen was still capable of doing stuff like this. Returning to Amsterdam when he knew he was wanted there. Breaking into the NSPCC offices in the belief that he would find an easy route down into the bank branch below, only to be shocked to find a 'massive metal door' blocking his path. Using a cheap battery-powered angle-grinder to try and cut through the metal bars protecting a bank window. Employing a disguise that made people stop, point and laugh as he walked by. What, you can't help wondering after a while, did he really think was going to happen?

And the answer is . . . he thought it would work. He had to. He was obsessed with carrying out these crimes and inhabiting the Robin Hood role he had created for himself. But if he approached these crimes with perfect, unflinching rationality, there was going to be a problem. And that problem was that he would see, very clearly, that it was not going to work: that robbing banks on his own in order to create a start-up fund for the foundation of a pan-global, supra-governmental philanthropic New World Order was simply a dream. He was going to get arrested and he was going to go to jail. So instead, he allowed himself to believe that tinfoil could scramble X-rays and all the rest of it. Because if he didn't believe it, then he wasn't going to try. So he made sure he believed it.

It was the reason why so many of his crimes seemed like 85 per cent smart, pragmatic, patient planning and then 15 per cent total fantasy. Once he had reassured himself that the blank-firing pistol he accidentally bought in Istanbul would be perfectly adequate for his purposes, why even take the risk of smuggling it through customs? He could just come back to the UK and order one online. That isn't cynicism. It's blind faith. It's fire-walking. And he kept going and going. Until he finally got burned.

* * *

The last time Stephen and I meet, in March 2019, it is for a meal at a vegan curry house in north London. It is a dark, drizzly night. He says that he has been spending more and more time doing farm work in different parts of southern Europe. It seems an austere and solitary life. He says he enjoys doing manual labour in the outdoors, staying in small, anonymous villages, going on long runs in the evening and then sitting down and writing at night.

He is not the boyish figure with the uncertain squint whose photo had made the papers ten years earlier. His dark eyes seem deeper-set, his face careworn. He explains that he is writing a book about his experience of the UK justice system, about his journey as an inmate with Asperger's, spending time in almost twenty different prisons. He does not say as much, but his life is difficult. He is isolated. His mother died in 2018, which left him 'devastated for weeks and weeks'. Since his crimes were uncovered, he says that none of his extended family have been in regular contact with him. Lisa, his half-sister, admits that he has emailed her about the possibility of him paying her a visit up in Liverpool, but that she feels uncomfortable with the idea and it has never happened.

Slowly and reluctantly, he has come to understand how 'debilitating' Asperger's is. He upsets people without realising. He struggles to find common ground with others. He sets himself goals which are not realistic, but which he finds impossible to veer from. He knows he can seem difficult, stubborn and pedantic when he really does not mean to be. Seeing the perspective of another individual and empathising with how they may be feeling is still a guessing game. For a long time following his formal diagnosis by Dr Suleman, he just accepted his condition or was at least able to shrug it off. These days he finds that he feels a constant resentment towards it. If he had a choice he would rather be in a wheelchair than on the autism spectrum. 'The fact is, it prevents people from living in society, from being accepted and integrated into society, and we're talking about a species that is, by definition, social. It's like being a fish without fins.'

The role played by Stephen's Asperger's in his crimes cannot be quantified or neatly calculated. It is almost impossible to imagine him robbing banks in the way he did had he not been on the autism spectrum. But nor did he rob banks simply because he is on that spectrum. What it is possible to say, I think, is that Stephen's social isolation did as much as anything to lead him down the path he took. And the irony – the tragedy, really – is that social isolation is not a symptom of Asperger's. Or at least, it doesn't have to be. By the time he had reached adolescence, he desperately wanted to be included in normal, day-to-day life. Only, he wasn't. So he drifted further and further away, retreating into the echo chamber of his own thoughts, beliefs and anxieties.

There is a temptation to assume that Stephen was somehow let down by 'the System'. And while an early diagnosis in his childhood or teens would have certainly helped, this is not necessarily to blame the various doctors, social workers and community nurses who monitored Stephen and tried to shepherd him through a childhood they had already identified as traumatic. He was under a child protection plan and passed GCSEs and A levels at the special school in which he had been placed. He did not slip through any net. He was always there.

What so much of Stephen's story shows is that we cannot simply expect psychiatric professionals or clinicians to somehow deal with people like Stephen, or his mother and father, on our behalf. To worry about them so that we don't have to. Stephen only had one real friend in Sidmouth, Ben Weaver.

But what if there had been two Ben Weavers? What if there had been three? How many interwoven friendships, or even just friendly acquaintances, would it have taken before Stephen begun to feel a part of something and started to look outwards rather than inwards? Would he have slowly begun to learn more about the emotions of others? Would there have come a point when he wouldn't need it explained to him that aiming a fake gun at a stranger might, in fact, be a terrifying ordeal for them long after the moment had passed? And even if the idea of becoming the new Robin Hood had entered his mind, would one or more of his friends have been able to say to him, 'Look, Stephen, that's just a really bad idea and it's not going to work'?

It is not society's fault that Stephen committed his crimes. Nobody made the decision to rob banks for him. But the Jackleys were nevertheless excluded by society because of psychiatric conditions which were not their fault. One of the reasons they moved around so much during Stephen's early years was for this very reason. Stephen knew enough to fret about asking his classmates to come round and play at Manstone Avenue because he feared how they would respond to his mother and father. It is not a coincidence that Ben Weaver's father worked with autistic people and that, as a result, Ben knew that some people were different and that while this may come with certain challenges, it was nothing to be squeamish about and certainly nothing to end a friendship over.

This is not a book with a message. But what I hope it shows is that people like Stephen do not arrive fully formed. They are shaped by the world in which they live, a world we happen to share with them. We have, therefore, a responsibility to understand and accept the reality of the different conditions we will inevitably encounter in others, whether its schizophrenia, bipolar, social phobias, Asperger's, whatever. And while it is not always an easy thing to show patience or empathy towards someone who has a condition you cannot see, nor is it the hardest thing in the world either. Far from it. It's one thing to encourage openness and honesty when we talk about it. It's another thing – a much more valuable thing – to not flinch or check the time more than you would otherwise do when somebody who does struggle with a difference is right in front of you.

At the vegan curry house where we have our last meal together, Stephen has with him a copy of Greta Thunberg's book, *No One Is Too Small to Make a Difference*. It is, I suppose, the closing of a circle. In 2018, Thunberg was a socially isolated teenager with Asperger's who had an intense anxiety about impending ecological catastrophe as well as a determination to do something about it. Following a social media campaign and series of emphatic speeches issuing calls to action over climate change, the Swedish teenager went on to become the world's most recognisable and influential activist on climate change. She has been named *TIME* Magazine's Person of the Year, has over four million Twitter followers and is considered a Nobel Peace Prize winner in waiting. The same stubbornness, determination and sense of injustice that was present in Stephen is present in her, and much of the world loves her for it. Stephen presents me with Thunberg's book a little bashfully. He says that he hopes I'll find the time to read it.

Sometimes he looks at the state of the world and feels an overwhelming pessimism. 'I'll feel that the world has reached a point where the course is already set and there is nothing anyone can do.'

More often, though, he tells himself that there is still a future

BEN MACHELL

worth fighting for. Over the course of hours and hours of conversation, Stephen only ever makes one very tentative suggestion about this book. He says that, despite everything that he has been through, he hopes that people still manage to find a positive message in his experiences. Stephen had seen that the world was in trouble and he had wanted to do something about it. What he did was wrong, and he knows that. But he had still done *something*. Which is what we have to do if we want to give ourselves a fighting chance. A train is coming rumbling down the track. We can either choose to hear it or not.

'The world is in a very precarious place. And it could get a lot worse. We can all take action and we can all take small steps to make it more sustainable and fair,' he says, before smiling shyly. 'Just not by robbing banks.'

Author's Note

When I first sat down to interview Stephen Jackley for *The Times* in the spring of 2016, the possibility that I might write a book about the quiet young man in front of me never crossed my mind. By the time we parted three hours later, I knew that I would eventually run out of excuses not to.

Writing about Stephen's life and his crimes has been strange, sad and exhilarating, and *The Unusual Suspect* would not exist – or at least not in the form it does now – if it had not been for his involvement and cooperation. I have, over the course of my job, encountered many people who relish the attention that comes with being a subject, even if they pretend not to. Stephen is not one of them. During the hours of interviews I conducted with him and over the dozens and dozens of emails I kept sending demanding more and more information – names, people, places, feelings – I was often left with the sense that he felt himself to be engaged into a process that was wearying but somehow necessary. There were many times I was sure that my next question would be the one that would finally cause him to simply walk away from memories that were painful, shameful and raw. He never did. For this I thank him.

Stephen had no editorial control over this project beyond consenting to the replication of his diary entries, other written materials and psychiatric reports. Dialogue, where it appears, is presented as he or other interviewees can best recall. Stephen would often provide the names or contact details of individuals he felt sure would have nothing good to say about him, only to voice his surprise when that turned out to not quite be the case. Equally, I approached a good many family members who simply did not want to talk about him and what he had done.

The diary entries included in this book are only snippets of the inner world Stephen documented throughout his adolescence and then on into the period of his crimes. I have some of these notebooks and entries, the West Mercia police hold others, some are shared between us in the form of photocopied evidence bundles used in his trial and still more may well have been lost or destroyed while Stephen was serving his jail sentence in the UK. I have tried to use the written material available to me in a way that does not editorialise. By quoting selectively from his diaries, it would be possible to cast Stephen as either a sinner or a saint. He was, in his own way, both these things, and so I have tried to make the quoted entries reflect that complicated reality.

A great deal of information relating to Stephen's crimes exists in the form of local news reports, CCTV imagery and court records from both sides of the Atlantic, all of which I relied upon throughout the course of my research. There are also moments when we have to rely on Stephen's version of events and nobody else's. As in any such circumstance, there is always the possibility that the teller, consciously or not, omits or embellishes or otherwise presents a reality they feel would either have been better then, or that serves them better now. Nevertheless I have tried, as much as possible, to take Stephen at his word. My intention had never been to place him on trial a second time and, in any case, it is my belief that far more has come to light as a result of him being given the benefit of the doubt than not.

I must thank a number of law enforcement agencies, particularly the Devon and Cornwall Police, the West Mercia Police, the ATF and the US Marshals. All the officers I interviewed were patient, thoughtful and professional, remembered Stephen's case with interest and bore him no ill will. But they all stressed that his crimes had real victims. It is for this reason that I am incredibly grateful to Luke Twisleton for talking so honestly about the long-lasting trauma of being robbed at gunpoint, and I would encourage everyone to consider that he was just one of dozens of people who found themselves caught up in Stephen's actions through no choice of their own.

I would like to thank the Vermont Department of Prisons as well as Mark Potanas and Cameron Lindsay, former warden of MDC Brooklyn, men who both provided a great deal of valuable information about the realities of the United States penal system. Similarly, Dr Sajid Suleman was a huge help in better understanding the nature of Asperger's in general and in Stephen in particular. My appreciation goes to the Arkbound Foundation for allowing the reproduction of Stephen's mother's poems, and also to Ben Weaver, not just for sharing his memories, but also for being a good friend to a young Stephen, a fact I cannot help wanting to thank him for.

Finally, I have to thank Nicola Jeal, my editor at *The Times Magazine*. When I first told her that I had heard about this geography student from Devon who developed an obsession with Robin Hood and then robbed a load of banks in order to give to the poor, she agreed that it was a story worth pursuing. Four years on, I know the reality is a little more complicated. But it was still a story worth pursuing. I am glad that I did.

Ben Machell, August 2020

Acknowledgements

This story would still exist in fractured pieces across a dozen different notepads and Microsoft Word files if it were not for the care, patience and professionalism of many different people, all of whom I owe a huge debt of gratitude. I would like to thank everybody at Canongate, but particularly Simon Thorogood, my editor. Simon's enthusiasm for this story was matched only by his sensitivity and perceptiveness when dealing with its complex morality, and I cannot thank him enough. Thank you also Francis Bickmore, Leila Cruickshank, Vicki Rutherford, Alice Shortland, Lucy Zhou and Anna Frame.

It's impossible for me to imagine any of this happening without Richard Pike at C+W. Richard not only managed to make the prospect of writing a book seem possible, but also even vaguely enjoyable and rewarding. I now accept that he was probably right. Throughout this entire process Richard has been a constant source of reassurance, good humour and deep professional knowledge that I could not have managed without. I am very fortunate to have him as an agent. I'd like to thank everyone at C+W as well as Luke Speed and Anna Weguelin at Curtis Brown, and Zoe Sandler and Heather Karpas at ICM, who have all been instrumental in bringing this story to as wide an audience as possible.